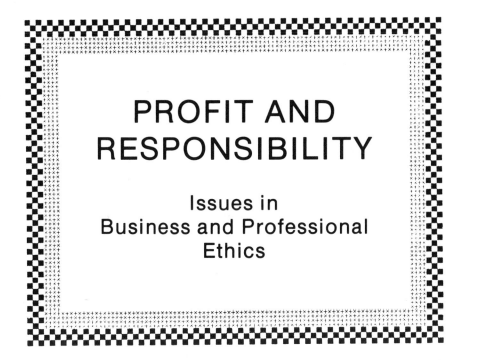

PROFIT AND RESPONSIBILITY

Issues in
Business and Professional
Ethics

Edited by
Patricia Werhane
and
Kendall D'Andrade

Studies in Religion and Society
Volume 12

The Edwin Mellen Press
New York and Toronto

Library of Congress Cataloging in Publication Data
Main entry under title:

Profit and responsibility.

(Studies in religion and society ; v. 12)
Includes bibliographical references.
1. Business ethics--Addresses, essays, lectures.
I. Werhane, Patricia Hogue. II. D'Andrade, Kendall.
III. Series: Studies in religion and society (New
York, N.Y.) ; v. 12.
HF5387.P75 1985   174'.4   84-27279
ISBN 0-88946-862-1

Studies in Religion and Society
ISBN 0-88946-863-X

The Edwin Mellen Press
P.O. Box 450
Lewiston, New York 14092

Printed in the United States of America

Profit and responsibility can come together because profit is one of business's responsibilities, but only one of many.

—from the introduction

CONTENTS

PREFACE

From a subject which was hardly more than a name for a joke ten years ago, business ethics has blossomed into a popular, even trendy, specialty. In one of the earliest collections of original essays in this field,[1] the editors thought it prudent to promote their book by pointing to the high costs of being caught acting unethically. Ethics, they were in effect warning us, was too important to one's personal and corporate success to be ignored any more. And they were right, of course; so clearly right that we no longer need remind ourselves of this obvious truth, whether we be members of the business or the academic communities, or simply part of the interested general public. We all believe in ethics, or at least feel we must pretend to support ethical behavior "for the record." Similarly, the job of the professional philosopher has evolved during this time. Ten years ago most of us were content to articulate our view of one or more of the major ethical traditions, leaving it to others to make the transition into practice. Now most of us have acknowledged that acting morally is not simply a matter of obeying the traditions, that there are fundamental theoretical problems in the move to applications. These problems are also interesting, as both this book and the continued interest in the subject attest. We are even taking seriously problems of persuading others to follow what are admitted to be morally correct paths. (The second section of our book -- Alternative Contexts for Business Ethics -- focuses on this issue.)

---

1. *Ethics, Free Enterprise, and Public Policy,* edited by Joseph Pichler and Richard DeGeorge (Oxford University Press, 1978).

Most of the essays started life as part of a Conference on Business Ethics which we hosted at the University of Illinois, Chicago while I was there. Two others[2] are revised versions of talks presented to the Business Problems and Public Policy series at UIC. It is with pleasure that we thank those who funded those events. Dorothy Grover, chairperson of the Philosophy Department at UIC provided generously from the Departmental funds. Alice B. Hayes, Associate Academic Vice President at Loyola University of Chicago and a grant from the Loyola-Mellon Fund covered the other half of our costs and have continued to support us in the preparation of this manuscript. Tom Bennett, Director of Research Services at Loyola also helped with preparation costs. The UIC Honors College has been a regular sponsor of the Business Problems and Public Policy series of talks for the past ten years; Sam Schrage was a continuing source of support and encouragement, both professional and personal. And Ralph Westfall and Al Star (dean and associate dean respectively) helped foster an atmosphere favorable to business ethics at UIC, thus ensuring the cooperation of numerous members of the business college. During his tenure as Chairperson, Myles Brand provided the same type of support in the Philosophy Department. Cynthia Rudolph and Ruby Murchison typed the manuscript, and were invaluable in its preparation.

Mark Pastin and Michael Hooker had just published their article, "Ethics and the Foreign Corrupt Practices Act" *Business Horizons* when we were organizing our conference. It is reprinted here with the permission of the authors and *BH*. Michael Philips wrote and published (in *Ethics*) his article, "Bribery," independently, but has kindly consented to its inclusion here. Three of the speakers at the Conference published their papers in specialized journals; they and their respective journals have graciously allowed us to print them

---

2. The articles by Barry Chiswick and Barrett and Verastegui.

here as well. They are: Michael Keeley's article, "Organizational Reality," originally published under the title, "Realism
in Organizational Theory: A Reassessment," in *Symbolic
Interaction*, Larry May's "Vicarious Agency and Corporate
Responsibility," published in *Philosophical Studies*, and Kenneth Alpern's "Moral Dimensions of the Foreign Corrupt
Practices Act" which originally appeared in *Ethical Issues in
Business*, edited by Thomas Donaldson and Patricia Werhane,
then in Michael Hoffman and Jennifer Moore's *Business Ethics*.

Finally, we would like to thank Vivian Weil; she was virtually the third co-host of the Conference that generated so
many fine papers, and whose products form the core of this
book.

K. D'A.

September 7, 1984

INTRODUCTION

Patricia Werhane

There is one and only one social responsibility
of business--to use its resources and engage in
activities designed to increase its profits so long
as it stays within the rules of the game, which is
to say, engages in open and free competition,
without deception or fraud.[1]

--Milton Friedman

The relationship of profit to responsibility in a capitalist
economy is a topic of interest not merely for economists such
as Milton Friedman, but is of great concern in business ethics as well. Friedman's famous edict, often lauded, often
criticized, has had the solubrious effect of alerting businesspersons, economists, ethicists, and theologians to the
importance of this issue. By identifying social responsibility
with profitability Friedman seeks to morally justify the normal activities of business in a free enterprise system and
challenges critics to explain how such an identification might
be misleading or indeed at fault. Meeting Friedman's
requires demonstrating that business responsibilities are not
merely economic ones and that the relationship between profit
and responsibility has an ethical as well as an economic component. The essays in this volume take on this challenge,

---

1. Milton Friedman, *Capitalism and Freedom* (Chicago:
University of Chicago Press, 1962), p. 133.

and in so doing the authors not only devise creative approaches to moral issues in business, but also prompt businesses and businesspersons to adopt moral as well as market responsibilities in their conduct of economic activities. In terms of the topic of this book, profit and responsibility, the essays in this collection both develop and use appropriate ethical theories to discuss profit and responsibility and, conversely, analyze particular situations in business where the relationship between profit and responsibility is at issue. The essays in the first sections of this book take up the first task, while the essays in the later sections focus on more specific business contexts.

Thomas McMahon's overview of the evolution of business ethics as a distinct discipline, and his analysis of the state of the subject today provides a valuable introduction to the rest of the book. McMahon shows how the emphasis in business ethics has shifted from a focus on the personal behavior of managers towards broader issues, such as the question of corporate responsibility. There has also been a shift from the analysis of practical guidelines for businesspersons to a discussion of the more abstract notions of rights, power and justice in the context of business. Additionally, there has been a split between philosophers and business theorists concerning the proper conceptual framework for business ethics. Business theorists tend to concentrate on the economic, social and cultural aspects of corporate responsiveness, sometimes in what is supposedly an ethically neutral context. William Frederick's essay is an example of this approach, and an ethically neutral context is implied in Friedman's identification of social responsibility with profit. Philosophers and theologians, on the other hand, focus on moral responsibility and on the notions of rights and justice. Philosophers tend to argue that because businesspersons are *persons*, and because corporations are run by them, managers and the businesses they control have *moral* obligations. These are not just the negative responsibilitiy not to do harm or merely to respond to social pressures. As McMahon points out, these responsibilities include positive obligations to respect human rights and to contribute to the society in which business is allowed to operate. Essays by Michael Hooker and Mark Pastin, Kenneth Alpern, Michael Philips, and Larry May in this book illustrate this type of approach.

McMahon points out that the philosophical study of ethics in business often borrows from the methodology of traditional ethics. This body of work by and large takes classical ethical theories and applies them to business contexts. The two most widely cited theories are forms of deontological ethics and teleological ethics, and later we shall see three very different applications of these theories to a specific issue: the implications of the Foreign Corrupt Practices Act for businesspersons and the business operations of transnational corporations.

Although many ethicists use versions of these two classical theories in approaching ethical issues in business, other thinkers on the frontiers of business ethics question the validity of such an approach as a general methodology. Specifically James Valone, William Frederick, and William Penn query whether theoretical ethics alone can serve to develop a complete analysis of ethical issues in business. Without committing himself to any particular moral position, James Valone analyzes some of the essential factors in moral decision-making, factors which are important whatever one's ethical perspective. These include the relativity of each situation, the distinction between understanding a situation and providing a moral justification of it, the nature, motives for, and consequences of a moral act, and the hierarchy of values. Valone's point is that moral decision-making in business is a complex process, not merely an extension of certain ethical principles to a socio-cultural position. A variety of factors come into play in any such decision and the astute manager must take all of them into account in a truly authentic ethical decision.

The kinds of factors which might enter into a moral decision in business are carefully spelled out by William Penn. Penn utilizes Lawrence Kohlberg's well-known theory of the stages of moral development to analyze the ways in which people reason about moral issues in business, and he adopts what Kohlberg calls "post-conventional moral reasoning" to discuss case studies in business ethics. Penn finds Kohlberg's analyses useful in evaluating the stages of decision-making procedures through which managers may go in making a business choice. The study of these stages is also helpful in equiping managers with skills necessary for making complex value judgments in business. More controversally, Penn suggests that post-conventional moral reasoning is useful for moral agreement or consensus on an issue. Penn uses a case study of a transnational corporation which is engaged in a bribery scheme in a foreign country to illustrate how moral consensus might be arrived at by Kohlberg's method. One has only to look at the debate in the next section between Michael Hooker and Mark Pastin who, with qualification, defend such bribery in specific instances, and Kenneth Alpern's sharp moral criticism of such activities to wonder whether moral consensus on very serious issues is as easily achieved as Penn, and perhaps Kohlberg, imagine. However, what is important in Penn's analysis is the emphatic demonstration that the study of moral development is of value in sensitizing managers to ethical issues in the marketplace in initiating a move towards consensus.

The approaches of Penn and Valone are useful in analyzing ethical dilemmas facing individuals in business. William Frederick stresses the importance of methodologies of the social sciences in examining ethical issues in business, in particular those issues facing corporations. Specifically, a determination of the value orientation of each participant in an ethical dilemma as well as the origins of and reasons for value differences are often the most fruitful ways to get at the heart of ethical puzzles. This approach, which evaluates an ethical issue within its social context, is superior to an analysis of the issue in terms of rights or social justice according to Frederick. The latter methods, while of interest to theorists, are non-contextual and neglect the details of the situation and its socio-cultural context that give rise to a particular dilemma. To discern how values operate in business one needs to examine carefully how value formation and the socialization of values takes place in our culture. Frederick discusses various modes for analyzing value formation, value preference, and value changes in individuals who are affected by societal constraints. Thus, in discovering the relation of profit to responsibility, one studies how value formation influences ideals which are or are not embedded in corporate culture and how these in turn affect the perception of social and moral responsibilities of businesses and those who must make business decisions.

Frederick is highly critical of ethical theorists who impose abstract categories of moral reasoning upon business and business activities without considering the societal, cultural and ethnic factors. This method has the danger either of reinforcing dominent value systems or of ignoring aspects of society's value experiences and thus being irrelevant. However, Frederick's criticisms of theoreticians in ethics overlook an important aim of business ethics which is to analyze and evaluate, rather than merely to describe, dominent cultural and business values. One does not merely study how businesses tend to equate social responsibility with profitibility, for example. Rather, one judges the moral viability of that position from a broader ethical perspective. But Frederick's emphasis on the importance of examining embedded values already in place in our society and in business is an important contribution to the field.

Tal Scriven and Christopher Morris introduce yet another, and a more quantitative, approach to business ethics by taking the mathematical model of the prisoners' dilemma and applying it to the process of business decision-making. The prisoners' dilemma may be described as any situation in which two individuals, two corporations, two nations, etc. are competing against each other under conditions that effectively prohibit their cooperation, because it is in each player's short-term interest to back down on any promise of cooperation. This is a dilemma, because both parties could maximize their personal payoffs if they could discover a reliable method of enforcing cooperative action; yet without the intervention of some third party, the two antagonists will correctly view each other as adversaries, because there is even more profit to be gained by feining cooperation with a "partner" who one then deceives than in a genuine partnership.

Scriven questions the thesis that cooperation is always the proper sort of action to take in prisoners' dilemma situations, at least in business. The fact that two companies compete because they cannot trust each other to fix prices, for example, may give us lower prices than under a model of "cooperation." From the point of view of the two companies involved in this dilemma not cooperating does not maximize profits. But from a societal point of view competition rather than cooperation is desirable. In fact this may be a mathematical model of what Adam Smith had in mind in describing his famous "invisible hand" in the marketplace. One can be self-interested and socially responsible simultaneously in

business, according to this view. In market situations, acting on one's own self-interest, i.e., maximizing personal
profit, rather than adopting a more benevolent perspective,
may in fact have positive side effects for society.

Morris is well aware of the social advantages of prisoners' dilemmas for business. But he is very conscious of the
problems either of following this simple market analysis or,
alternatively, of advocating some simple coercive mechanism
wherein we force individuals to cooperate. In the latter
instance one might legislate cooperation, justifying this by
an appeal to what Morris calls "Prisoner's Dilemma norms"
(PD norms) to achieve an optimum result for the parties to
the competition and to society without assuming the unreli-
ability of either party. A third alternative, according to
Morris, is to conceive of PD norms not as constraints but as
goals for business. According to this view, the social
responsibility of corporations should include a responsibility
to the public interest. This alternative avoids the difficulties of externally imposed norms which are restrictive to
corporations. These sorts of constraints violate whatever
rights corporations have to conduct business competitively
and freely, and sometimes   these constraints achieve the
undesirable result of favoring one business or one group of
businesses over another. Morris does not fully develop this
third alternative., But his theory suggests that if business
wants to operate freely and competitively without governmental restraint, businesses and businesspersons need to take
seriously their moral as well as economic responsibilities to
norms suggested in the prisoners' dilemma. PD norms are
enforcement mechanisms in that they change the payoffs of
various actions to make the desirable choice (from the regu-
lator's perspective) the most profitable for each player.
Unfortunately, the distinction between profit and responsibility is lost in these models, because there is only a single
standard for payoffs and losses, usually a monetary unit or
other quantitive measure of satisfaction. Focusing on PD
norms, in fact, any use of this type of model, literally
forces us to ignore the moral dimensions of our choices.

The preceding essays concentrate on the role of moral
decision-making in the activities of business managers and
corporations as if these were similar. However, to compare

corporations to individuals and to conflate corporate moral decision-making with individual moral decision-making are highly questionable procedures. A central issue in the study of business ethics is the proper delineation of the nature of the modern business corporation. While this question might appear to be of only esoteric value to theoreticians, it turns out to be crucial in the correct allocation of moral responsibility to corporations and the identification or nonidentification of these organizations with the individuals who comprise them. If corporations are distinct agents, then they are capable of moral activity and one can ascribe to them moral responsibility. On the other hand, if all corporate action can be redescribed as individual actions of boards of directors, managers, and other employees of the corporation, then the responsibility for business actions must be ultimately individual responsibility.

Now it would seem at first glance that to talk about corporations as moral agents is silly. No one sees a corporation in action nor shakes hands with it. Michael Keeley supports this view of the corporation, by criticizing what he calls a "realist" theory which views corporations as independent autonomous entities. Realist theories, in brief, assume that a corporation is a actual goal-oriented entity. But this sort of analysis of corporations is fallacious according to Keeley. To make his point Keeley notices that there is a distinction between goals *of* a corporation and goals *for* a corporation. What appear to be "intentions" of the corporation are in fact the intentions of managers and boards of directors. The realists' mistake is in treating the series of different goals various individuals or groups of individuals in the corporation have projected for the corporation as if they were also the goals of some further abstract entity, The Corporation. It is not clear whether or not Keeley himself is a nominalist in regard to corporations such that when one is talking about corporations in any context one is only talking about individuals who comprise the organization. But at the least, Keeley holds that any predicate which derives its meaning from or is parasitic on, persons (including so-called mental as well as moral predicates) cannopt be applied to corporations.

The failure of realist theories accurately to describe the nature of the corporation has serious implications for the corporate moral responsibility and for any claims that corporations have any rights, according to Keeley. If we erroneously treat a corporation as if it were a single moral agent we often ascribe to it rights such as the right to free speech. If Keeley is correct, this ascription does nothing for the corporation since it is not an entity at all. But it extends the enjoyment of rights of managers when they exercise these rights in the name of the corporation, giving them undue powers which can be misused to the detriment of other individuals.

In contrast, Larry May points out that even though corporations are not analogous to human moral persons, nevertheless there is a sense in which corporations are distinct entities. This is because the actions of corporations cannot be always redescribed successfully as actions of managers and boards of directors acting on behalf of the corporation. This is particularly true when one is ascribing blame or trying to hold a corporation liable for some action. The reason that actions of corporations cannot be ultimately traced to some individuals or group of individuals in every instance is in part because, when acting on behalf of the corporation managers often act anonymously in terms of goals set out by the board of directors rather than on their own personal behalf. Thus, while it is obviously true that corporations do not have intentions, beliefs or desires so that a corporation could be called a full-fledged moral person, it makes sense to ascribe to corporations a qualified sort of agency, which May calls "vicarious agency," to account for the ways in which corporations, and not merely managers, act and are held responsible.

The debate between Keeley and May has reprocussions for the relationship of profit and responsibility. For if corporations are in no sense real agents, then much of what the law ascribes to corporations in the way of rights and liabilities needs to be redefined. But if a sense of agency *is* appropriate to describe corporations, then their responsibilities extend beyond profitability since they are capable of ethical choices, and thus they can be morally culpable.

The development of various approaches to ethical issues in business and the proper analysis of the business corporation as a moral agent are important theoretical tools in business ethics. However, they are empty concepts without their application to particular business dilemmas. Using these approaches the second set of essays in the book analyze specific ethical issues in business. The first of these deal with the recurring debate over the ethical responsibility of transnational corporations. How should American corporations and businesspersons act when they are in another country? Business is conducted differently in various countries so that from a practical point of view one must adopt different operating procedures when doing business in a foreign lands. If one does not adopt the mores of that country one risks insulting the host country. Yet sometimes even the minimum requirements for operating a business transnationally are ethically questionable, or at least ethically questionable from our perspective. This has most clearly come up in countries where bribery and extortion are common practices in doing business. Should American transnational corporations participate in these ethically questionable acts in order to do business in those countries? Can bribery be condoned where it is an acceptable practice?

Michael Hooker and Mark Pastin discuss this problem in the context of the Foreign Corrupt Practices Act (FCPA), the statute which forbids American companies to bribe or pay extortion to officials of foreign governments. Hooker and Pastin argue that the act should be abolished, because less harm is created and positive benefits in terms of jobs and profits accrue, from engaging in business practices consistent with the practices of the country where one is operating. Through a modified utilitarian approach Hooker and Pastin argue that bribery and extortion in foreign countries can be justified in certain business circumstances (a) if it does not create harm and (b) if the benefits to the corporation, consumers and employees outweigh any liabilities of bribing or paying extortion.

In contrast, Kenneth Alpern takes a deontological approach to this issue. He claims that if bribery is in and of itself wrong, it cannot be justified in foreign countries. Alpern recognizes that bribery may still be justified in extraordinary instances, or when the background system renders it the lesser evil, e.g., when it is absolutely necessary for one's very survival. But since American transnational corporations are not in desperate straits one cannot morally permit bribery, and certainly not as the general rule as Hooker and Pastin contend. Alpern also questions the

utilitrian case against the FCPA, a position developed further by Tom Calero. Where Hooker and Pastin emphasize the
costs to a single business which refuses to pay bribes,
Calero notices that the evidence for these costs is only anti-
dotal and not systematic.   Thus, he says, we just do not
know what bribery costs and what it profits.   The whole
argument defending bribery has been swept away by the
FCPA, because the Act forces all American firms to stand
together in resisting extortion. If no one is paying bribes
or extortion, the cost to a single firm of refusing to pay will
go down.   Thus it may be possible to act morally and pursue
profits simultaneously.   Calero very much wants American
businesses to investigate this possibility before lobbying for
the abolishment of the FCPA.

Hooker and Pastin on one side, and Alpern and Calero
on the other, represent the traditional debate over bribery.
Michael Philips breaks new ground, namely by appropriating
a new metaphysical analysis of bribery in terms of three
parties: the original bribe-offerer, and the bribe-taker, plus
the person betrayed by the bribe-taker.   This shifts the
problem to a discussion of the relative strength of the
bribe-taker's obligation to be faithful to her first principal
versus the obligation to accomplish whatever good she seeks
by taking the bribe *and* following the bribe-offerer instead.
Sometimes bribe offers will promote a morally superior outcome, so some bribes will be desirable, and thus may be
properly offered and accepted.   Philip's consequentialist
evaluation of the worth of actions produced by bribes should
be a challenge to those who approach this issue from a more
deontological point of view.   All parties will have to work
out the implications of this new analysis of the meaning (and
mechanisms)· of bribery.   The debate is surely not over,
although it has entered a new phase, as illustrated in these
essays.

John Haddox's presentation of the "Twin-Plants" dilemma
illustrates another issue often facing transnational corporations operating in foreign countries where wages and
working conditions are substantially different from those in
the United States.   Corporations often build plants in countries where labor is cheaper and where laws regulating

working conditions are, at best, lax. Should workers at these plants receive the same wages and benefits as their American counterparts? This might disrupt the economy of that country, but can one justify lower wages and bad working conditions when operating in poorer countries? One of the difficulties is that companies operating in countries with cultures and economies quite foreign from their own often pay little attention to these problems. But if corporations or at least their managers are morally responsible, they have these responsibilities everywhere, even when doing business in foreign countries.

In partial defense of "twin-plants" companies, it might be the case that they are working from the Friedman ideal that everyone has the right to do as they please so that workers too have the right to seek their own economic advantage by trading increased risk for better remuneration. Haddox's strong position criticizing transnational business operations which engage what are viewed as exploitive practices needs to be examined carefully.

Barry Chiswick and Michael Barrett each examine a specific problem within their profession, noting that the traditional wisdom is inadequate to deal with these issues. As an economist, Chiswick begins by wondering why the nursing home industry does not seem to obey the normal laws of supply and demand. It does, of course, but we have been fooled because we have not isolated the real consumer. The true purchasers of nursing home care are not the residents but their relatives who see the home as providing superior care to that which could be provided within the family. The scandals occur when this purchase is also treated as the shifting of all responsibility for good care onto the institution. There are two possibilites for reform: institutional (professionalism or governmental intervention) or individual. Chiswick is highly sceptical of the value of institutional solutions. Rather, he advocates continued monitering by relatives who so clearly demonstrte their concern for the elderly family member that the institution finds it profitable to provide optimal care. Chiswick knows that this is not a perfect solution, but he argues that it is cheaper and more effective than any proffered solution, and it places the moral obligation for care of the elderly in the hands of those responsible: the family.

The claim that moral responsibility is always a matter of

individual obligation reflects the position of Michael Keeley in
his analysis of corporations.   If Keeley and Chiswick are
correct,   then   neither   corporations   nor   government   has   a
decisive   role   in   improving   the   moral   climate   of   business.
This places all the responsibility on individuals: employees,
managers, corporate directors, and stockholders.   Yet not
all   individuals   recognize,   much   less   exercise,   their   moral
obligations.

What   is   the   accountant's   job?   This   question   does   not
originate   from   philosophical   musings   outside   the   business
community but from a practicing accountant and professor of
accounting: Michael Barrett.   His article with Verastegui
argues that we are not clear about the ultimate audience for
audited   statements,   that   we   have   far   too   vague   standards
about   what   financial   information   should   be   disclosed,   and
that we lack even a basic measure of a firm's financial
health.   Further, it is a mistake to try to separate financial
issues from other considerations. Stability of management is
not thought relevant to financial disclosure, but it may be
more important than the firm's net worth or last four quar-
ters'   performances   in   determining   where   that   business   is
likely to go.

Barrett and Verastegui are certainly in favor of institutional change in a way Chiswick is not, but it would be a
mistake to push this difference too hard.   The accountants
feel that an enlightened public will demand better disclosure
policies, thus invoking the market mechanism.   The economist (Chiswick) argues that the current market will work if
only the true consumers recognize their own role and act on
a real desire to provide quality care for institutionalized relatives.   The   stress   on   individual   initiative   is   tempered   by
the reliance·on the "institution" of the market to bring most
parties into line with what is desirable at the margin.   For
this   to   work   some   governmental   regulation   is   obviously
desireable; for example, the requirement that nursing homes
be open for inspection at least twelve hours every day, thus
providing the interested relatives *access* to information about
the institution.   Chiswick's position is not that givernment
plays no important role, but that it has played its part well
so far, better than the relatives.

The analysis of the market, what it can do, and what
mechanisms it uses should remind the reader of the controversies between Morris and Scriven, and Hooker, Pastin and

Alpern.   Can individuals, operating freely in the marketplace restrain their self-interest to the benefit of society?   Are PD norms built into a free enterprise system, or is legislation necessary to reinforce these norms in the public interest? Or are most of us too short-sighted so that external constraints are necessary to control behavior in business?   The debate cannot be settled here, but many of the essays in the volume address the intricacies of the problem.

The book concludes with an essay directed specifically at the relationship of profit to responsibility.   Ronald Cordero puts the role of profit in business in its proper perspective. If the only responsibility of business is profitability, business could justify a number of morally questionable acts which businesspersons would in reality seldom consider. Through a careful choice of examples, Cordero shows that a business can exist not only when profit is not the major goal, but also where profit has no place whatsoever in the operation of business.   The essence of business is not the search for income; it is regularly charging for a product or service provided on a recurring basis.   Profit, then, is only one of the goals of business, ans so it cannot have absolute weight.   Cordero asks business to rethink its goals and set them in a rational order.   It may turn out that efficiency in achieving profitability may be counterproductive in achieving moral aims which are also important to business.   Cordero's essay seeks to liberate the business theorist from her preoccupation with profits, for it is only after noticing that business have goals other than profit that one can begin to compare the relative importance of several goals in a given context and then make a truly rational decision about the interests of business.   Here profit and responsibility can come together because profit is one of business's responsibilities, but only one out of very many.

The State of Ethics in Business

SOCIO-ETHICAL ISSUES: TWO CONCEPTUAL FRAMEWORKS

Thomas F. McMahon, C.S.V.

Business ethics, as a distinct discipline in schools of higher education, evolved from reaction to three separate events: the Electrical Scandal in 1960; social legislation starting in 1964; and Watergate in 1972.

The first event was the publication of the electrical industry price fixing scandal of the early 1960's. During the post-World-War II development of the Eisenhower years, business enjoyed high respectibility. Its legitimacy as a social institution was never questioned: business pulled the United States out of economic depression and provided jobs and upward mobility through what was considered to be a conscious contribution to society by providing goods and services. American "international" companies grew beyond expectation. Among the most sought-after American exports from foreign countries was American managerial expertise. The era of the organization man (few women were "in busi-ness," as the saying went) had an aura of goodness-social goodness, ethical goodness, moral goodness and even relig-ious goodness. The electrical industry price fixing scandal of the early 1960's shocked the world. As an antitrust vio-lation, price fixing is illegal. It is also unethical, according to many business persons and ethicians. Revelation of long-term and widespread use of price fixing in the electrical industry raised questions about the ethics of executives and business managers in other industries. And it also triggered inquiries about the teaching of ethics in business schools throughout the United States. The Commerce Department established a Business Ethics Advisory Council which sent an open-ended questionnaire to undergraduate and graduate business schools to determine what was being

taught in business ethics, if at all. Courses in business
ethics began to proliferate. Most of them, however, dealt
with the personal ethics of businessmen. Under the broad
notion of social justice, the impact of corporate activity on
the different segments of society was limited to specific
issues, such as plant shutdown. Father Raymond Baumhart,
S.J., President of Loyola University of Chicago, wrote the
classic treatise on personal business ethics. In his empirical
study of business persons, he showed that unethical business behavior was not limited to the electrical industry but
could be found almost in every industry. Both business and
society reacted to his findings, primarily with academic solutions. Although university courses, executives' seminars,
and business writing on the ethical dimension of business
decision-making raised the issue of the personal values system of business managers, they rarely touched the structure
within which these decisions were made. Thus, they asked
the question: *who* (*viz.,* superior, sales manager, etc.) did
what (*viz.,* pad an expense account, conspire to fix prices,
etc.)? Given the assumption that each business person was
responsible for his (in 1961 there were few women in business) own personal conduct within an acceptable institutional
structure (*viz.,* corporation), this reactionary approach of
business managers to business ethics was the logical outcome
of an individualistic approach to responsibility. It was also
consistent with the social role of business "to provide goods
and services for society." The Eisenhower years of enhanc-
ing the material needs of society assumed that an increase in
quantity in goods meant an automatic increase in the quality-
of-life. The "invisible hand" theory of Adam Smith had
ardent supporters in the proponents of the individual, personal business ethic.

The second event to trigger interest in the ethical
dimensions of business education was the 1964 Civil Rights
Act. Subsequent social legislation, such as the Clean Air
Act (1970), Federal Water Pollution Act (1972), Toxic Sub-
stances Control Act (1976) and other laws attempted to deal
with problems which had direct social implications. Expectation shifted from quantity-of-goods to quality-of-life.
Towards the end of the 1960's business schools began to
offer courses on corporate social responsibility, primarily
under the title of "Business and Society." These courses
stressed the obligations of business corporations to the

different segments of society and the claims of these private or public interest groups against the corporation.[1] Social responsibility meant balancing the interests of the various claimants of the corporation according to some kind of priority (which was not always clear--nor consistent): shareholders, employees, local communities, governmental agencies, consumers, and so forth. Nor was it clear, furthermore, whether the *rights* or the *power* of the claimants was the reason behind corporate response to the all-encompassing demands of competing interest groups.

A problem which arose with the shift of emphasis to quality-of-life and social issues relates to identifying the source of the decision. On the one hand, it was relatively easy to pinpoint the source of the decision which led to the antitrust violations of price fixing and collusion in the 1961 Electrical Scandal. On the other hand, it was very difficult to determine *who* made the decision for U.S. Steel to pay a fine for environmental pollution rather than install anti-pollution equipment. The "corporate veil" covers up the actual decision-maker and places the blame on the whole corporation, so that slogans, such as "U.S. Steel pollutes," identify the culprit as the corporation rather than the individual within the corporation. Thus, in order to find out whose ethical and social values determine corporate decisions, the second issue should raise the question *who* told *whom* to do *what?* The actual question which the different interest groups asked, however, was too limited to reveal the source of ethical and social values. They merely asked: *which company* did *what?* The underlying assumption seems to be that corporate values pervade the corporate ladder. The increase in "whistle-blowing" on corporate conduct, on the contrary, proved this assumption wrong.

The 1972 Watergate scandal set the stage for raising the

---

1. Prakash Sethi's *Up Against The Corporate Wall*, (1971, Englewood Cliffs: Prentice-Hall) typifies this approach, which was primarily rhetorical questioning of corporate insensitivity to the social impact of business decision-making.

issue of personal responsibility within an institutional setting.   The questionable conduct of the Watergate break-in
penetrated deeper than the corporate veil and sought to find
a person--not an institution--who was responsible for giving
orders.   Watergate--and questions of corporate behavior
since Watergate--asked the question to get at the *ultimate*
decision-maker: *who* told *whom* to do *what*.   The corporate
mirror image of Watergate took the form of payoffs to
national and foreign politicians and their parties.   The Gulf
Oil case became the prototype when Mr. B. R. Dorsey,
Chairman and Executive Officer resigned upon revelation of
his payoffs.   The Gulf Board of Directors commissioned an
impartial panel to investigate the allegations.   A 298-page
report revealed the pervasive use of payoffs to obtain favorable decisions for Gulf: throughout the report it became
clear that Chairman Dorsey actively participated in the illegal
and/or unethical conduct (depending upon the involvement
and country).   Indeed, since Watergate, *who* told *whom* to
do *what* is a basic issue discussed in courses on business
ethics.

Social Responsiveness

A closer look, however, suggests another change:
change from rhetorical to empirical studies, from corporate
social *responsibility* to corporate social *responsiveness*.   The
shift from the rhetorical exposition of the early 1970's to
empirical reporting of corporate programs first appeared in
The Social Challenge to Business by Robert Ackerman.[2] Ackerman presented studies on discrimination and pollution from
two large corporations.   His position, however, was that
".... socially responsive corporations are ...managerial in
nature rather than ethical or ideological,"[3] that "...even if

---

2.   Cambridge: Harvard University Press, 1975.

ethical (sensitization of top management) were a prime requirement, it would not be sufficient in itself to provoke responsive behavior in the corporation;" and that "...emphasis will inevitably fall on the implementation of pro-grams responsive to social needs rather than on the philo-sophical rationale for corporate responsibility."[4] Notice that Ackerman employs the phrase "social responsiveness" rather than "social responsibility." "Social responsiveness" reflects the notion of power rather than rights. "Corporate social responsiveness," states William Frederick, "refers to the capacity of the corporation to respond to social pressures."[5] In a later publication co-authored with the late Raymond Bauer, Robert Ackerman further claimed that responsibility "...places an emphasis on motivation rather than on perform-ance and that 'social responsiveness' is a more apt descrip-tion of what is essential."[6]

The more current position has gone a step further: social responsiveness is pro-active (*viz.,* active intervention) rather than reactive. Pro-action, which assumes a leader-ship role, requires some form of social scanning or social forecasting to anticipate social change. In *Private Manage-ment and Public* Policy[7] Lee Preston of State University of New York at Buffalo and James Post of Boston University pushed the reactionary notion further in proposing "public policy" in place of social responsibility. More recently, Rogene A. Bucholz published a textbook[8] on the external

---

3. *Ibid., p. 1.*

4. *Ibid., p. 4 and p. 10.*

5. University of Pittsburgh Graduate School of Business Working Paper No. 279, (1978), p. 6.

6. *Corporate Social Responsiveness: The Modern Dilemma,* (New York: Reston Publishing Co., 1976), p. 6.

7. Englewood Cliffs N. J.: Prentice-Hall, 1975.

8. *Business Environment and Public Policy* (Englewood

environment using the

> concept of public policy throughout as an integra-
> tive concept. Environmental influences are dis-
> cussed in terms of their impact on public policy
> rather than on the corporation directly, issues are
> discussed as public policy issues rather than social
> issues, and management's response to the changing
> environment of business is seen as participation in
> the public policy process rather than being viewed
> from the perspective of social responsibility. [9]

Furthermore, these authors prefer "social involvement" rather than "social responsibility" because the term "involvement" is "ethically neutral." Indeed, Lee Preston complained in a letter to *MBA* magazine that these questions are not ethical at all:

> References to ethics and morals generally suggest
> distinctions between good and bad, right and
> wrong, with respect to individual behavior.
> Important as such distinctions are--in all areas of
> personal life, both private and professional--they
> are not the key aspects of current managerial con-
> fusion or likely future change. On the contrary,
> the important questions are: What does society at
> large expect from corporate (and other) managerial
> units? And how can these expectations be ana-
> lyzed and dealt with in the process of managerial
> decision making? [10]

These are not "ethical" questions. They are analytical problems involving a combination of economic, political, social, legal, and managerial disciplines.

Cliffs: Prentice-Hall, 1982).

9.   Bucholz, p. xiii.

10.   November 1975, p. 13.

Rights and Power: Basis for Teaching

Business school courses on socio-ethical issues also reflected the changes in the demands of society upon corporations and their managers by using one or more of the following approaches to the topic:

1) Personal ethics of the manager (no corporate social policy);

2) Negative rhetorical challenge to the corporation (social criticism);

3) Positive social responsibility (involving corporate obligation);

4) Reactionary social responsiveness (ethically neutral);

5) Pro-active social responsiveness (non-ethical problem).

It should be noted that the first three approaches include the notions of rights and responsibility, both personal and corporate. The remaining two approaches imply the application of power, both reactive and pro-active, rather than a source of obligation derived from respecting the rights of the different segments of society.

The distinction between *rights* and *power* thus became crucial to the teaching of business and society courses. On the one hand, when the question of corporate involvement with segments of society relied upon the issue of rights, corporate obligations were founded upon ethical, or even legal, foundations. Regardless of the size and political clout of the interest group or economic disadvantage to the corporation, a right imposes a corresponding obligation on the corporation to respect that right. On the other hand, if the question of corporate involvement is limited to reacting to the power which different segments of society display, corporate obligations will be reactionary, depending upon size, political clout and other power-centered faculties of the interest groups. If interest groups do not gain power, lose their power, or lack initial power, corporations can legitimately deny any so-called social responsibility. Up to 1975 when my study on the teaching of social-ethical issues was published[11] courses on business and society stressed either rights or power as their conceptual frameworks.

Questionnaires were sent to 847 undergraduate and graduate programs listed in the 1972 Sigma Delta Pi Biennial Survey. Sixty-five percent responded. Sixty percent of the respondents (334) offered no special course on socio-ethical issues. (The use of "special" is to distinguish from those programs in which socio-ethical issues are included in every business course.) However, of those who offer a special course, almost 28% had offered a course for more than five years and almost 12% for more than ten years. For 40% of the respondents the special course on socio-ethical issues pre-dated Watergate; thus, it was more than a reaction to pressure from outside sources to "teach ethics."

The study also showed that the special course on socio-ethical issues followed one of two conceptual frameworks or general orientations:

1. *Values of participants* in socio-ethical decision-making: 18.5% of the courses followed this approach, which was *rights-related*.

2. *Implication of business activity for society*: 22.7% followed this approach, which seemed to be *power-related*.

The importance of a choice between these two conceptual frameworks becomes clearer in the following observations:

1) The course on socio-ethical issues has either a value-oriented framework based more-or-less on rights and justice (distributive) or has a response-related framework based more-or-less on the power of the firm and the power of the different segments of society.

----

11.   University of Virginia, 1975.

2)   The rights-oriented framework is usually taught out of philosophy or theology; the power-related framework is taught in business schools.

3)   The role of *ethics in business* has been assumed by philosophers; business school theorists now tend to approach corporate social responsiveness as ethically neutral. According to some (like Preston), personal ethics has no place in corporate social responsiveness. Indeed, a number of these theorists (*e.g.*, Buchholz) even prefer the terms "public policy" to social responsibility or to social responsiveness.

4)   Some progress towards developing a more acceptable conceptual framework seems to be appearing in those courses on business and society which have a team-taught methodology: *i.e.*, combining a philosopher with a business theorist in a course offered through the management department of the business school (or vice versa).

5) The personal values of the executive, in terms of resolving role conflicts, seem to have been relegated to case situations without providing a method or structure or format for resolving these problems. In a recent issue of *The Public Interest*,[12] *Peter Drucker warned us that* business ethics under the guise of social responsibility leads to casuistry--a disreputable form of problem-solving which lacks integrity and historically led to the term "jesuitical." Nonetheless, it appears that the opposite is occuring now; namely, that the emphasis on institutional ethics has almost preempted the role of the personal ethic of the individual executive or manager. The power-related framework of business theorists has even questioned the role of a personal ethic in business decision-making.   The power approach to socio-ethical issues has institutionalized once again the "corporate veil" which had been torn open during the reaction to Watergate: by closing the corporate veil under the pretense of social forecasting and similar techniques, society will not find out *who* is

---

12.   Spring, 1981.

exercising power--the gamesman, the organization man, or
the jungle fighter.

Perhaps what I am trying to say has already been said
by Charles Powers and David Vogel in *Ethics in the Education of Business Managers*[13] *in their distinction between professional and* managerial ethics. While I do not agree
entirely with their positions I am impressed with their
insight: Where as the profession is an instrument of the
practitioner on a one-to-one personal relationship, the man-
ager-- as an instrument of the organization--contributes
indirectly to the social good. For understanding the manager's ethical problems requires an understanding of the purposes of business institutions and constraints placed upon
them by society. The primary ethical assignment at this
stage is to ascertain when, and how, and which circumstances work together to make an agent morally rsponsible for a
given action. The challenge is not simply to know what
ought to be done but to specify who is responsible for doing
it.

CONCLUSION

1. The shift in business theorists from corporate
social responsibility to corporate social responsiveness
became the fork in the road towards different conceptual
frameworks for business ethics and corporate socio-ethical
issues.
2. Philosophers and business theorists *appear* to be
further apart in 1984 than in 1975.
3. Systems approach and scanning, social forecasting,
issues management and similar managerial functions are crucial to corporate social responsiveness but apparently have
little relationship to business ethics.

---

13.   Hastings-on-the-Hudson: The Hastings Center, 1980.

4.   Rights and justice (especially distributive justice)
are paramount in business ethics; power and its different
dimensions are intrinsic to corporate social responsiveness.
5.   The widespread interest in business ethics, social
responsibility and responsiveness, public policy, quality-of-
life management, public affairs and related aspects of corporate impact is reflected in many departments of colleges and
universities--not just in the business schools.   And there
are many indications that the interest in socio-ethical issues
will continue even in these changing times.

Alternate Contexts
for Business Ethics

A GUIDE FOR THE PERPLEXED:

AN ETHICAL MATRIX FOR THE MODERN MANAGER

James J. Valone

Managers want to develop some notion of what are morally acceptable practices and prepare guidelines and principles which can aid in ethical decision-making. In effect, they seek to develop their own ethical position. In forming their own position the hope is that they can learn from the different schools of thought, if not accepting one of them as their ethical home base. But managers, like others, can become baffled and frustrated with the smorgasbord of ethical theories. We can choose from among Utilitarianism, Relativism, Deontologism, Situationism, etc.

The difficulties are enhanced by the belief that there can be no single correct moral code. Yet to claim there is no single correct moral code is not to argue that there is no way to validate moral codes or philosophies against competitiors. While a certain amount of pluralism and toleration in matters of morality may be necessary and prudent, there is also the equally pressing need for managers to reaffirm their fundamental moral order. A perfect ethical position may be unattainable, but this is no reason to totally abandon the pursuit of a partial clarification of the values which characterize free activity, nor is it reason to abandon reflection on the nature of moral activity.

What follows is an analysis of some essential factors which must be considered and which are operating in any moral decision irrespective of one's ethical system and position. Such a matrix can serve to clarify the components in the moral decision-making process and supply a gauge to judge how adequate an ethical system is in accounting for these elements. More concretely, Aristotle and common wisdom teach that one ought to turn to the good person to discover what is moral and immoral. Concrete human models are chosen as the criterion for acting well, not so others can imitate their actions, but so we can learn the process of acting well. Analysis of the factors of moral activity furnish guidelines by which to judge who the good person is.

I. The Relativity of Each Situation

The character of human existence and the differences in moral values among people and cultures suggest that morality is relative. But despite its sensitivity to the contingent character of the human condition, relativism, no matter what its form, is not without its difficulties.

Perhaps the most apparent difficulty with the claims of relativism is that the variation in moral positions and cultures is not a compelling basis for taking up the relativist's position. Universal agreement or disagreement does not itself count as the criterion for universal and common moral principles. There is also a practical inconsistency in holding the position. No matter how convinced we may be of the relativity of all norms and standards of choice, we must nevertheless choose, which is always a manifestation of a preference.[1]

One could argue that the practical inconsistency notwithstanding, morality is clearly related to self-interests, personality, and society. But again it seems these relationships are not ones of necessity. Morality may have begun in the need for social harmony and cooperative living, but it does

---

1. cf. Henry Veatch's discussion of this problem with relativism. *Rational Man: A Modern Interpretation of Aristotelian Ethics* (Bloomington: Indiana University Press, 1962), pp. 37 ff.

not follow that every ethical rule is formed or performed
with the intent of supporting the social order. Moreover,
socially and personally useful acts are not necessarily
instances of ethical behavior. For example, there is no
moral necessity for the useful role of cab driver nor for the
existence of a credit system in the economy.

Articulation of the problems with ethical relativism does
not eradicate the variations in personalities, cultures, and
ethical positions, nor does it eliminate the relativistic dimension of every situation. Moral decision-making involves discovering what the moral thing to do is at *this* time and
under *these* particular circumstances. Any satisfactory
interpretation of morality must account for the relativity of
each situation and for the moral judgments found in all cultures and differing personalities.

The strength of relativism is to accept that the person
of practical wisdom cannot depend solely on knowledge of
moral principles. The moral individual must also depend on
concrete ends. Once the end(s) is chosen or given, the
task is to choose the means to achieve *this* end in *this* case
in respect to *this* end.

There is an art and skill, a practical wisdom, but this
too is not merely bound and subject to the contingencies of
the moment and the culture. This practical wisdom is
underpinned by our character as a human subject in a community, a character persisting throughout every situation.
Existential uniqueness of time, place, and personality does
not jettison our membership in the human community. Resolution of concrete moral issues affects the community of
ends. Even in the face of the relativity of each circumstance we bear the responsibilities of our humanity.

II.   The Distinction Between Understanding and Justification

The first component in the ethical matrix, relativity,
brings with it a corollary, the importance of the distinction
between understanding a moral act and justifying it. Justification and validation go beyond understanding. No matter
how sympathetic one is or how "understandable" an action or
set of actions is, moral validity must be anchored in accurate

judgment of the facts, and one must be willing to abide by the judgment and have others do so.

In short, it is important in any moral decision or development of a moral philosophy not to confuse the relevance of contending alternatives with their validity. The causal understanding and motivational understanding of an action is no normative justification for the behavior. One cannot and should not draw inferences about the ethical justification of an action in any simple way from the understanding of that action.

III.   The Consequences, Nature, and Motives of a Moral Act

Once we begin taking stock of important distinctions a number of other features of moral action present themselves for scrutinty. These factors include the consequences, motives, and nature of a moral act.

In determining whether an action is right or not, one needs to ask what its consequences will be. Ethicists dispute whether the rightness of an action rests exclusively on its consequences or not, but it certainly depends in part upon them. This dependency flows from the fact that the effects of an action are an integral part of its performance, if not temporally and/or intentionally, at least in the sense that the consequences owe their existence to the performed act.

Aside from consequences, the morality of an act is certainly influenced by the subject performing the act. An additional factor, then, is *whether* an act possesses a moral character and *what* this character is. This means determining *why* the agent performed the act and on whom or what the act was performed. Finally, factors relating to the act itself must be considered, including the *way* it is performed and the *time* and *place* of its performance.

Surely, different moral philosophies and various moral circumstances call for assigning varying weights to these features, but no moral position or judgment can afford to overlook any of these features.

IV.   Ends, Means, and the Hierarchy of Ends (Values)

Perhaps central among all moral distinctions is that between means and ends. Again, the place and importance assigned to the means and ends in moral activity varies. Nevertheless, a number of general points can be made which can serve as parameters in the ethical matrix.

First, the end or goal of any moral act has priority in the exercise of moral judgment. It is the end which shapes, defines, and totalizes human action. This does not mean, however, that the content of the end is known or can be known absolutely. Second, the means are relative to the end. Means have a reality of their own but they derive their value from the end to which they are means. Third, this basis and rootedness in the end issues in a sense of obligation and justification. Obligation is a sense arising from the end to be realized. Since choice is a concern with means to an end, moral justification turns on this relation in terms of the end sought. Fourth, there is a dialectical relation of means and ends in the concrete exercise of moral judgment. Every good in human history is an end and simultaneously a means for the good life.

But the importance of the distinction lies not in merely what we regard as an end, but on what grounds we prize it and what place it has in a hierarchy of values and objects. These grounds, of course, are determined by what we consider an end in itself and not merely as a means, e.g., wealth, power, happiness, or duty. The hierarchy and prioritizing of ends and values is equally significant in the means/ends schema and should likewise find a place in moral action and moral philosophy.

V.   The Moral Act as Free

Co-important with the preceding factors is an assumption that has remained unquestioned up to this point. Any discussion or reference to an act as having moral significance assumes the act to have been or as being the result of

free choice.   To take a completely deterministic stance is to
make non-sense of morality.   One cannot be held accountable
for what one is not in some way free to do or refrain from
doing.   Freedom means having some control and self-determi-
nation.   The free act is one which is dynamic and thereby a
response from within the agent; one that the person decides
for him/herself.

What can we say is the essential role of freedom in morality?   The most common response to this question is that
unless humans were free we could not justifiably praise and
punish others or ourselves.   Certainly praise and blame play
a role in morality, but they are not the center of the moral
situation.   What is even more basic is the human attempt to
achieve and realize possibilities which are regarded as best
for oneself and the world.   The moral task involves the discovery of what each of us is to make of ourselves and the
"world" in which we are engaged.   This human project is
what makes freedom essential, otherwise each of us could not
see ourselves and our world as having possible values and
alternatives, the realization of which depends on our choices
and decisions.

VI Responsibility for the Moral Act

Responsibility is the constant companion of freedom.
The origin of this term points to its meaning as an answer-
ability *for* a task defined in advance *to* the people for whom
the task is performed.   Responsibility is the consciousness
of being the incontestable author and source of an action or
event.

In order to make a beginning of characterising the
nature and parameters of responsibility, we take our cue
from Henry Veatch's work in this area.   Veatch explores this
topic by examining the major reasons for and sources of our
mistakes: ignorance, bad choices, bad luck and the force of

circumstances.[2]

The first of these categories, ignorance, faces us with the question of our responsibility for our foolishness. To unravel some of the complexities in determining to what extent we are responsible for our ignorance an analogy from the legal world will help. In the Western tradition of common law and civil law to plead ignorance of the law is no excuse whereas ignorance of the facts sometimes is. An example will help explain. Take the case of an engineer who works for a manufacturer of airplane parts. The firm in question has acquired a contract with the Air Force for a brake system of special design. Our engineer has been placed in charge of running the required tests and seeing that they meet the required standards. After testing the brakes under the required conditions the brakes are found inadequate proving the design to be faulty. The final report is doctored to ensure the contract and thereby misleading the Air Force as to the specifications of the brake tests and the safety of the system. In this fraud is the engineer responsible in any way even though there were superiors involved in determining the status and content of the final report?

Let us assume that knowing full well the dangers and consequences involved the engineer monitored the test without taking the appropriate measures to guarantee the existence of the required test conditions. Or let us say that under the pressure of making the contract good and out of fear and eagerness to please his superiors the engineer changes the results of the tests to read as if the brake system met the standard requirements. In the first case he is negligent and didn't bother to take the proper precautions and is thereby responsible. In the latter case his deceit certainly makes him responsible. In these kinds of situations the engineer is responsible. But what of the case where the engineer performs the required tests and records the results accurately even though the outcome will lead to redesigning the brake system or the loss of the contract,

---

2.   Veatch, pp. 125-179.

both resulting in huge financial losses for the company? Unknown to the engineer his superiors change the results to meet contract specifications. Since the engineer took all reasonable precautions and recorded his results honestly he could hardly be held legally responsible. He was ignorant of the facts. If we move to the moral sphere, the analysis would not be essentially different. If we are responsible it is because our ignorance is due to a lack of moral virtue, e.g., we are lazy, reckless, careless, negligent, or deliberately avoid the possibility of knowing the facts. Whenever we should know something or could have known but didn't take the time or effort to do so, we are certainly responsible for our mistaken actions.

But while ignorance of the facts *may* be an excuse, ignorance of the law is not. This also holds true for moral virtue; ignorance of the moral law is no excuse. This premise is somewhat of an embarassment to lawyers, legal theorists, and moral theorists since the explanation of it is not obvious. Although it is now an unpopular term this is what has been known as the natural law theory of morality. There are, in this conception, laws of human nature to which all are responsible. Without defending or analyzing the natural law theory, let us suppose there are recognizable moral norms which determine what the right life is for humans. How can all people be expected to know what they are? It seems that there are cases where the conditions of human life are such that anything like responsibility for ignorance of the so-called moral law of human existence cannot be fairly attributed to the individual involved.

However, it is easy to exaggerate the interference of these conditions in an absolute way in one's ability to judge proper from improper activity. Despite the differences in individual and cultural circumstances, the requirements of human excellence are discernable. Most of us have at least some idea of the kinds of claims which our human nature makes upon us. The criteria of bravery, honesty, or stupidity may vary, but the distinctions between bravery and cowardice, honesty and dishonesty, wisdom and folly will nevertheless be recognized and maintained almost universally. If all humans do have such powers of mutual appreciation, an ability to recognize and respond to human folly and excellence, the ignorance of those values and moral norms appropriate to human nature is an ignorance for which all of us are in some measure responsible.

Bad choices quite as much as ignorance may be the source of failures. Some of our ignorance is due to bad choices. We may be ignorant simply because we did not choose to take the trouble to learn. It seems true enough to say that when each of us chooses we choose only that which seems best at the time, but this does not mean we are choosing what we think or know is best. We sometimes know what the right thing to do is, or think we know, but we select the wrong alternative anyway. For these bad choices we are responsible.

Ignorance and bad choices aside, it appears that human success or failure is ultimately a matter of good luck or bad luck. Employing the legal analogy once again, the relevant questions in any legal situation have to do first with whether the circumstances were such as to leave the person any choice, and secondly, whether, assuming one had a choice, the choice was one that a reasonable person, or a morally good person might be expected to make in such circumstances. Adding to this, there are also those circumstances for which we are not responsible yet once thrown into them we are obliged to choose the lesser of the evils. In such circumstances we choose to perform undesirable actions not because we prefer them in themselves but because no better alternative seems open to us. As long as any choice is open to us, whether in a moral or merely legal context, our choices are ones for which we may properly be held responsible.

VII Human Nature and Morality

Discussion and analysis of moral activity involves both direct and oblique reference to human nature. As with the topic of freedom, there are continuing controversies among philosophers regarding the existence and character of such a phenomenon. Since there is always the danger of reifying what is existentially dynamic, much of the debate centers on the tendency to treat human nature as a thing or object. But these conceptual hazards should not overshadow the realities these concepts are meant to illuminate.

Human nature refers to those features, tendencies, capabilities, and conditions present wherever and whenever humans are present. But why study human nature and why is it important for moral activity? What is not understood cannot be managed intelligently. The status of moral values and what is good is a determination which we can make only when the self is examined so as to ascertain its essential features with respect to value. Basing morality on the realities of human nature will no more simplify life than it would eradicate moral struggle. All action is an intrusion on the future and into the unknown, making conflict and uncertainty normal characteristics. But morals founded on facts and the tendencies of human nature would at least derive guidance from this knowledge and secure available resources in their service. Knowledge of human nature enables us to traverse otherwise uncharted territory and find our way intelligently through the complexities of economics, politics, religious beliefs, etc.

The importance of what it means to be human and how best to live one's life is never so urgent than in those moments we attempt to or are forced to face the question of what our life means. No one sets out to simply waste his/her life. Such a goal makes no sense and that is precisely the point. Humans desire to lead a meaningful life, a life worthwhile and worth living. We are naturally coaxed to find out in some way what will best satisfy us, our ideals and aspirations. Life thrusts upon us this need to disclose the source of these ideals and aspirations. We return, therefore, to the relation between ethics and human nature, a relation long ago recognized in the Socratic motto, "Know Thyself."

VIII Self-Deception: The Apparent and the Real Good

Self-knowledge falls in the category of "easier said than done." Even when some discernment of right from wrong is correctly made, there is no guarantee that the person with this knowledge will choose what is good. The human capacity for self-deception complicates ethical decision-making and reflection on morality. In self-deception, as in lying, a truth is being hidden. But the situation is not entirely the same. Self-deception is a hiding of the truth from oneself rather than from another. *The duality of the deceived and the deceiver does not exist here.* Since the person deceived and the deceiver are one and the same person, one must know the truth which is hidden from oneself. In fact, the truth must be known very exactly in order to conceal it more carefully. The more traditional distinction between the apparent and the real good covers the same territory. We have the uncanny ability of making what is a known evil appear as a good or a lesser evil appear as the greater good. It is not too difficult to conjure up examples from our daily life, particularly those instances in which comfort and convenience win the day over the more difficult but more correct choice. Professionals who make illegal or questionable payoffs under the rubric of good business (i.e., leading to large contracts, more employment, better balance of payments, etc.) exemplify this form of consciousness.

The possibility of self-deception does not mean we must view each and every act as infiltrated by self-deceit. Yet moral philosophy can ill afford to overlook the realities and complexities of the human psyche. It is imperative to recognize the capacity for self-deception and determine the patterns and role of self-deception in moral action and development.

IX Passions and the Emotive Dimension of Moral Activity

Our next to last component in the ethical matrix, the human passions, has a checkered history in moral philosophy. The passions either suffer at the hands of rationalists or unduly receive attention when reason gets bad press. The affective dimension of man, in any case, must receive a balanced account in any moral philosophy. One's affective states are part of the very fabric of ethical matters. These states range from feelings and moods, to sentiments, temperament, and emotions. We can give an umbrella term to all these states and call them passions.

The common feature of our diverse human passions and

emotions is not that they tend to disturb the sane and intelligent conduct of life. Rather, our passions are the very
motive and emotive forces of our activity, moving us toward
what we need and what is beneficial and away from the
harmful, dangerous, and evil. Our passions help provide
our lives with meaning. The passions are *implicit* judgments
constitutive of our reality, giving it shape and structure.
Intelligence and feelings are unified; reflection and the passions are compatriots in the constitution of the world. The
implicit and immanent judgmental character of emotions signals the essential relation between reason and passion,
reflection, and emotion.

All the passions are important and all are more or less at
work in the course of moral activity. The emotions, however, are of special importance because they have a more
direct relation to a meaningful stimulus situation and are also
characterized by a set of physiological changes peculiar to
emotion. Emotions bring a concern for the world. The concern is not only with the way the world is but also with the
way the world ought to be. As a thrust into the future our
emotions are laden with the intention to act. The expression
of an emotion is generally an action, gesture, or utterance
that will satisfy the emotion. In moral indignation, for
example, injustice requires some effort at personal vindica-
tion and retribution.

Evaluation of our emotions exposes their intelligibility
and their purposive character. This is what may be termed
the proto-logic of our affective life, a logic which can be
rendered explicit through reflection. There is, however, a
normative sense in which emotions may be rational; those
that are appropriate and effective and do so well are
rational. But not all emotions are rational in this sense.
There are irrational emotions. Not all passions and emotions
are to be equally valued. We do not always do what we
want or what we feel like doing. None of us gives in to
every impulse. Common sense tells us that we must cancel
or postpone some of our wants and desires. As part of our
own *doings* we are responsible for our emotions and passions
to the extent they are the result of freely chosen behavior.
On what basis are we to detemine which emotions and passions to value? Emotions require some appeal to standards
since they involve implicitly value judgments. Our prere-
flective emotional experiences are often quick and

oversimplified, and sometimes disloyal to the facts of the circumstances.   And, perhaps of most importance, the evalua-
tive dimension of many of our emotions has a moral thrust.
The moral question is never "What do I feel?" but always
"What am I *doing* and why am I doing it?"   Emotions alone,
however, cannot account for obligation.   We cannot implore
emotions to answer the questions raised by our affective
states.   Our final element in the ethical matrix, reason, ush-
ers in the chief agent of direction for human action.

X Reason in Moral Activity

In everyday life we continually face questions of what
to make or do.   These concerns in common sense practices
employ intelligence besides habit, impulse, passions, convention, and caprice.   We commonly speak of living well as
opposed to ruining one's life.   None of us likes to think we
are a fool.   We want, at least, to think we are wise.

Yet, learning seems to have little bearing on how one
lives.   Perhaps Socrates was wrong in assuming self-knowledge was actually a matter of knowledge, that it is possible
for human beings through investigation and reflection to discover the way in which they should live.   A response to this
challenge plunges us into a brief examination of the role reason can play in moral activity.

Why is reason important to morality?   The very historical
character of human existence gives reason a role to play.
Bound to temporal conditions where each of us is affected by
the past and seeking ways to live the future, reason enables
us to determine and develop alternatives of behavior in light
of one's past and the possible future.   Reason allows us to
transcend the boundaries of the present.   Furthermore, each
of us is affected and influenced by those activities by which
we affect others and external circumstances.   Reason lets us
weigh the significance of one's acts on oneself.

Reason plays a constitutive role in distinguishing among
goals   that   ought   and   ought   not   to   be   pursued,
distinguishing among frustrations that are superficial and
ought to be avoided and those frustrations that cover up
fulfillments that should be pursued.   Reason is part of the

very network of moral experience, and moral experience is neither extrinsic to reason waiting to be disclosed by it nor is reason the a priori source of morality. The involvement of reason in human action and transactions makes them different than they otherwise would be. In fact, the world and our actions would not matter to us without the presence of reason. The capacity to grasp possibilities in human affairs accounts for the tension reason produces in moral decisions, a tension between what is, the world as given, and what this world *could be* and *ought* to be if the situation is to be consistent with the character of the human community.

The determination of principles and practices through reason and experience helps us get where we want to go. Intelligence can provide order and direction. Discernment of these principles enhances our chances of fulfilling our desires and achieving our goals. Without the knowledge of what it takes to be a truly human being, all the good intentions in the world will *not* make one's actions the actions of a good person. To do good means to act intelligently. Yet even with such understanding, one still needs moral virtues whereby one will actually want and come to choose actions which are requisite in an intelligent, examined life. Fully practical knowledge is present when the will to use a capacity is joined with that capacity and thereby one's judgment is made true with practical truth.

Conclusion

The litany of factors in the ethical matrix concluded, it seems prudent to inject a note of caution and reaffirm the message of the introductory comments. Schematizing the components of ethical decision-making should not cover up the fact that moral actions are not a checkerboard of these factors. Moral action is an integration of the needed and appropriate components. An analytic approach tends to distort the real character of moral existence and, if this tendency is acted upon, morality takes on the character of being restrictive and regimented. Managers cannot and do not, while under the pressure of decision- making and policy formation, rehearse this tapestry of components in all its detail. Nevertheless, business decisions often do in fact approach and embody such a matrix in an abbreviated and habituated form. Managers can and should habituate themselves to sound patterns of thinking and acting, and where time allows, take advantage of the benefits an ethical matrix can provide. We must not lose sight of the fact that reflective analysis is in the service of enriching our understanding and practice of an integrated moral character.

Needless to say, the previous analysis is neither complete nor likely to quiet the debates among competing schools of thought. Utilitarianism, Absolutism, Deontologism, Situationism, etc, will remain strong and effective forces in the community of discourse about morality. But managers will still have to make moral decisions and decide among these competing claims and the moral implications of each. The ethical matrix is offered as an additional way of grasping the significance and adequacy of contending moral philosophies. Moreover, the hope is that this brief characterization of the ethical matrix articulates something of a common ground for the continuing dialogue about moral activity.

Even though all we can claim to have done is indicate the factors that play a role in the moral person's decisions and increase awareness of the complexity of moral activity, this modest task is nonetheless crucial. Analysis of the ethical matrix brings attention to those factors important in any moral problem. To meet the moral demands of our existence and historical period we must develop our intellectual capacity to grasp the concrete moral significance of a situation as well as the principles embodied. The reflective efforts of moral theory aid in giving moral principles and values the meaningful efficacy of tools that can be employed in dealing with concrete situations.

EMBEDDED VALUES: PRELUDE TO ETHICAL ANALYSIS

William C. Frederick

What does science, especially social science, tell us about the ways in which values are formed within the life history of individuals, of organizations, and of culture generally? Without an answer to this question, as well as a willingness to employ it in ethical analysis, all attempts will fall short of touching the vital core of understanding needed for clarifying right and wrong, moral and immoral behavior.

Consider the following episodes. A construction worker who operates heavy equipment refuses a work assignment on grounds that legislatively mandated safety precautions and procedures have been ignored by the construction firm. After a long struggle with the company and his union to get the situation corrected, he is fired. He and his family suffer economically over a period of several years while the struggle is going on; after it is over, he has difficulty obtaining steady work, claiming that he has been "blackballed" throughout the construction industry.

In another instance, a woman is attracted to a sales job with a large newspaper, which holds out the prospect of an advancement into management ranks after a trial period. Although highly successful in her sales work, she encounters obstacles to the promised management job. Favorable assignments are given to others, her work is denigrated, and her superiors turn a cold shoulder to her insistence that she be evaluated for a managerial position. After years of frustration during which great organizational pressures are brought to bear against her, she leaves the organization and sues on grounds of sex discrimination. [1]

In both of these examples, we have an almost classic struggle between an individual and an employing organization, as each entity pursues its self-perceived rights amid a rising tide of recriminations and charges of unethical behavior, unjust outcomes, and the ultimate triumph of an unfeeling bureaucratic organization over the relatively weaker voice of humane reason. An ethicist is strongly tempted to assess such episodes in terms of the respective rights of the two entities, with a nod toward the utilitarian consequences that flow from the struggle, and to find a "solution" that incorporates a notion of social justice.

A social scientist, on the other hand, would be inclined to view contests of this type between individuals and their organizations as a manifestation of differential value commitments by the involved entities. The construction worker would appear to have ranked his own safety and that of his fellow workers at a high point on his personal value profile; the company and union appeared to downgrade safety relative to other values such as organizational loyalty, obedience to superiors' orders, and, by implication, economy of operations (that is, it would presumably be costly to comply fully with mandated safety standards). The woman sales representative's values appeared to encompass personal ambition, professional competence, social recognition, and a sense of accomplishment, while the newspaper and its managers were committed to the principles or values of organizational loyalty, preservation of the organizational status quo, unequal opportunities for women employees, and, if the sales representative is to be believed, a pathological desire to retaliate against a hapless employee who dared to challenge traditional procedures and rules.

In both cases, as well as in countless others that are similar, the values of one party are pitted against the values of another. What the social scientist sees is a clash of

---

1. Details of both cases are in Alan F. Westin, *Whistle-Blowing! Loyalty and Dissent in the Corporation* (New York: McGraw-Hill, 1981), pp. 55-68, 75-82.

values and an ensuing contest for the dominance of one set
of values over another.   More basic than the question of
whether the construction worker or the sales representative
have, or should be accorded, certain rights that the organization has disregarded--a debatable matter that can be the
subject of long and contentious reasoning--is the indisputa-
ble fact that each person manifests identifiable values and
value commitments that are at odds with equally identifiable
value-sets of their respective employing organizations.   Similarly, the complex and often indeterminate search for a balance between the reciprocal rights of the contending parties
such that a condition of social justice is established with
least harm to all parties provides a far less fundamental, as
well as a less satisfactory, explanation of the ethical dimensions involved than would a clear delineation of the origin
and reasons for the existence of the differential value commitments that led to and subsequently sustained the respective struggles.

To the question, Are not "rights" and "values" only different ways of referring to the same phenomena? the answer
is, "Not quite."   Rights are typically made to appear as
non-contextual (i.e., abstract) assertions of privilege.   Values, by contrast, are treated as behavioral traits, beliefs,
and intellectual orientations that are thoroughly and completely contextual in their origin and subsequent development.   Rights tend to be imposed upon a context of human
action, with the language itself being suggestive of a coercive or insistent privilege not to be gainsaid.   Values grow
out of a given context and its history, and the (moral) reasoning that employs values likewise has a life history that
can be, and has been in fact, observed and documented.
Values may and usually do become firmly embedded in individuals and organizations, and in that sense they resemble
the coercive, insistent, imperative character ascribed to
rights; but values are not usually assigned, and do not
deserve, a superior claim in the overall range of human
behavior traits that one often finds to be the case with
"human rights."   Values are a fact of human existence and
they play a key role in human behavior.   But aside from
their functional role, they are not put forward as being
"superior to" other behavioral phenomena such as attitudes
or motives.   It is possible to maintain that rights are deriva-
tive from values and therefore need to be seen in this

functional sense rather than from a perspective that assigns
a hierarchically superior meaning to them.

Our interest, then, in grasping the fundamentals of
value formation in individual persons, human organizations,
and the culture process generally turns us away from the
byways of philosophic discourse and toward explanations
provided by the social sciences. From such a perspective,
human behavior, including those features we call values and
valuation, appears to be a blend of culturological and ethological phenomena, activated and made dynamic through social
interaction, and focused in each one of us by a distinctive
patterning of traits that we call "personality."

1. The role played by culture in the formation of the
human person has long been acknowledged. The version
that appears to be closest to the mark is the view that we,
as humans, owe our humanity to an ability to engage in symbolic behavior.[2] Symboling is made possible by the compre-
hensively developed and elaborated neurological system, particularly the structure and functioning of the brain,
possessed by the human species alone. By virtue of this
unique advantage, humans have been able in the course of a
long evolution to learn more quickly, to store information in
memory more successfully, to imagine and foresee more com-
prehensively, to extend the use of tools further, and to
accumulate and transmit the species' fund of experience in a
more enduring fashion than has been possible for other
species. While this fund of human culture has thus been
amassed over the years, individual members of the species
unavoidably take their behavioral cues from it. Entering the
human community as a behavioral, motivational, emotional,
and intellectual cipher (according to this view), the infant is
encapsulated within the cocoon of human culture and tradition. We thus become what our culture defines for us as
falling within the scope of accepted belief and behavior. To
the extent that human culture contains within itself dicta of

---

2. Leslie A. White, *The Science of Culture* (New York:
Grove Press, 1949).

right and wrong behavior and belief, to that extent will the
individuals who are nurtured within its folds gain some
understanding (not always perfectly grasped or developed)
of the meaning of right and wrong. Due to the vastness of
time during which human evolution has taken place, as well
as to the diversity of circumstances under which humans
have lived, an enormously elaborated pattern of human culture and an equally configured design of rights and wrongs
present themselves to the observer of the human scene.
Human behavior and human values are thus said to be relative to time, circumstance, and culture pattern.

2. Less clear but not to be dismissed is the probable
role played by genetic factors in the determination of human
behavior.[3] Cultural determinists are inclined to denigrate
genetics on two grounds. Methodologically, it becomes difficult, perhaps impossible, to design and carry out experi-
ments that clearly separate and distinguish between genetic
and cultural influences; but even if that might be accom-
plished in such a manner to establish a role for genetics as
an influencing factor, culture's influence is said to be so
pervasive and all powerful that it overrides and renders relatively unimportant the underlying structure of genetically
determined behavior. Some ethologists are quick to acknowledge both the methodological difficulties and the dominance
of culture over genetic inclinations.[4] Yet the tantalizing, if

---

3. For an ethological view, see Konrad Lorenz, On
Aggression (London: Methuen, 1966) and Konrad Lorenz,
Evolution and Modification of Behavior (Chicago: University
of Chicago Press, 1965); and Irenaus Eibl-Eibesfeldt, The
Biology of Peace and War: Men, Animals, and Aggression
(New York: Viking, 1979). For other, related views, see
George H. Kieffer, Bioethics: A Textbook of Issues (Read-
ing, Mass.: Addison-Wesley, 1979), Chapters 1, 2, and 11;
and C. H. Waddington, The Ethical Animal (New York: Athe-
neum, 1961).

4. Eibl-Eibesfeldt, op. cit., Chapters 1, 6, and 7.

(for some observers) disturbing, possibility lingers that the human organic creature has not by any means been entirely cut off and insulated from the phylogenetic traits that brought the species to the threshold of culture. In a logical sense, such a leap beyond one's selectively adaptive phylogenetic origins would seem not only to violate the experiences of all other organisms and species but is not required as a condition of accepting a culturological explanation of human behavior. Anthropologists, though lacking a firm conceptual and experimental basis for incorporating biological elements into their cultural analyses, have not been entirely hostile to the idea[5] and as noted, ethologists have freely admitted that genetic dispositions necessarily mingle with learned cultural orientations. Child psychologists, particularly those concerned with the evolution of cognitive, emotional, and judgmental skills, also have acknowledged that biological maturation (a process heavily influenced by genetic factors) is unavoidably involved in an explanation of the developmental and normative behavior of children.[6] Again, in a logical sense, it seems unrealistic to assume that children, once having ceased "growing" in a biological sense, somehow or other turn off the genetic switches and thenceforth guide their behavior during adulthood by a strictly cultural compass. This kind of discontinuity is not generally observable in nature. The basic ethical implication of ethology is that

---

5. A careful reading of even such a confirmed cultural determinist ·as Leslie White reveals his recognition of the behavioral consequences of underlying organic (genetically determined) processes. See Chapters VI and VII of *The Science of Culture*.

6. For a comment on Piaget's position concerning the importance of biological factors in normative behavior, see John C. Gibbs, "Kohlberg's Stages of Moral Judgment: A Constructive Critique," in *Stage Theories of Cognitive and Moral Development: Criticisms and Applications*, Reprint No. 13, Harvard Educational Review (Cambridge, Mass., 1978), p. 43.

phylogenetically determined behaviors are selectively adaptive for the human species, thereby creating a fundament--an underlying structure--of ethical predispositions that contribute to the species' survival and continued growth. In this formulation, ethologists maintain that culturally-derived ethical systems that separate the species into contending societal groups may impel humans to engage in behavior that is contrary to their inherent, genetically determined (adaptive) predispositions. Hence, some learned cultural value systems may prove to be selectively mal-adaptive for the species considered as a whole.[7]

3. Socialization is the process by which individual persons acquire the culture of their group or society, including approved behaviors, attitudes, motives, and values. According to anthropologists and sociologists, socialization does not operate willy-nilly. Rather, we are socialized into an existing structure of roles, role behaviors, organizations, and institutions.[8] From the perspective of the individual person, there is a "something" that is "there" which we are expected to learn about and to become successful in functioning within. That is the meaning of "becoming an adult." The process is not easy or lacking in pain, as most parents (and their children) can testify. Well known is the fact of diversity in social structures that is observable from society

---

7.   Eibl-Eibesfeldt, *op. cit.*, pp. 188-196; Kieffer, *op. cit.*, pp. 38-39 and Chapter 11. See also Waddington, *op. cit.*, and H. J. Eysenck, "The Biology of Morality," in Thomas Lickona, ed., *Moral Development and Behavior: Theory, Research, and Social Issues* (New York: Holt, Rinehart & Winston, 1976), pp. 108-123.

8.   Ralph Linton, *The Study of Man* (New York: D. Appleton-Century, 1936), Chapters VII and VIII; Ralph Linton, *The Cultural Background of Personality* (New York: D. Appleton-Century, 1945), Chapter III; and Florence R. Kluckhohn and Fred L. Strodtbeck, *Variations in Value Orientations* (Evanston, Ill.: Row, Peterson, 1961).

to society and from one era to another. Equally well established are the diversity and relativity of the value-sets that
are found in social structures. An individual's acquired values, and the manner in which he/she employs them in moral
reasoning, are largely a function of the particular social
structure into which that person has been inducted from
childhood on.

4. Value formation and socialization to moral reasoning
that occur in the life cycle of individual persons have been
elucidated by child psychologists, sociologists, social psychologists, and anthropologists.

Jean Piaget and Lawrence Kohlberg tell us that individuals develop their moral reasoning capacity by progressing
through a series of "stages" or stair-steps beginning in
infancy and continuing on into early (and perhaps middle)
adulthood.[9] These stages are distinguished from one another
by the principal justifications given for, or used by, an
individual in assessing a situation that involves ethical
choices. According to this view, we move continuously and
invariantly from an ego-centered to a group-centered ethic,
from a specific to a generalized concept of morality, from an
externally imposed authoritarian source of moral reasoning to
one based on internalized, self-principled notions of justice,
and (in the "ideal" case?) from societally-bound moral systems of reasoning to moral concepts embracing humankind at
large within a broad cosmos. This sequence has been
observed in all cultures and is in some sense independent of
the specific content and meaning assigned to right and
wrong behavior by a particular society's cultural traditions.
To reach the higher stages of moral reasoning is to have

---

9. Jean Piaget, *The Moral Judgment of the Child* (New
York: Free Press, 1965); and Lawrence Kohlberg, "Moral
Development," *International Encyclopedia of the Social Sciences,* Volume 10 (New York: Crowell Collier & Macmillan,
1968), pp. 483-494; and Lawrence Kohlberg, "Moral Stages
and Moralization: The Cognitive-Developmental Approach,"
in Lickona, *op. cit.,* pp. 31-53.

escaped the strictures imposed on one in childhood and adolescence and early adulthood by specific portions of the
social structure, thus becoming in some cases an admired (as
well as perhaps a villified) moral leader capable of seeing the
human moral predicament writ large within the totality of
human experience.   Few persons, according to Kohlberg,
advance this far; in fact, he finds that most remain at the
fourth, law-and-order, stage of moral reasoning, with stage
five, six, and seven populations becoming increasingly
sparse.
    The important sociological finding is that adult, as con-
trasted with childhood, socialization concerns itself less with
values and motives than with behavior.[10] In a sense, society
seems to "give up" on changing a person's values once he/
she has passed through a society's basic socialization process
and attained the status of adulthood.   For grownups the
problem becomes one of finding a niche (or perhaps a whole
series of niches) within the social structure where one's values are compatible with those that are part of the roles, role
behaviors, organizations, and institutions comprising the
social structure.   Within varying degrees of flexibility and
tolerance, most societies manage to attain at least a "rough
fit" or a "match" between the values inculcated through
childhood socialization and the values embedded in that society's social structure.   Those for whom this socialization
process failed may be relegated to special institutions--pris-
ons and mental hospitals are two types--where re-socializa-
tion may or may not be attempted.   By and large, though,
values-socialization--including the learning of proper behavior and of how to reason in right-and-wrong terms--tapers
off remarkably once adulthood has been achieved.
    Milton Rokeach and his followers have produced another
body of knowledge that gives useful insights into value

---

10.   Orville G. Brim, Jr. and Stanton Wheeler, *Socialization after Childhood: Two Essays* (New York: John Wiley,
1966).   See also Orville G. Brim, Jr., "Adult Socialization,"
International Encyclopedia of the Social Sciences, Volume 14,
op. cit., pp. 555-562.

formation as manifested in individual persons.[11] Value profiles that reflect a person's preferred ordering of a set of
terminal and instrumental values have been gathered, analyzed, and compared for various populations; and correla-
tions of these profiles with various demographic characteristics have been made. From this work it is apparent that the
total number of values held by all people everywhere is relatively small, that they rank them differentially within varying societal contexts, that value change is initiated when a
person perceives an inconsistency between one's self-concep-
tion and an ordered array of socially-approved values, and
that value change in the sense of a reordering of one's value-set may occur from time to time but that the amount of
value change that occurs over the life cycle tends to be
modest and (as demonstrated in one study)[12] occurs to a
greater extent in younger than older persons. Some values,
it is argued, are "higher" (he seems to mean "better") than
others that are "lower" (i.e., "less good") according to their
ability to provide a person with ego-defensive, socially-ad-
justive, and self-actualizing experiences.[13] Additionally, it is
proposed (arguably, I would think) that value change in
individual persons can occur only in a direction that moves
that person toward a high ranking for the values of freedom, equality, and a world of beauty, such that no person
can be moved against the grain of her/his own self interest
or self esteem within a given societal context.[14]

5. We are brought, then, to the following set of

---

11. Milton Rokeach, *The Nature of Human Values* (New
York: Free Press, 1973) and Milton Rokeach, *Understanding
Human Values: Individual and Societal* (New York: Free
Press, 1979).

12. Rokeach, *Understanding Human Values*, Chapter 7.

13. Rokeach, *The Nature of Human Values*, pp. 16-17.

14. *Ibid.*, pp. 328-329.

conclusions about values and value phenomena generally:

  a. Values and valuing behavior are sociocultural phenomena, conditioned by genetic predispositions that
  are selectively adaptive for the human species.

  b. A society's social structure is a repository of
  right-wrong phenomena, providing ethical behavior
  guidelines for individuals who are socialized into it.
  Penalties are imposed on those who fail to heed these
  ethical orientations.

  c. Value commitments are formed primarily in childhood, adolescence, and early adulthood, with relatively little change occurring in later life. Some kind
  of "value formation ceiling" is observable, whether
  one speaks of value rankings or the manner of moral
  reasoning employed. Few appear to go beyond this
  ceiling, once adulthood is achieved.

  d. Value change *for an individual person* may be initiated when a sense of self-dissatisfaction emerges
  from observing an inconsistency between expected
  (socially approved) behavior-and-belief and one's own
  value preferences. [15]

  e. Value preferences and modes of moral reasoning
  evolve toward, but do not usually attain, progres-
  sively universal, abstract, generalized, humanistic,
  and cosmic status. [16] A strong implication is that societal systems impose limits on the ability and

---

15. *Ibid.*, Chapters 8 and 12.

16. Lawrence Kohlberg, "Continuities and Discontinuities
in Childhood and Adult Moral Development Revisited," in
Kohlberg & Turiel, eds., *Moralization, the Cognitive Development Approach* (New York: Holt, Rinehart & Winston,
1973), Chapter 45.

willingness of individual persons to exceed the value
orientations and ethical principles embedded in the
social structure.

6. If we seek knowledge of how these general processes
of value formation manifest themselves within the business
and management sphere, the work of two scholars is particularly useful.

George England and his followers have described the
value characteristics of managerial behavior, demonstrating
that distinctive types and directions of behavior are a function of a given manager's value preferences, that different
societal and cultural traditions produce differential patterns
of values in managers, and that it is possible to distinguish
between managers and groups of managers on the basis of
their orientation toward pragmatic, moralistic, affective, or a
mixture of the three types of evaluation.[17] These studies
also tell us that only some, not all, of a manager's total value-set is brought to bear as organizational decisions are
made: some values are directly operative; some are intended
to be but may be submerged to other contextually determined
operative values; others are adopted values somewhat
removed from personal preference but capable of being activated by situational (organizational) factors; and still others
are weak values falling within the manager's overall philosophic outlook but not often actually employed.

American managers' values, it turns out (probably to no
one's surprise), are operatively oriented toward pragmatic
considerations, acceptance of organizational goals, competence, realization of the importance of other reference
groups (e.g., labor unions), and achievement; with humanistic orientations being intended, not operative, values; and
an outright rejection of organizational egalitarianism. One
can conclude from England's studies that managers, like
other societal actors around them, have been subjected to a

---

17. George W. England, *The Manager and His Values*
(Cambridge, Mass.: Ballinger, 1975).

socialization process that has driven or channelled them in
the direction of these kinds of value preferences rather than
some others.

The process by which these managers and their values
have found their way into business organizations has been
described by a number of scholars, but the work of Neil
Chamberlain is especially worthwhile as a model of how a
value consistency is established and enforced between individual and organization.[18] The story is reasonably familiar.
Each firm exhibits a "strategy-set" (others have referred to
such sets as "corporate culture") which is to some extent a
function of the personal value preferences of its primary
managers. Organizational norms and values are derived from
this strategy-set. Both strategic (planning) decisions and
routine (operating) decisions flow from and are consistent
with the organization's norms and values. Organizational
behavior and performance appraisals also are carried out
with reference to the firm's accepted norms and values.
Neither behavior nor policy can wander far from the directions embedded in the company's strategy-set or culture. A
recent article describes the outcome of some attempts to
change a company's directions without heeding the constraints of its culture.[19]

Chamberlain also tells us, as have many others before
him, that business firms pursue a generalized objective of
profit and that this quest conditions the nature and character of a company's culture. It is a matter over which the
firm exercises little or no discretion. Being in business
means pursuit of profit. It is the chief goal, the highest
good, the primary value, firmly and deeply embedded in the
company's culture.

But unlike others who have been willing to leave the

---

18.   Neil W. Chamberlain, *Enterprise and Environment*
(New York: McGraw-Hill, 1968), Chapter 4.

19.   "Corporate Culture: The Hard-to-Change Values
that Spell Success or Failure," *Business Week*, October 27,
1980, pp. 148-160.

matter there, Chamberlain takes the analysis out into the broader realms of society and culture--out to the locus of value formation that runs through the culture process generally.[20] Thus, we are able to link up what we know of values-socialization that operates within the life cycle of individual persons with the perceived value preferences of their organizations. The conclusion is not surprising: both firm and individual manager are constrained by the society's dominant value-sets. The quest for profit or any other organizational goal is heavily conditioned by prevailing societal and cultural values. Not only are managers within the firm limited in what they can or wish to do by their own embedded personal value systems and the equally embedded value systems of the organization itself, but the entire firm is constrained by the society's long ingrained and widely accepted value systems that have brought it to this point in its evolution. One might refer to this situation as a triple value bind: human action in the value sphere is thrice bound, each time by the outcome of distinct though interrelated values-socialization processes: one occurs within the individual person, one within organizations, and one within the culture.

(One needs, at this point, to pursue the analysis of how organizational and societal value-sets are related to one another. Of particular significance is the question of overlap and consistency between the two, when contrasted with separation and competition between value-sets. Chamberlain sees overlap and mutual reinforcement between American values and corporate values outweighing competition and conflict, with the dominant value pattern yielding only incrementally to variant value preferences being expressed by diverse interest groups.[21] But these matters cannot be

---

20. Neil W. Chamberlain, *The Place of Business in America's Future: A Study in Social Values* (New York: Basic Books, 1973).

21. Neil W. Chamberlain, *Remaking American Values* (New York: Basic Books, 1977).

pursued further in this paper.)

Having now laid down the foundations of social science knowledge about values, value formation, and the patterning of values within organizational and societal structures, let me now turn to consider the more traditional, philosophic approach to business ethics. One notable fact stands out from the beginning: standard philosophic ethicians pay little or no attention to the insights and perspectives that have been developed by social scientists. A widely used text on business ethics has no mention of Piaget, Kohlberg, Rokeach, or England, although there is brief acknowledgement that ethical notions first appear in our lives during childhood and that they come to us from the society.[22] Three reports on the teaching of business ethics have been circulated nationally in recent years; none of the model curricula, the recommended bibliographies, or the discussion of various ways to approach the teaching of business ethics makes any reference to the major research on value formation, moral development, or managerial values.[23]

There is a decided tendency for standard ethics theory to impose abstract and logically consistent categories of philosophic discourse upon the field of business and management

---

22. Tom L. Beauchamp and Norman E. Bowie, eds., *Ethical Theory and Business* (Englewood Cliffs, N.J.: Prentice-Hall, 1979), p. 1.

23. Richard T. De George, *Moral Issues in Business: An Outline of a Course in Business Ethics* (Lawrence, Kas.: University of Kansas, 1979); *Report of the Committee for Education in Business Ethics*, Sponsored by a grant from the National Endowment for the Humanities, June 1, 1977 - May 31, 1980; Charles W. Powers & David Vogel, *Ethics in the Education of Business Managers* (Hastings-on-Hudson, N.Y.: The Hastings Center, 1980). Of these three, only the latter acknowledges the importance of explicitly introducing the notion of institutionalized values and corporate "character" or culture into business ethics courses; see p. 53 and footnote 59 on p. 71.

action without considering the societal, cultural, and ethological factors involved. As such, it is a good example of
culture-binding, for its analytic categories, even though
derived from a long tradition of philosophic thought, reflect
the value orientations of a selective (narrow) band of cultural experience. Because it does not incorporate the goals,
purposes, functions, and ends of value formation or of moral
reasoning understood as culturological and ethological phenomena, standard ethics theory can make only limited contact
with or contributions to the genuine ethical/value issues and
dilemmas that confront managers, business professionals, and
their organizations.[24]
    A danger is that, being culture-bound, standard ethics
theory may simply serve either (1) to reinforce the dominant
value systems embedded in the prevailing culture or (2) to
avoid a true confrontation and analysis of a society's values
that do not serve a positive (i.e., selectively adaptive)
human purpose or experience. Given time and space limitations of this essay, these two charges will have to stand as
simple assertions rather than proved fact, but let me draw
the distinction between a social science and a philosophic
approach to ethics by returning to the plight of the construction worker and the sales representative.
    These two whistle blowers are symbols, as well as
agents, of social value change occurring in American society.
They act as channels through which differential values and
value orientations flow and are expressed in their respective
companies. In effect, our society has begun to rank-order
occupational safety and equal occupational opportunity relatively higher than formerly, but these new value orientations
are not firmly embedded in the social structure. The

---

    24. Steps are being taken by some philosophic ethicians
to acknowledge the importance of social science perspectives
in their discussion of business ethics, and to see ethical
issues within the broader realms of society and culture.
See, for example, Manuel Velasquez, *Business Eth-
ics:Concepts and Cases* (Englewood Cliffs, N.J.: Prentice-
Hall, 1982).

counter values that *are* in place are economy of operation and hierarchical control by males. Within the scope of traditional moral reasoning, the managers of the two firms are "morally correct" in insisting that embedded organizational values take precedence. By what (other) warrant should they depart from these embedded values? Careful socialization has brought them to this point of moral understanding. Would not a reckless abandonment or subjective interpretation of these organizational values be likely to bring on a state of social disorder generally, as well as isolating the two firms from the profit-oriented value-sets that enable them to function and survive within the prevailing social structure?

When the bell of social-value change tolls within the halls of a given firm, should the firm assume it tolls for all or for it alone? How should it answer the summons? How can it know whether a complaining employee or group of employees, or an external interest group, is simply a poorly socialized person/group (a "troublemaker") or whether the complainants are riding the crest of a swelling wave of social-value change? (General Motors once faced this question with Ralph Nader, a then unknown and obscure New England lawyer, and wound up giving the wrong answer.)

The heralds of social-value change--in this case the construction worker and the woman sales representative--are typically treated harshly, much as the king's messenger who, having brought bad tidings, was promptly executed. But they, too, are the products of a long socialization process who have been brought to this point of values confrontation by a different route and who are now marching to a drummer whose moral cadence is dissonant with respect to the dominant chords of organizational loyalty and fealty. How expect the herald to act differently, when driven by a value-set firmly embedded in personality and being?

Clearly, the behavioral and socialization realities on both sides lead unavoidably to confrontation and clash of embedded values. Exhortation directed toward either side is notably ineffective. Each party digs in--one for a prolonged siege, the other for guerrilla warfare. Moral brickbats fill the air.

Now enter the philosophic ethician, speaking the voice of sweet reason and urging the adoption of abstractly attractive ethical principles and categories. As well ask Niagara to

stop falling or the salmon to stop spawning. Embedded values *will drive* organizations and individuals along certain
pathways. Neither drive is likely to be deflected by an
appeal to philosophic reason or wisdom, however attractive
the alternatives may appear to be. Here we find the real
difference between a philosophic and a social science
approach to ethical analysis. The latter deals with the reali-
ty--the observed fact--of value conditioning within a sociocultural context, not with the wishfulness that humans committed to one set of values would yield to another, more
attractive, set or to the moral reasoning or principles inher-
ing in philosophic categories. For social science, the locus
of the ethical problem is in the value systems that drive
individuals, organizations, and societies along certain pathways and toward certain destinations and to reason ethically
in certain ways and according to certain culturally- and
genetically-induced principles. For this reason, most ethical
problems, issues, and situations have an *a priori*, not an *a
posteriori*, character.

Given these differences, then, how might we direct our
thinking if we are to marry the best of both philosophy and
social science in the service of greater ethical understanding
of business? My answer would run along the following lines.

From social science we need to accept and further
develop an understanding of the major value orientations
embedded by accumulated experience and genetic predisposi-
tion in the human culture process--the value channels that
have directed human culture to this point in its long evolution. We need to focus upon and highlight those value orientations that have proved to be the most adaptive and the
most liberating of human potentialities. We shall have a
truer picture of the ethical dilemmas, as well as the ethical
possibilities, faced by organizational actors if we grasp the
grim truth that a largely unyielding socialization process
leads the actor and the organization to perpetuate value orientations beyond their control which are mal-adaptive in
their cultural function and purpose, while simultaneously
nourishing other value principles capable of carrying both
parties toward selectively adaptive goals.

What can philosophy, particularly applied ethics theory,
contribute? Rather than imposing upon this confrontation of
competing and clashing value systems a set of abstract cul-
ture-bound analytic categories--utility, rights, duties,

obligations, justice--and asking culture (and managers) to
yield to reason, philosophy can perform a more important
function. It can refurbish its analytic categories by relating
them to those cultural and genetic processes that lead to
value formation in individuals, social groups, and human culture generally. Utility, rights, and justice contain hints of
value orientations and moral principles that have proved, in
the course of cultural evolution, to be more selectively adaptive than their opposites. If ethicians could, and would,
help to identify and highlight the somewhat shadowy value
orientations that lurk behind their principal categories of
discourse, a more operational--if perhaps more painful and
controversial--ethics/values paradigm could emerge.

Organizational actors--managers and whistle blowers
alike, along with all others between these extremes--might
then have in full view--thanks to social science--the panoply
of possibilities and limitations created and sustained by culture. They might also have--thanks to philosophy--a rea-
soned way, not *out* of the grip of cultural reality, but
rather a way to understand how actors and their organizations might achieve those adaptive value orientations embedded (but still partially concealed) within the principal analytic categories of utility, rights, and social justice.

My essay leaves many questions unanswered. My choice
of language sometimes implies a rigid and unyielding outcome
to the values-socialization process, but clearly values change
over a person's life cycle and within organizations. What
stimulates, governs, and nourishes these changes? Are
there ways to break through the values-socialization ceiling
which seems to be imposed on individual and organization
alike? Must whistle blowers alone bear the brunt of social-
value change? Can the decisions of pragmatic managers be
deflected into more humane organizational purposes without
jeopardizing the adaptive gains made possible by large-scale
undertakings?

No enduring answer to these questions is possible absent
an understanding of the values and valuation processes
embedded in persons, organizations, and culture. From that
base, and that base only, can ethical analysis proceed on its
difficult quest for moral clarity.

KOHLBERG AND BUSINESS ETHICS

William Y. Penn, Jr.

For over two decades Lawrence Kohlberg of Harvard University has been doing sustained and illuminating cross cultural research into the way moral reasoning develops in children, adolescents and adults.[1] He has provided a model

---

1. Over the past ten years there have been significant advances both in Kohlberg's theory and in the scoring system for identifying moral stages. For a current formulation of the theory, a review of the cross-cultural research, and a response to major critics of the theory, see L. Kohlberg, C. Levine, A Hewer, *Moral Stages: A Current Formulation and Response to Critics* (Basel; New York: Kager, 1983). For an excellent general introduction see, R. H. Hersh, D. P. Paolitto, J. Reimer *Promoting Moral Growth, From Piaget to Kohlberg*, Second Edition (New York: Longman, Inc., 1979). All references to *Promoting Moral Growth* in this essay are to the first edition. For a comprehensive introduction to the history of the scoring system and to the philosophical and theoretical issues underlying the measurement of moral judgment see A. Colby and L. Kohlberg, *Measuring Moral Judgment*, Vol. I (Cambridge: Cambridge University Press, in press). Much of Kohlberg's own work formerly available only through journals or the Center for Moral Education at Harvard, is now available in Lawrence Kohlberg, *The Philosophy of Moral Development* (New York: Harper and Row, 1981) and L. Kohlberg, *The Psychology of Moral Development*

for moral education which is respectful of the pluralistic values of modern societies.[2] His research provides substantial
evidence that there is an innate six stage developmental pattern of moral consciousness common to all human beings.[3]
(For a definition and enumeration of these stages, the reader
is referred to Appendices I & II.) While the longitudinal
sample upon which he based his original research was small
(consisting of 58 American males, half upper middle class,
half working class), there are now over 1,000 studies which
support the correctness of his theory.[4] To a large degree

(Harper and Row, 1983).

2. See Lawrence Kohlberg, "Stages of Moral Development
as a Basis for Moral Education," in *Moral Education*, eds. C.
M. Beck, B. S. Critenden, and E. V. Sullivan, (New York:
Newman Press, 1971), pp. 23-92.

3.   Although much of Kohlberg's work has reference to
six stages of moral reasoning, the sixth stage has been
dropped from his scoring system.   This has been done
because the longitudinal data have not provided the empirical
material "necessary to a) verify our hypothesis or b) construct a detailed scoring manual description which would
allow reliable identification of the sixth stage." Kohlberg,
Levine, Hewer, *Moral Stages*: *A Current Formulation and
Response to Critics*, p. 60. Kohlberg does not seem to
doubt that there is stage 6 moral reasoning. However, neither he nor his co-workers have ever encountered it apart
from individuals with formal philosophical training. If Kohlberg's argument as to the superiority of Stage 6 over the
other five stages of moral reasoning is correct, it supports
the traditional claim that formal philosophical training is necessary for an individual to attain the highest level of human
ethical wisdom.   It is worth noting that out of the original
longitudinal sample of 58 individuals, the only subjects who
reached Stage 4 or higher were individuals with a college
degree.

4.   For a review of the research see James Rest, "Moral-

the results and implications of his research have either been ignored or inadequately understood by educators preparing courses in ethics for adults and professionals. For instance, in the *Report of the Committee for Education in Business Ethics* (CEBE Report), prepared by representatives from six major universities, there is no indication that any use was made of the important data discovered by Kohlberg and his associates regarding the facts of moral development.[5]

In this essay, I wish to share my perceptions and the perceptions of an older than average and international group of MBA students on the practical value of a business ethics course which made extensive use of Kohlberg's theory. The course was offered as an elective in the MBA program at St. Edward's University in the Spring term 1980. Twenty-five of twenty-seven students completed the course. Of these twenty five, eight were international students. Four of these were from Nigeria, one from Italy, one from Jordon, one from the Philippines and one from Venezuela. Three of the class were retired field grade military officers pursuing second careers in business. Most of the class members were persons already well into professional careers in business,

---

ity," in (J. Flavel, E. Markman, vol. eds.) *Cognitive Development*, Vol. III in (P. Mussen, gen. ed.) *Handbook of Child Psychology* (New York: Wiley & Sons, 1983), pp. 556-629.

5. The CEBE Report was the result of a study funded by NEH from 1977-1980, and is available through the American Philosophical Association. The participating institutions were California State University at Long Beach, Northwestern University, University of Delaware, University of Minnesota/Morris, University of Pennsylvania, The Wharton School, and the University of Pittsburgh. There is a great deal of valuable material in the report. However, had the analytical tools provided by Kohlberg been utilized I strongly suspect that the students at The Wharton School would not have found the course offered there "a 'soft' course which contributed little to their analytical skills and understanding of complex issues." CEBE Report, p. 17.

government and the military.   The average age was thirty-
five.
     Two principal objectives in   using Kohlberg's theory
were, first, to assist students in developing the analytical
skills necessary to make sense of the various ways people
actually reason about moral issues, and second, to develop
skill in applying what Kohlberg terms "post-conventional"
moral reasoning" to case studies in business.
     Central to Kohlberg's theory is the thesis that specific
individual attitudes about moral issues are not the product of
irrational, purely emotional factors, but are due to the
interaction between assumptions of fact and nonfactual cognitive moral assumptions.[6] This thesis requires one to draw
upon a distinction similar (but not identical) to the distinction between what is and what ought to be first clearly made
by the 18th century empiricist David Hume.[7] The point of
similarity between Kohlberg and Hume is the agreement that
nonmoral premises, i.e., assumptions about what is, do not
of themselves logically entail a moral conclusion, i.e., a conclusion about what ought to be.   The point of the difference
is that Hume regards the foundations of morality as non-ra-
tional while Kohlberg does not.   The point of the distinction
drawn by Kohlberg between assumptions of fact and nonfactual cognitive assumptions is not that assumptions of fact are
irrelevant to moral conclusions, but that to understand correctly an individual's moral conclusion, it is necessary to
understand both his view of the facts and his understanding
of how human affairs ought to be governed.   It is a claim
about the relevant facts together with a general understanding of how human affairs ought to be governed which logically generate a concrete moral judgment, i.e., a judgment

---

6.   L. Kohlberg and D. Elfenbein, "The Development of
Moral Judgments Concerning Capital Punishment," *American
Journal of Orthopsychiatry* 45(4), July 1975, p. 617.

7.   David Hume, *A Treatise on Human Nature*, Book III,
Part I, Section 1, ed. L. A. Selby-Bigge (London: Oxford
University Press, 1968) pp. 469-70.

about what ought or ought not to be done.

For example, to understand correctly someone's attitude towards the morality of capital punishment, it is necessary to understand both his assumptions about the facts (e.g., whether capital punishment is in fact a deterrent to murder) and his assumptions about the moral justification of the punishment (e.g., whether it is understood primarily in terms of retribution -- an eye for an eye, social utility -- the greatest good for the greatest number, or inalienable individual rights). The individual who is convinced that capital punishment does deter acts of murder and that the moral purpose of such punishment is to protect society is very likely to believe strongly in capital punishment. In contrast, the individual who is convinced that it is not a deterrent, but who shares in the moral assumption that the purpose of such punishment is to protect society is likely to be opposed to it. In this case, the individuals share common moral assumptions but arrive at different moral conclusions because they have a different understanding of the facts. In such a case, the basis of their disagreement is on factual rather than on strictly moral grounds.

The exact relation between the factual and the moral components in moral judgment is often exceedingly complex since the moral assumptions also affect what facts are regarded as important. Thus, for an adult who holds a retributive conception of punishment, the only relevant fact is likely to be whether the individual committed an act legally defined as murder. Such a person would find evidence as to the ineffectiveness of capital punishment as a deterrent to murder irrelevant, while a person who holds to a social utility conception of punishment could not logically ignore the relevance of such facts.

Given the interaction between assumptions of fact and moral assumptions in determining specific moral judgments, all ethical disagreement can be reduced to the following three categories: 1) disagreement about moral assumptions, 2) disagreement about factual assumptions, 3) disagreement about both moral and factual assumptions. Failure to attend to the importance of the moral component in addition to the factual, leads to what has been called "the naturalistic fallacy," i.e., the fallacy of assuming that one can logically derive moral conclusions from factual assertions alone. Depending on whether the basis of a disagreement is

predominantly moral or predominantly factual, different methodologies are required rationally to resolve the dispute. If
the dispute is essentially moral, no amount of facts can
resolve it.

Required for attaining rational consensus on disputes
which are essentially moral are: 1) a methodology which
enables one to identify the structure of the moral reasoning,
and 2) a systematic way to assess the moral adequacy of that
reasoning. Kohlberg's theory meets these requirements.

Kohlberg's research focuses on the structural and developmental relation between the various cognitive moral
assumptions which empirical research has shown to be present in people's moral reasoning. He argues that these nonfactual cognitive components are not culturally derived but
"are best understood as deriving from particular stages in
moral reasoning in a developmental sequence validated
through twenty years of research."[8] This research has
resulted in substantial evidence that these stages are culturally universal[9] and "qualitatively distinct structures (which
form) an invariant sequence."[10] The theory predicts that
since the stages are structural wholes, there will be internal
consistency of moral reasoning across different moral problems, i.e., "generality of stage usage across moral issues or

---

8. Kohlberg and Elfenbein, "The Development of Moral
Judgments Concerning Capital Punishment," p. 618. For
results of the longitudinal study Kohlberg began in 1955 see
A. Colby, J. Gibbs, M. Lieberman, "A Longitudinal Study of
Moral Judgment," *A Monograph for the Society of Research
in Child Development* (Chicago: University of Chicago Press,
in press). This paper presents the data on the reliability of
Kohlberg's standard from scoring of moral judgment. Test-
retest reliability was in the high 90's, as was inter-rater
reliability.

9. "The Development of Moral Judgments Concerning
Capital Punishment," pp. 618-19.

10. *Ibid*, p. 621.

dilemmas."[11] This prediction has been confirmed by the data
gathered by Kohlberg and other researchers.[12]

Kohlberg also argues that these stages are hierarchically
related with each higher stage demonstrating greater power
to produce rationally equilibrated resolutions of moral conflict. The later stages are considered more rationally equilibrated because of their increasing power to distinguish accurately different elements in the social world (e.g., persons
and things, the divergent perspectives of different individuals and generalized roles, law and morality, assertions of
facts and assertions of moral ideals) and to integrate these
elements into increasingly coherent conceptual systems.
Because of the greater rational adequacy of the later stages,
Kohlberg maintains that the higher the stage of moral reasoning "the greater the likelihood that individuals at that
stage will agree... in the content of their moral judge-
ment."[13] The motive force for the development from the
lower to the higher stages is the rational inadequacy of the
lower stages and their inability to generate fair or even
determinate resolutions of moral dilemmas.[14] As Carl Bereiter
has expressed the Kohlbergian perspective, "morality, like
logic, is neither 'taught' nor 'caught' but is inexorably
developed out of each individual's moral struggle to make
sense of the world. Customs and climates may differ, but
the underlying sources of cognitive conflict remain the same
and, interacting with universal stages in biological maturation, produce a uniform sequence of mental growth.[15]

---

11.   Colby, Kohlberg, Gibbs, and Lieberman, "A Longitudinal Study of Moral Judgment," p.5.

12.   See "A Longitudinal Study of Moral Judgment" and
Rest, "Morality."

13.   Kohlberg and Elfenbein, "The Development of Moral
Judgments Concerning Capital Punishment," pp. 629-30.

14.   *Ibid*, p. 634.

To say that the process is inexorable does not mean that it is inevitable, for Kohlberg's research clearly shows that only a small percentage of individuals ever advance beyond the conventional level of moral thinking.[16] In the context of Bereiter's comment, inexorable must be understood as meaning that the sequential dynamic from which this development unfolds is innate and that provided with the proper environment and stimulus it will proceed in and of itself so long as the individual continues his personal struggle to make sense of the world.

This has profound implications with regard to adult and professional education. The popular belief is that one's morals are determined by upbringing and early training. Thus moral development is conceived primarily as something restricted to youth and largely determined by external factors. However, if Kohlberg's theory is correct, then this popular belief is in error. Rather than being a process restricted to youth, some of the most interesting and challenging aspects of moral development only begin after a person reaches adulthood and has experienced more profoundly the practical exigencies of life in an imperfect and often brutal world.

Kohlberg's research indicates that most American adults only reach stages 3 or 4 of the five stage developmental sequence. The research also indicates that individuals are most attracted to reasoning that is one stage above their own.[17] Thus adults who are capable of stage 4 reasoning are ideal candidates for the next step in the developmental sequence, the move to post-conventional moral reasoning.

---

15.   Carl Bereiter, *The Hasting Center Report*, Vol. 8, No. 2, April 1978, p. 20.

16.   Kohlberg and Elfenbein, "The Development of Moral Judgments Concerning Capital Punishment," p. 619 and "A Longitudinal Study of Moral Judgment," p. 7. See also, Rest, "Morality."

17.   Hersh, Paolitto, and Reimer, *Promoting Moral Growth*, p. 104.

The response of students in the Business Ethics and Values course strongly supports the correctness of this thesis.

I began the course with the normative/descriptive distinction and a discussion of the naturalistic fallacy. In general, students find this distinction very difficult and thus are often initially unable to see how the issue "Capital punishment is/is not a deterrent to acts legally defined as first degree murder" is quite different from the issue "Individuals convicted of an act legally defined as first degree murder ought/ought not to be executed." Familiarizing students with this distinction and developing their skill in applying it enables them to look critically at the different kind of mental processes at work in their own thinking when they attempt to verify empirical claims as distinguished from claims about how things ought to be. After they had begun this kind of critical self-reflection, I introduced them to Kohlberg's theory.

My purpose in teaching students Kohlberg's empirically based developmental model is to further the processes of ethical reflection in ways which directly correspond to their own experiences. This is in contrast to the usual approach in introductory ethics classes (whether on the graduate or undergraduate level) which begin with highly abstract and complex ethical theories. Students generally find it difficult to relate these theories to how people actually think about and deal with moral dilemmas in the "real" world. This experience of a lack of connectedness between what is taught in the ethics class and what is perceived in the "real" world is, I believe, a significant source of the debilitating pessimism some students develop after taking an ethics class. In contrast, approaching ethics in terms of an empirically based developmental model provides students with a unified theory of ethics and ethical development which moves them through a rational progression from familiar patterns of thought to the unfamiliar patterns of philosophical ethics. Simultaneously, it enables students to observe and understand their concrete operating procedures in moral decisions and to see where the abstract principles they are learning call for change.

Students were introduced to Kohlberg's theory by means of lectures and reading assignments in *Understanding Stages and Moral Development: A Programmed Learning Workbook* by

Susan Pagliuso[18] and Lawrence Kohlberg's and Donald Elfenbein's article, "The Development of Moral Judgments Concerning Capital Punishment."

The special value of the Pagliuso workbook is the programmed way it assists students in developing the analytical
skills necessary to identify the formal stage progression of
moral reasoning in nine different areas: social perspective,
role-taking, exchange, interpersonal relationship, gover-
nance, rules, sanctions, property, and life.[19] Special
emphasis was placed on the progression of role-taking ability
as one moves from the lower to the higher stages, for the
core of morality and of the moral stages is the concept of
role-taking. (For the progression of moral reasoning from
stage 1 through stage 5 in the areas of role-taking and
rules, see Appendix II.) As Kohlberg and Elfenbein put it,
"Each higher moral stage is logically more advanced in the
sense that movement to each higher moral stage presupposes
movement to a new logical stage as defined in Piaget's work.
Moral judgment, however, is not simply logical reasoning
applied to moral problems. In the first place, moral judgment involves role-taking, taking the point of view of others
conceived as *subjects* and coordinating those points of view,
whereas logic involves only coordinating points of view with
respect to *objects*. Secondly, moral judgment, unlike logical
reasoning, rests upon principles of justice or fairness.
Moral development consists in the gradual equilibration of
role-taking structures and principles of justice. Following

---

18.   Paulist Press, 1976.

19.   The workbook has some limitations. It is not well
edited or printed, and it sometimes fails adequately to dis-
criminate conventional and post-conventional thinking.
Nonetheless, I know of nothing comparable to it in assisting
students in analyzing the formal stage progression of moral
reasoning in these various areas. The standard for assessing the adequacy of an analysis of the stages is Anne Colby
et al., *Standard Issues Scoring*, Form A and Form B, Center
for Moral Education, Harvard University, May, 1982.

Kant and other formalists we have argued at length elsewhere that rational moral judgments must be universalizable,
consistent and reversible. Each higher moral stage meets
these formal conditions better than its predecessor by virtue
of being a more equilibrated role-taking structure and a
more equilibrated principle of justice."[20] By a fair or equilibrated solution of a moral dilemma is meant a resolution "in
which everyone whose interests are at stake is 'given his
due' according to some principle that everyone can recognize
as fair. That is, a fair resolution is one that would be
judged to be right by everyone involved, given each person's willingness to consider his own claims impartially and
to put himself in the shoes of the others."[21]

In these comments a framework is provided for analyzing
a problem often encountered when persons of considerable
logical competence and technical skill are elevated to managerial positions. As a student who holds a mid-level management position with a major computer company expressed it,
"These individuals often have little, if any, role-taking ability (i.e., ability to understand the perceptions of subjects[22]
as distinguished from understanding a logical relationship
among objects). They come to their new management
position with great enthusiasm and ideas, then discover that
staff (i.e., subjects) in other units resist their plans and
will not fall into line (i.e., like objects capable of technical
manipulation). They then become frustrated and because
individuals in other units have failed to cooperate, they
cease being cooperative in turn (Stage 2: I'll scratch your
back, if you scratch mine). Then the organization as a

---

20.   Kohlberg and Elfenbein, "The Development of Moral
Judgments Concerning Capital Punishment," p. 634.

21.   *Ibid*.

22.   What distinguishes a subject from an object is the
former's capability for feeling, desiring, reasoning and
choosing.

whole has problems."[23]
     The value of equipping managers with the analytical tools
necessary for discerning stages of moral reasoning with the
consequent increase in their ability to understand the thinking of others is self-evident. For "it is axiomatic that individuals cannot manage well that which they poorly compre-
hend."[24] But does a practiced familiarity with Kohlberg's
theory increase an individual's ability to do this? There was
consensus among the students, whether Nigerian, Philippine
or North American, that it does. After we had worked for
approximately one month with Kohlberg's theory and developed some of the analytical skills necessary for discerning
moral stages, a student who holds a management position in
a state agency came to me before class to express his appreciation for what we were doing. He told me that he could
now see and understand interpersonal dynamics among his
staff which before had been invisible to him. Several other
students in managerial positions told me essentially the same
thing. The Nigerian students were also adamant in their
insistence that what they had learned from Kohlberg was of
immense benefit in seeing and understanding business practices and the socio-political environment of their own country. Such comments from culturally diverse and practically
experienced individuals (while not scientific evidence) give
support to the thesis that the theory is practically applicable
both at home and abroad, and give strong indication of the
theory's value as a cross-cultural teaching tool.
     In addition to the value my students and I found in the
theory as a descriptive tool (descriptive in the sense that it
helped us to understand better others' moral reasoning), we
also found it had significant power as a normative instrument, i.e., an instrument which helps one see not merely

---

     23. This is not an exact quote, but as close as I can get
from memory. The material in parenthesis is my translation
of his comments into the Kohlbergian structure.

     24. *Modern Values in Business and Management: Pro-
ceedings from the 1979 AACSB Annual Meeting*, p. 36.

how things are, but how things ought to be. In part we gauged the test of its normative power in terms of how well it helped us to come to a rational consensus on moral issues.

As noted above,[25] Kohlberg's research indicates that the higher the stage of moral reasoning "the greater the likelihood that individuals at that stage will agree not only in their mode of moral reasoning but in the content of their moral judgments as well." The form or mode of moral reasoning concerns the logical structure of the reasoning, e.g., whether it is pre-conventional, conventional or post-conventional. The content of the moral judgment is the specific attitude an individual holds on a particular issue. At the lower or middle stages of moral reasoning, e.g., the conventional level, individuals often hold radically opposed attitudes on specific issues even though the formal structure of their reasoning is the same. For example, a conventional subject from the western or southern states who strongly identifies with the small businessman will probably regard the establishment of right to work laws as a moral imperative. Another conventional subject from the industrial northeast and the strongly pro-union working class will probably find right to work laws unjust. Insofar as these two individuals are locked into the perspective of their own particular group, it is unlikely that they will be able to arrive at a resolution of their differences which seem just or fair to both. Thus one of the ultimate goals of ethical reflection is frustrated, i.e., the development of a methodology or perspective which increases the probability of agreement among rational individuals (regardless of cultural background or group identification) on specific issues. This goal is unlikely to be obtained so long as individuals of diverse background and group identification do not advance beyond the conventional level of moral reasoning.[26]

---

25. Above, p. 5.

26. An alternative way to work toward this goal is through "The Just Community Approach," *Promoting Moral Growth*, pp. 233-43. The emphasis here is on working to

The difficulty of arriving at agreement on substantive ethical issues in our society is a phenomenon Kohlberg's theory predicts given the great number of diverse interest groups and the small percentage of individuals who ever advance beyond a conventional level of moral thinking in our society. The theory likewise predicts that the development of post-conventional moral reasoning in a larger percentage of adults in our society will significantly increase the probability of these individuals coming to rational consensus as to just or fair resolutions of these issues, irrespective of their particular group or regional loyalties.

Kohlberg's theory, supported by empirical data and rationally coherent moral arguments,[27] points to the innate presence in the human person of the capability for arriving at just resolutions of moral dilemmas. As was stated earlier, these are resolutions "in which everyone whose interests are at stake is 'given his due' according to some principle that everyone can recognize as fair. That is... a solution... that would be judged right by everyone involved, given each person's willingness to consider his own claims impartially and to put himself in the shoes of others."

---

help individuals (primarily in the secondary school context) to a moral consensus which is stage 3-4 through the development of a sense of trust and of loyalty to a shared democratic community where all participate in making community decisions.

27. For an excellent discussion of the underlying theoretical issues and a review of the psychological research see Rest, "Morality." For the philosophical argument see L. Kohlberg, "The Claim to Moral Adequacy of a Highest Stage of Moral Judgment," *Journal of Philosophy*, 40 (1973), pp. 630-46. See also L. Kohlberg, "From Is to Ought: How to Commit the Naturalistic Fallacy and Get Away With It in the Study of Moral Development," in *Cognitive Development and Epistemology*, T. Mischel, ed., (New York: Academic Press, 1971). Also "The Development of Moral Judgments Concerning Capital Punishment." Updated versions of these essays are in Kohlberg, *The Philosophy of Moral Development*.

The outline for a method to achieve this goal, the method of ideal role-taking, is stated by Kohlberg and Elfenbein[28] and based on the work of John Rawls.[29] Rawls' conception of valid principles of justice are "those which would e adopted as the governing principles of a society by rational persons in an 'original position,' i.e., behind a 'veil of ignorance' as to who in society they are to be and have an equal (or unknown) chance of being the least advantaged member of society.[30] Kohlberg and Elfenbein have articulated this concept of "the original position" as a concrete procedural rule which involves three steps:

1.) To imagine oneself in the position of each person in the situation and to consider all the claims he could make (or which the self could make in his position).

2.) Then to imagine that one does not know which person one is in the situation and to ask which claims one would uphold and which claims one would relinquish.

3.) Then to formulate a moral judgment in accordance with fully reversible claims (those one would uphold not knowing who one were to be).[31]

---

28. Kohlberg and Elfenbein, "The Development of Moral Judgments Concerning Capital Punishment," p. 635.

29. John Rawls, *A Theory of Justice* (Cambridge, Mass: Harvard University Press, 1971). For an excellent introduction to Rawls see, *John Rawls Theory of Social Justice: An Intorduction*, eds. H. G. Blocker, E. H. Smith (Athens, Ohio: Ohio University Press, 1980).

30. Kohlberg and Elfenbein, "The Development of Moral Judgments Concerning Capital Punishment," pp. 635-37.

31.

Kohlberg and Elfenbein then make the remarkable claim, "If all the parties involved in a moral dilemma follow this hypothetical three step procedure, they will almost inevitably reach agreement with one another as to what the fair resolution of the situation is... Many of our most secure moral convictions can be accounted for in terms of our stage 6 ideal role-taking. An example discussed by Rawls is our intuition that the fair procedure for dividing a cake between two persons is to have one person cut the cake and the other choose the first piece. This procedure is fair because it is the one to which anyone would agree not knowing which person he was to be..."[32]

The latter half of the course centered around the effort to make use of this method as a way to analyze cases and to arrive at a moral resolution of the dilemmas these cases presented.[33] The intent was to see to what extent this method would enable the class to reach a consensus as to the most just resolution of a given ethical conflict. In employing the method of ideal role-taking it was stressed that its effectiveness would in large measure depend upon the extent to which we were first able to reach agreement as to the pertinent facts. It was soon discovered that this is often more difficult than the analysis of the purely moral dimensions of the problem.

The initial issue presented to the class concerned the use of bribery and pay offs by transnational corporations and raised the question whether these practices should be rationally regarded as objectively immoral or simply as a different but acceptable way of doing business in accordance with the conventions of some cultures. Before giving my presentation I made the claim that by first determining the likely social consequences of such practices and then

---

Ibid. p.30.

32. *Ibid.* p. 31.

33. Most of the cases were taken from *Ethical Issues in Business*, eds. T. Donaldson and P. H. Werhane, (Englewood Cliffs, N.J.: Prentice-Hall, Inc., 1979).

applying the method of ideal role-taking, our highly hetero-
geneous class would come to a consensus that bribery and
pay offs as standard ways of doing business were objectively
immoral, whether these practices occurred in the Third World
or in the United States. This prediction was greeted with
considerable scepticism.

Making use of an unpublished report "An Assessment of
the Issues in Prevention of Corrupt Practices of Transnational Corporations"[34] prepared by Jack Behrman for the
U.N., I focused my presentation on what he terms decision
altering payments and systems altering payments. Decision
altering payments were defined as payments made to alter
decisions which otherwise would be adverse to the company,
e.g., payments to a purchasing agent for a contract, to a
regulatory agency to obtain an exception, or to the judiciary
to obtain a favorable judgment. Systems altering payments
were defined as those which seek to alter the decision making process itself, e.g., to alter the composition of the judiciary, legislature, board of directors, or managment. These
are payments to alter the way decisions are made rather than
payments for a particular decision. The discussion of bribery and pay offs was limited to these two types of payments.
The students were then asked to consider four likely effects
(as outlines by Behrman) of this way of doing business.

1) The warping of the social and economic objectives of
the countries affected through over-buying and the purchasing of inappropriate items.

2) The disruption of the statutory and political processes
by buying special favors for moneyed interests.

3) The undermining of national security through persua-
sion of purchasing agents to buy inappropriate arms or to
pay dearly for those they do receive.

---

34. Copies of this report are available through Jack
Behrman, Luther B. Hodges Distinguished Professor, University of North Carolina.

4) The frustration of the development of a more equitable economic order by preventing more equal distribution of opportunity and benefits.

I maintained that most of these effects were present in countries where decision and systems altering payments were standard ways of doing business. The international students agree with this assessment. I then asked what it could mean to say that practices with these effects are morally good.

Employing a stage structure analysis it could be said that they are perceived as "good" at a stage 2 for the individual taking the bribe and the company receiving the requested favor. They could also be understood as "good" at stage 3 because of the benefits they obtain for the privileged group with which one identifies. They certainly could not be considered "good" from a stage 4 or higher perspective which considers the good of the society as a whole, precisely because of the four major effects of such practices stated above.

I then asked if anyone in the class would willingly contract into a society which accepted such practices as standard operating procedures, not knowing in advance whether he would be a member of the privleged or disadvantaged group in that society. There were no takers. I asked if we had a consensus that such practices were universally unjust and therefore, wherever they exist, whether in South America, Africa or the U.S.A., such practices ought to be eliminated. The show of hands indicated we had our consensus.

Such a consensus does not, of course, address the issue of how such practices can be eliminated. Nor does it provide certainty that those "consenting" would never engage in such practices.[35] Nonetheless, it demonstrates that

---

35. There are, however, a growing number of studies which "link moral judgment test scores with real-life decision making and behavior. One of the more intriguing studies for instructors of applied ethics reports a significant link between moral judgment scores and the clinical performance of pediatric house staff as rated by medical faculty." James

practically experienced persons of diverse nationality and background can come to a verbal moral consensus on an issue many consider immune even to that sort of agreement. In this instance, at least, the method of ideal role-taking resulted in the agreement predicted by Kohlberg and Elfenbein. I regard it as especially significant that it did so in a class composed of mature individuals of exceedingly diverse cultural experience, sectional and group loyalties.

The same procedure was used in other cases, not always with equal success. In part I am persuaded that this was due to the students' and my lack of skill in applying the method cases. Nonetheless, at the conclusion of the course there was a strong consensus among the students that the method was useful and enabled them to arrive at significantly greater clarity in their treatment of ethical issues than they could have reached without it. In subsequent offerings of the course the method has been used in ways which designate more clearly the key roles/parties involved in a moral conflict, and has used both considerations of utility and the formal principles of universalizability and consistency to reach a resolution. The explicit use of utility considerations and formal ethical principles in ideal role-taking enables one to meet the criteria of reversibility in a more rationally articulated and less intuitive way.[36]

Rest, "A Psychologist Looks at the Teaching of Ethics," *The Hastings Center Report*, Vol. 12, No. 1, Feb. 1982, p. 32. See also, Augusto Blasi, "Bridging Moral Cognition and Moral Action: A Critical Review of the Literature," *Psychological Bulletin*, Vol. 88, No. 1, July 1980, and L. Kohlberg and D. Candee, "The Relationship of Moral Judgment to Moral Action," Center for Moral Education, Harvard University, 1983.

36.   There is an interesting discussion of the philosophical limitations of the method of ideal role-taking in paper by David Cooper, "A Cognitive Developmental Approach to Teaching Business Ethics," pp. 15-18. The paper is to be published in the *Journal of Business Ethics* sometime in the winter of 84/85.

For a research project, students were asked to apply Kohlberg's theory and the method of ideal role-taking to an area of ethical conflict in business, government or some other social context which was of especial interest to them. Topics chosen included "Profits and Ethics in a Semiconductor Product Line Pricing Structure," "Historical Cost Accounting," and "How to Make Employee Performance Evaluations More Ethical." Virtually all of the papers were able to make significant use of the descriptive and normative tools provided by Kohlberg's theory.

Evaluation forms to be filled out anonymously were given to the students after the final; twenty of the twenty-five forms handed out were returned. The first three questions and the break down of the answers were as follows:

1) "After taking this course, do you think a business ethics course should be a part of the education of all business students?" Nineteen of the students answered with an unqualified "yes" and eighteen of these with strongly affirmative comments. One student qualified his answer by saying that business students should be "exposed" to ethics, though he was not convinced that a full semester should be devoted to it. It is interesting to note that this student also commented, "Whenever an issue comes up the ideal of ideal role-taking comes to my mind even though I decide at the stage 3-4 level. The ideal role-taking aspect is a very interesting one to me."

2) "Has this course changed how you think about ethical issues?" Sixteen students answered with a clear "yes," two responded by saying that the course had "broadened their perspective," and one responded "maybe" and one with "not exactly, although now I'm more informed and can explain myself a lot better."

3) "Has this course helped you to be a more ethical person?" Thirteen students answered "yes," six answered "no," and one, surely the honest man Diogenes was searching for, "I don't know yet."

In a subsequent offering of the course Kohlberg's Moral Judgment Interview (MJI) was administered at the beginning and the conclusion of the course. Test results support the perceptions of students that the course significantly affected how they think about moral issues. Pre- and post-course MJI scores showed that while 36% of the MBA students at the beginning of the course were at a transition point between conventional and post-conventional reasoning, none demonstrated a solid post-conventional framework. This data is consistent with other research which indicates that only a small percentage of the individuals graduating from our universities and professional schools have developed the capacity for post-conventional moral reasoning. At the end of the course 37% of the students (7 out of a group of 19) moved into a post-conventional framework. Four of these students moved up from the transition between stages 4 and 5, and three moved up from stage 4. 52% of the students showed a significant gain in moral judgment scores (a minimum advance of one-third stage), with the average gain for this group being two-thirds stage. The average gain for the class as a whole was 30 points, which was slightly under the one-third stage required for the change to be regarded as statistically significant.[37] In Kohlberg's original longitudinal study, on the average, one third of a stage is the equivalent of four years natural movement.[38]

Harvard's President, Derek Bok, addressing the issue whether separate business ethics course taught by specialists

---

37. Six of the moral judgment interviews were sent to the Center for Moral Education as a check on the reliability of my scoring. The average difference on scoring done at the Center and my own (on a scale of 500 points) was 18 points. This is well within the third stage which is considered the limit of the instrument's reliability. For a discussion of the use of psychological testing to assess ethics courses see Rest, "A Psychologist Looks at the Teaching of Ethics."

38. Rest, "Morality," p. 583.

should be incorporated into the curriculum, remarks "If a
professional school divides the responsibility for moral education among a large number of faculty members, most
instructors will not have a knowledge of ethics that is equal
to the task. Many of them will give shortshrift to the moral
problems and concentrate on other aspects of the course
materials that they feel more equipped to teach. The difficulties are clearly illustrated by the findings of a recent
report from a prominent business school. After listing a
wide variety of moral issues distributed throughout the curriculum, the report described the reactions of a sample of
students and faculty: 'Almost without exception, the faculty
members indicated that they touch on one or more of these
issues frequently but while they were certain they cover the
issues, they often had second thoughts about how explicit
they had been. Almost equally, without exception, students
felt the issues are seldom touched on and when they are,
are treated as afterthoughts or digressions.'"[39]

Why this general lack of an explicit and sustained focus
on ethics in the business school curriculum? Partly at fault
is surely a scepticism about the possibility of teaching ethics
in a way that can significantly improve individuals' ability
and willingness to deal ethically with complex moral issues in
business. If this is so, then a careful reading of the
research by Kohlberg and his colleagues on moral development should remove a major obstacle to incorporating ethics
courses into the business school curriculum.

----

39. As cited in *Modern Values in Business and Managment, Preceedings from the 1979 AACSB Annual Meeting,* p.
55.

APPENDIX I
KOHLBERG'S LEVELS AND STAGES OF MORAL
DEVELOPMENT[40]

LEVEL I. PRE-CONVENTIONAL MORAL REASONING.

This form of moral thinking reflects an ego-centric per-spective before group ways are accepted. The individual is responsive to cultural rules and labels of good and bad, right and wrong, but interprets these labels either in terms of the physical and hedonistic consequences of action (pun-ishment, reward, exchange of favors) or in terms of the physical power of those who enunciate the rules and labels. Right and wrong are determined by physical consequences, not by the human meaning of an action. Any exchange must carry a guarantee of getting as much as is given. There is a severely restricted sense of time and space. A person's worth is defined by what he owns or controls. The level is divided into the following two stages.

Stage 1. Punishment and Obedience Orientation.

The physical consequences of action determine its good-ness or badness regardless of the human meaning or value of those consequences. Avoidance of punishment and unques-tioning deference to power are valued in their own right, not in terms of respect for an underlying moral order sup-ported by punishment and authority (the latter being stage 4). There is little ability for abstract thought or seeing situations from another's perspective. At this stage the individual thinks only in terms of physical problems and physical solutions. This stage of reasoning is inevitable at a certain age, perhaps five to eight years, but usually does

---

40. Most of the material for this description of the stages was taken from the following sources: Lawrence Kohlberg, "Stages of Moral Development as a Basis for Moral Education," in *Moral Education,* eds C. M. Beck, B. S. Cri-tenden, E. V. Sullivan (New York: Newman Press, 1971), Appendix I, pp. 86-88; *Promoting Moral Growth,* pp. 65-82; *Understanding Stages of Moral Development,* pp. 78-91.

not continue in our society beyond the years of pre-adolens-
cence.

Stage 2. Instrumental Relativist Orientation.
    Right action consists of that which instrumentally satis-
fies one's own needs and occasionally the needs of others.
Human relationships are viewed in terms similar to those of
the market place. Elements of fairness, of reciprocity, and
equal sharing are present, but they are always interpreted
in a physical pragmatic way. Reciprocity is a matter of "you
scratch my back and I'll scratch yours," not of loyalty,
gratitude or justice. Fairness is defined very concretely in
terms of getting one's own fair share. This is the type
thinking reflected in child's moral outrage when he perceives
a sibling getting a cookie slightly larger than his own. At
this stage the individual begins to be able to perceive things
from the view of one other person at a time, but cannot step
outside the two-person relationship and look at it from a
third-person perspective. At this stage the hypothetical in
the Golden Rule -- Do unto others **as you would** have them
do unto you -- is understood in terms of the concrete reciprocity of -- do unto others **as they do** unto you. Stage 2
begins to develop in our society among seven and eight year
olds and remains the dominant stage throughout the grade
school years. Studies of adolescents show that among mid-
dle-class populations stage 2 reasoning recedes considerably,
but it remains a fairly dominant mode among working-class
and lower-class youth. Among adults it continues to per-
sist, but more as minor stage.

LEVEL II. CONVENTIONAL MORAL REASONING.
    This form of moral reasoning stems from group member-
ship. Maintaining the expectations of the individual's family,
group, or nation is perceived as valuable in its own right,
regardless of immediate and obvious consequences. The attitude is not only one of conformity to personal expectations
and social order, but of loyalty to it, of actively maintaining, supporting and justifying the order, and of identifying
with the persons or group involved in it. The group has a
structure within which people live. It is important to define
and maintain this structure; rules and laws help you do
this. There is much concern about the interaction between
people in a group context (be it large or small). There are

the following two stages.

Stage 3. Interpersonal Concordance or "Good Boy - Nice Girl" Orientation.

Good behavior is that which pleases or helps others and is approved by them. There is much conformity to stereotypical images of what is majority or "natural" behavior. Behavior is frequently judged by intention: "He means well" becomes important for the first time. One earns approval by being "nice." The person is able to perceive things not merely from the perspective of another concrete individual, but from the perspective of the abstract entity -- the group. The hypothetical in the Golden Rule is now understood in ways which enable the individual to empathize with the feelings of others and to be concerned about the human meaning of loyalty, friendship and general role obligations. This mode of thinking is often adequate for dealing with conflicts among people who know one another. Its inadequacy clearly surfaces when one must deal with conflicts between groups and problems on a societal level. This stage begins to develop during pre-adolescence; it is the dominant stage during adolescence and, along with stage 4, remains the major stage for most adults in our society.

Stage 4. The Social System and Conscience.

Right behavior is defined by its contribution to the social system as a whole. Social perspective is still based on shared empathy/or respect. The difference is in the size and complexity of the context. The societal point of view is differentiated from interpersonal agreement or motives. This stage takes the point of view of the system which defines the rules and roles, and considers individual relations in terms of place in the system. The individual is concerned to avoid a breakdown in the system which would result from the infraction of given rules or laws "if everyone did it." At this stage there is a sophisticated understanding of the complex network of cause-effect relations and interdependencies throughout the social system and of the resultant vulnerability of such systems. Insofar as persons at Stage 4 conceive of morality as a fixed system of laws and beliefs (whether Marxist, capitalist or religious), they can grant little validity to other views without threatening their own. Thus the limits of stage 4 reasoning are most noticeable when a person at that stage must deal with diversity outside his own system. Stage 4 reasoning begins to develop during mid-adolescence.

LEVEL III. POST CONVENTIONAL MORAL REASONING.
This reflects an individual rather than a group orientation. What distinguishes it from the egocentric perpsective of Level I is the individual's advanced logical and social sophistication and emphasis on ethical universals. Through a broader and deeper conceptual development, consideration is given to much more abstract principles, rights, and duties. There is a clear effort to define moral values and principles which have universal validity and application apart from the authority of the groups or individuals holding these principles and apart from the individual's own identification with these groups or individuals. This level also has two stages.

Stage 5. Social Contract/Legalistic Orientation.
Generally this stage has utilitarian overtones. Right action tends to be defined in terms of general individual rights and in terms of standards that have been critically examined and agreed upon by the whole society. There is a clear awareness of the relativism of personal values and opinions and a corresponding emphasis on procedural rules for reaching consensus. Aside from what is constitutionally and democratically agreed upon, the right is a matter of personal "values" and "opinion." The result is a focus upon the "legal point of view," but with an emphasis upon the possibility of changing law in terms of rational considerations of social utility and fundamental human rights. Outside the legal realm, free agreement and contract are the binding elements of obligation. This is the "official" morality of the United States government and constitution. The major limitation of Stage 5 is in dealing with situations where legal mechanisms and democratic due process generate rsults contrary to substantive justice.

Stage 6. Universal Ethical-Principle Orientation.
Right is defined by the decision of conscience in accord with self-chosen *ethical principles* appealing to logical comprehensiveness, universalizability, consistency and reversibility. These principles are abstract and ethical (Kant's Categorial Imperative, Rawls' two principles of justice, the

second order conception of Golden Rule represented by the method of ideal role-taking); they are not concrete moral rules like the Ten Commandments. At heart, these are universal principles of justice, of the reciprocity and equality of human rights and respect for the dignity of human beings as individual persons. The rationality of these abstract principles and rights is best understood from the hypothetical perspective of a rational individual who is able to determine the basic principles of the society in which he is to live, but without knowing in advance his own socio-economic status, personal capabilities and family connections. Thus the moral authority of those basic principles is understood in terms of the basic protection they provide for all the members of that society and not because of one's own identification with any particular individuals or group.

APPENDIX II
STAGE PROGRESSION IN MORAL REASONING

ROLE-TAKING: the ability to understand different points of view.

Stage 1: Very limited ROLE-TAKING ability.

Stage 2: ROLE-TAKING ABILITY needed to recognize that others have ideas or attutudes of their own, but tends to think others' ideas are just like his.

Stage 3: ROLE-TAKING ABILITY allows putting oneself in others' shoes and understanding of group ideas.

Stage 4: ROLE-TAKING ABILITY develops so that the perspective of any member of society, a member of a role class or an individual can be taken.

Stage 5: ROLE-TAKING ABILITY has developed so that a rational or moral perspective is possible.

RULES: the means through which the structure is made known.

Stage 1: RULES are set up by the Authority; the purpose of rules is to tell people what to do.

Stage 2: RULES are viewed as a means to one's end.

Stage 3: RULES are shared guides for being good and can be broken for a good reason.

Stage 4: RULES are made to protect society as a cooperative scheme.

Stage 5: RULES are a mechanism to preserve individual

rights.[41]

41. From Pagliuso, *Understanding Stages of Moral Development*, pp. 78-91.

Mathematical Models of
Business and Ethics

FORCED FREEDOM AND GOVERNMENT INTERFERENCE

Tal Scriven

Few, if any, believe that the marketplace should operate in a completely free and unrestricted manner. Even the most ardent supporters of laissez-faire capitalism think that practices like child prostitution and murdering for hire must be disallowed even if there is an economic demand for and willing suppliers of these services. In less obvious cases, however, state intervention in the marketplace is, for a growing number of people, held to be a very dubious enterprise. The preferred mode of regulation is the self-regulation of the "invisible hand."

The main point of this paper is to discuss a case where government intervention is justifiable even from the point of view of the competitive capitalist. This case is interesting for a couple of reasons. First, it bears the form of a wide class of cases where state intervention can be justified on the basis of the purely egoistic concerns operative in the marketplace. In fact, as we shall see, the consequences of this case are general enough to form the foundation of a social contract theory that is substantially different than and, in most respects, less controversial than other contract theories (for example, Rawls's). Secondly, the case places the capitalist in a very revealing paradox. Specifically, he finds himself being rationally compelled to resist the imposition of official constraints that it is in his own rational self-interest to have imposed.

I

At the heart of the matter is the prisoner's dilemma. Although the properties of this game are widely known it will be helpful here to briefly review the details of the standard interpretation for the dilemma. The story involves two prisoners who are being held in isolation from one another on suspicion of robbery. Each has the alternative of either cooperating with the authorities by confessing to the crime or refusing to confess. If only one of the prisoners confesses while the other refuses then the former will be rewarded for his cooperation by a very light sentence (1 year) while his accomplice will have the book thrown at him (10 years). If, however, neither prisoner confesses then the authorities will only have enough evidence to convict the pair on a lesser charge (which carries a maximum penalty of 3 years). If both confess then, although neither will have the book thrown at him for non-cooperation, there will be enough evidence to convict them both on the more serious offense (and send them away for 6 years). The situation is representable by the following matrix:

	B confesses	B doesn't confess
A confesses	-6, -6	-1, -10
A doesn't confess	-10, -1	-3, -3

where A's payoffs appear first.

The dilemma that A and B find themselves in is that, for each, the best possible strategy is to confess. For example, whether B confesses or doesn't confess, A comes out better if he confesses than if he doesn't confess. Given the symmetry of the situation, B's best strategy is also to confess. So, by acting in a fully rational manner in this case, A and B wind up getting 6 years each. The irony, of course, is that they would have come out better if they had both acted irrationally. Stated more formally, the paradox is that the equilibrium outcome (that which results from the independent actions of ideally rational individuals) is not Pareto-optimal.[1] The result of both prisoners confessing is the equilibrium outcome here since neither A nor B can change strategies without lowering their expected utility. However, the result of both prisoners refusing to confess is optimal since all of the three remaining outcomes (including the equilibrium) will disadvantage someone relative to the optimum.

One might think that if A and B were really fully rational then they would have foreseen the possibility of such a situation occuring and would have agreed in advance not to confess if captured. However, a simple promise would not avoid the dilemma, for as soon as they were captured and separated the rational thing to do would be to simply break the promise and hope that the other prisoner would be stupid enough to keep his word. If the dilemma is to be avoided then something stronger than a mere promise is required. What is needed is a prior agreement not to con-fess that is enforcible. In other words, what is needed is a *contract* backed up by an enforcible penalty stiff enough to outweigh any advantage that could be obtained by breach of the contract. For example, prisoner A could accept B's promise not to confess if A could make good on the following threat: "If you break the promise while I live up to it then my friends on the outside will make sure you're dead the minute you hit the street." If B could do the same then the dilemma would not have to be faced, for, in essence, the payoff matrix will have been changed as follows (assuming death = -10):

	B confesses	B doesn't confess

---

1. A social state of affairs is Pareto-optimal if and only if it is such that no one's position can be improved without thereby damaging someone else's position).

| | A confesses | -6, -6 | -10, -10 |
| | A doesn't confess | -10, -10 | -3, -3 |

Although the outcome brought about as a result of both prisoners confessing is still an equilibrium outcome, it is dominated by the outcome that results if both don't confess. Thus, the rational thing to do now is refuse to confess.

W. G. Runciman and A. K. Sen[2] have argued that the imposition of such a contract in order to free the prisoners from their dilemma can, in a generalized sense, be used to flesh out Rousseau's concept of "the general will." The prisoners are, in Rousseau's words, "forced to be free" while such a contract is in force. And, indeed, the prisoner's dilemma does help make more sense of Rousseau's notion of "forced freedom" than is often made from the following passage in the *Social Contract*:

> Therefore, in order for the social compact not to be an ineffectual formula, it tacitly includes the following engagement, which alone can give force to the others: that whoever refuses to obey the general will shall be constrained to do so by the entire body; which means only that he will be forced to be free. (Book I, Chapter VII)

and an even more paradoxical statement in the corresponding section of the *Geneva Manuscript*:

> By what inconceivable art could the means have been found to subjugate men in order to make them free; to use the goods, the labor, even the life of its members in the service of the state,

---

2. "Games, Justice and the General Will." *Mind* 74 (1965): pp. 554-562.

> without forcing and without consulting them; to
> bind their will by their own consent; to make their
> agreement predominate over their refusal; and to
> force them to punish themselves when they do
> what they did not want? How can it be that all
> obey while none commands, that they serve and
> have no master, and are all the freer, in fact,
> because under what appears subjugation, no one
> loses any of his freedom except what would harm
> the freedom of another.

The prisoner's dilemma seems to make perfect sense of the
following claims about the general will that occur at the
beginnings of the first two paragraphs of Book II, Chapter
III in the *Social Contract*:   "...the general will is always
right and always tends toward public utility.... There is
often a great difference between the will of all and the general will." How "public utility," "the will of all" and "the
general will" can differ is easily explainable in the language
of game theory. The will of all (the result of everyone's
"particular wills") is the equilibrium outcome. The general
will is the optimal outcome. The prisoner's dilemma shows
how they can conflict and how public utility is best served
by enforcing the optimal outcome.
    But whatever the merits of this interpretation of Rous-
seau the prisoner's dilemma does provide interesting inroads
to the rational basis of contract formation. In the first
place it locates the motivation for forming a contract in the
area of purely egoistic rational concerns (where, common
sense would seem to suggest, it belongs) rather than in the
area of concerns about fairness and justice (where Rawls,
for example, places it). Certainly fairness in enforcement is
an essential feature of contracts but the usual motivation for
entering into a contract is that it is mutually advantageous
for relevant agents to do so. A second, and closely related,
difference between the Runciman-Sen contract model and the
Rawlsian model is that the former does not lean on the dubious maximin principle that figures so prominently in Rawls's
theory and objections to it. Rather it relies simply on a
straightforward application of the minimax principle that figures so prominently in the theory of non-cooperative games.
From this follow other significant differences, for consent to
the contract that arises in cases like the prisoner's dilemma

will be unanimous whereas Rawls can secure consent to the
maximin principle only in the original position, and only then
in the face of controversy.[3] Furthermore, in freeing the
issue from the imposition of an original position, the Runciman-Sen model justifies the imposition of the social contract
on an ongoing basis, that is, it will be consented to even in
actual situations where the agents involved know their social
positions relative to the other agents.

One should not overgeneralize the significance of the
Runciman-Sen model, however. This model cannot, in my
view, replace Rawls's, for Rawls was out to do more than lay
a foundation for the social contract. He was also, and principally, concerned with giving substance to the notion of
justice, and this is a far broader task than the Runciman-
Sen model can handle. The epistemic context that arises in
the prisoner's dilemma simply cannot be extended to all the
cases where the concept of justice is intuitively applicable.

Nevertheless, the consequences of the prisoner's dilemma
extend far beyond a puzzling story about two robbers. The
point of the remainder of this paper will be to examine some
of these consequences as they relate to the justification of
government interference in a free market economy.

II

The standard story given as an interpretation for the
prisoner's dilemma is, of course, inconsequential to the formal characteristics of the dilemma. The situation arises in
any 2 x 2 game[4] with a matrix of the following form:

---

3.   See J. Hospers, "Rule-Egoism." *The Personalist* 54
(1973): pp. 391-395.

4.   The dilemma is not restricted to the 2-person situation. It can easily be extended to any n x 2 game.

$$
\begin{array}{c}
\text{B}\\
1 \quad\quad 2
\end{array}
$$

$$
\begin{array}{cc}
 & \begin{array}{cc} 1 & 2 \end{array}\\
\begin{array}{c} 1 \\ \text{A} \\ 2 \end{array} &
\begin{array}{cc}
m,m & k,j \\
 & \\
j,k & n,n
\end{array}
\end{array}
$$

where $j > m > n > k$ and $2m > j + k$. So, coming up with alternate interpretations is simply a matter of ingenuity. Coming up with interpretations that even roughly approximate real-life conditions is, however, a different matter. Whether or not a given social, political or economic situation is indeed a prisoner's dilemma is an issue that involves a lot of empirical information. Nevertheless, it is reasonably clear that the prisoner's dilemma is a basic mechanism in the competitive marketplace. It seems to fit, quite well, the description of an "invisible hand" that drives competitors to increase production to their own disadvantage but to the advantage of consumers. If all of the producers in a certain market could collude (i.e., contract) to restrain production thus causing product scarcity and price inflation they would all be better off than they would be if they produced at full capacity thus driving prices down. The dynamics of the prisoner's dilemma, however, will drive them all to full production. Of course, in most cases the consuming public has a strong interest in making sure that producers cannot contract their way out of the dilemma by forming cartels.

However, in some very important cases producers *and* consumers have an interest in avoiding the pressure of the invisible hand. Consider the following interpretation of the prisoner's dilemma involving two oil companies who, we will assume, are the only two companies operating in the market. The characteristics of this situation, however, can be generalized to situations where more than two companies are involved and where the relevant commodity is finite, diminishing and in high demand. Our two companies, A and B, have two available strategies: 1) to proceed with exploration and production at the highest capacity their available capital will allow and, 2) to restrain exploration and development thereby extending the availability of the diminishing resource further into the future.

Now, if both companies opt for strategy 1 then increased supply will drive the price of oil down and also put A and B

out of the oil business in a relatively short period of time.
Let us assign an overall net utility of 5 to A and to B if
they arrive at this outcome. If, on the other hand, both A
and B take strategy 2 then decreased supply will drive the
price of oil up and also keep A and B in the oil business a
relatively long period of time. Even if we suppose that the
tightening of supply and the attendant rise in price bring on
a strong public reaction in the form of fuel conservation, it
would still seem that A and B would be substantially better
off if they both pursued strategy 2 rather than strategy 1.
In fact, public conservation would just allow A and B to further restrict supply and, thus, extend the availability of oil
even further into the future. So, let us assign a utility of
6 to this outcome.

Suppose, however that only one company, say A,
decided on strategy 2 while B continued full-speed-ahead
with exploration and development. Then supply will be
slightly higher than if A and B take strategy 2 but lower
than if both take 1 and, thus, the price of oil will be at an
intermediate level. But, B will have a large amount of this
medium-priced oil to sell whereas A will have a fairly small
inventory. Thus, if things remain like this very long, B
would be cleaning up year after year while A would not be
doing nearly as well. Also, as B's profits piled up it would
be able to acquire remaining oil leases at a higher rate than
A, and so B would wind up running out of oil no faster than
A. Clearly, then, B acquires the best possible position in
the short or in the long run (7 for B) while A suffers (4
for A). The following matrix summarizes the situation:

$$
\begin{array}{ccc}
 & \multicolumn{2}{c}{B} \\
 & 1 & 2 \\
1 & 5,5 & 7,4 \\
A & & \\
2 & 4,7 & 6,6 \\
\end{array}
$$

This is a prisoner's dilemma, and the "invisible hand" will
make the wrong choice, for the equilibrium outcome here
(A1,B1) is sub-optimal, (A2,B2) is Pareto-optimal.

Let's continue the story. Why don't A and B have the
foresight to recognize their dilemma and simply agree to
restrain production? Because, as we saw before, a mere
agreement to pursue the optimal rather than the equilibrium

outcome is worthless in a prisoner's dilemma. It will pay both A and B to simply break the agreement and hope the other is stupid enough to live up to it.

Well then, why don't they appeal to the only apparent outside authority (the government) who can referee a workable contract which would force A and B to pursue the optimal outcome by penalizing pursuit of the equilibrium? Well, actually they did! An agency called the "Department Overseeing the Development of Oil" (DODO) was created to serve the interests of A and B and also those of the public. But any attempt to regulate oil production was met by fierce lobbying by A and B. The agency, solely on the basis of information provided by A and B, caved into loophole after loophole until every piece of regulation was reduced simply to a demand for pointless paperwork.

Why did A and B lobby the agency into uselessness? Why didn't they just stay clear and let DODO impose the regulations which were clearly beneficial to A and B (not to mention the consumer who, in the absence of regulation, is threatened with a quick depletion of all oil reserves)? Firstly, because they mistrusted DODO. But, primarily, because they were locked into lobbying by another prisoner's dilemma. They would both be better off if both stayed away than if they both lobbied. But, if, say, A lobbied but B didn't then A would get all of its loopholes built into the regulations while B felt the full force of government control. In short, A could get outcome (A2,B1) mandated by law.

While all this was going on, A and B, of course, constantly found themselves delivering an embarrassingly contradictory message to the public. On the one hand they were running advertisements encouraging conservation of a rapidly diminishing resource while, on the other hand, various high-level representatives were publicly calling for government to get off their backs so that they could have at all that readily available oil with both hands. They were, so to speak, getting the ideology of the optimum and the ideology of the equilibrium mixed up. This, in turn, just added to the public's suspicion that A and B were greedy and short-sighted connivers who simply wanted to pump all the oil fields dry as fast as possible to sell at ridiculous prices caused by frequent industry-manufactured shortage panics (an, ironically, contradictory assessment of A's and B's contradictory PR). Of course, greed and short-sightedness just have nothing to do with the situation. A's and B's own egoistic self-interests would be best served by contractual regulation, but, no matter how far-sighted their planning, they are trapped into a sub-optimal outcome.

Well, what really follows from this tale of economic tragedy--that controls ought to be imposed on all American oil companies immediately? Certainly not. Although I think the story provides an interesting interpretation of the problems we and the oil companies are facing these days, I have neither the intention nor the information necessary to make this interpretation stick in a totally convincing way. Nevertheless, some strikingly broad conclusions about the proper role of government regulation in a free market economy are in order. They are as follows:

1) There are cases (namely, prisoner's dilemmas) in which governmental interference is warranted and beneficial even from the point of view of the producers who would be regulated.

2) In such cases only *governmental* regulation will work. That is, the producers themselves, either individually or collectively, will be unable to regulate themselves to their own advantage.

3) These cases are possible in any situation where the raw materials involved are finite and diminishing and in heavy demand.

4) In many of these cases the consequences if they are mishandled will be extremely grave. Precious raw materials will be squandered to the advantage of no one.

5) *In order just to know whether or not such cases really exist the government must be in possession of independently researched, accurate and exhaustive analyses of prevailing market conditions.* This in itself would seem to justify the existence of substantial government bureaucracy and also government financing of industry-independent research facilities.

6) When the assessment is made that such a case really exists and that the relevant resources are valuable enough to warrant intervention, the government must move decisively, treating with *extreme* skepticism all analyses of the situation offered by the producers themselves and all of their protestations that the government's assessment of the situation is in error. It is, of course, in the interests of the producers to lobby for loopholes in the regulation that

will benefit them but it is not in their interests that they all
succeed and manage to reduce to the regulations to rubble
or to a collection of "guidelines." There is a point at which
they must be "forced to be free."

MORAL CONSTRAINTS, PRISONERS' DILEMMAS,

AND THE SOCIAL RESPONSIBILITIES OF CORPORATIONS

Christopher Morris

The debate over the social responsibilities of corporations is now a familiar one. The matter has been at the center of discussion in business and professional ethics for more than a decade. But it is still not clear what exactly is the subject of controversy. Studying the literature that has mushroomed around the issue, it is not easy to understand the exact nature of the disagreement between the various parties.

We may date the start of the current debate with the appearance of a paper by the well-known economist, Milton Friedman, with the provocative title, "The Social Responsibility of Business is to Increase its Profits".[1] Developing some of the positions defended in *Capitalism and Freedom*[2] Friedman argued that

---

1. *New York Times Magazine*, September 13, 1970, reprinted in Thomas Donaldson and Patricia H. Werhane, eds., *Ethical Issues In Business* (Englewood Cliffs, NJ: Prentice-Hall, 1979), pp 191-197.

2. *Capitalism and Freedom* (Chicago: University of Chicago Press, 1962), pp. 133-136.

In a free-enterprise, private-property system, a
corporate executive is an employee of the owners
of the business. He has direct responsibility to
his employers. That responsibility is to conduct
the business in accordance with their desires,
which generally will be to make as much money as
possible while conforming to the basic rules of the
society, both those embodied in law and those
embodied in ethical custom.[3]

Friedman undoubtedly thought that the call for the "social
responsibility" of corporations on the part of many political
groups required the restatement of his position.[4]
 The position that Friedman develops in this paper is now
known as the classical view of corporate social responsibility,
and it has been subject to criticisms on many fronts. Some
point out that "social responsibility" is in the long-term
interests of business anyway, so there is no incompatibility
between profits and responsibility.[5] Others invoke the

---

3.   Donaldson and Werhane, p. 192.   The earlier statement of this thesis is slightly different:

(In) a free economy...there is one and only one
social responsibility of business - to use its
resources and engage in activiities designed to
increase its profits so long as it stays within the
rules of the game, which is to say, engages in
open and free competition, without deception or
fraud. *Capitalism and Freedom*, p. 136.

This earlier statement (quoted in the 1970 paper) is ambiguous on the matter of ethical constraints on business.

4.   For instance, the 1969 "Project on Corporate Responsibility" See John Collins, "Case Study - Campaign to Make
General Motors Responsible" in Donaldson & Werhane, pp.
90-101.

existence of an "Iron Law of Responsibility" which will
snatch away power from irresponsible firms.[6] It is also often
claimed that the free competitive markets presupposed by
Friedman's analysis are long since gone, if they ever
existed.[7] Others argue that large corporations have enor-
mous power and ability which can and should be used to
solve social problems,[8] some of which business contributed to
or created in the first place.[9]

Some philosophers have analyzed notions of ownership
and corporate property and have found them more complex
than Friedman's analysis permits.[10] And yet others argue

---

5.   Keith Davis, "The Case for and Against Business
Assumption of Social Responsibilities", in Archie B. Carroll,
ed., *Managing Corporate Social Responsibility* (Boston: Little, Brown and Company, 1977), p. 36; Arthur A. Thomp-
son, Jr., *Economics of the Firm* (Englewood Cliffs, NJ:
Pretice-Hall, 1977), p. 327.

6.   Davis, p. 37. The text does not make it clear
whether this "Iron Law" is an empirical generalization, a
synthetic a priori truth, or a normative principle; in any
case, it appears to be Professor Davis' most prized discovery.

7.   James F. Stoner, *Management* (Englewood Cliffs, NJ:
Prentice-Hall, 1978), p.77.

8.   Keith· Davis, "Five Propositions for Social Responsibility", in George A. Steiner and John F. Steiner, eds.,
Issues in Business and Society, 2nd ed. (New YorK: Random House, 1977), pp. 182-183, 186-187; Davis, "The Case
For and Against...", pp. 39-40.

9.   Stoner, p. 77.

10.   Lawrence C. Becker, "Property Theory and the Corporation", in Michael Hoffman, ed., *Proceedings of the Second National Conference on* Busines Ethics (Washington, DC:
University Press of America, 1979), pp 257-267; Michael

that the "rules of the game" have changed and that the corporation should conform to "the new demands of society."[11]
   The problem with most of these criticisms is that they do
not actually challenge Friedman's stated thesis.   It is worth
noting the exact nature of his claim.   He is *not* arguing that
corporations have only legal obligations and thus may (morally) maximize profits subject only to legal constraints.
Instead he is arguing that corporations should maximize
profits subject to the basic rules of the society as embodied
in law *and* in ethical custom.   Thus, if we take Friedman at
his word, he grants that corporations are legitimately constrained by ethical norms in the pursuit of profit.[12]
   Now much ink has been spilled trying to show that corporations are and should be subject to moral constraints.
But can this really be the issue, since Friedman (and most
everyone else?) concedes the point ("...while conforming to
the basic rules of the society, both those embodied in law
and those embodied in ethical custom.")?[13] What then is the

---

Hoffman and James V. Fisher, "Corporate Responsibility:
Property and Liability", in Tom L.   Beauchamp & Bowie
eds., *Ethical Theory and Business* (Englewood Cliffs, NJ:
Prentice-Hall, 1979) pp. 187-196.

   11.   Melvin Anshen, "Changing the Social Contract: A
Role for Business," and Norman E. Bowie, "Changing the
Rules", both in Beauchamp & Bowie, pp. 141-147, and
147-150.

   12.   See also Theodore Levitt, "The Danger of Social
Responsibility", in Beauchamp & Bowie, p. 141: "In the end
business has only two responsibilities - to obey the elemen-
tary canons of everyday face-to-face civility (honesty, good
faith, and so on) and to seek material gain."

   13.   There is, of course, an issue concerning the ontolo-
gical status of corporations and whether they are the sort of
things that can have social responsibilities or moral obligations.   But I take it that this is not the central question of
the debate.

debate about? Management textbooks now announce the victory of Friedman's critics and the advent of a new, socially
responsible firm.[14] Are these celebrations warranted?

In a recent book, *The Moral Foundations of Professional
Ethics*, Alan H. Goldman analyzes and criticizes Friedman's
position, and we may turn to his account for an elucidation
of the issues at stake in the debate. Goldman sets up the
question in the manner customary to Friedman's critics:

> The question is not whether people in business
> should observe legal limits, but whether they
> ought to recognize moral obligations beyond
> requirements of law, when assumption of such obli-
> gations is incompatible with maximization of profit.
> Should managers sacrifice profits for moral reasons
> not incorporated into law, or can they assume that
> pursuit of profit within legal limits will tend
> toward a moral social outcome?[15]

Expressed thus, there should be no disagreement with Friedman in the event that Goldman should argue that there are
or ought to be some moral constraints on business over and
above ordinary legal constraints. But Goldman poses
another question, one which clarifies much of what is at
issue. The deeper question is whether

> those in professional - in this case, managerial -
> roles assess each decision in ordinary moral terms
> directly, or should they view it in terms of special
> professional norms?... My question here is whether
> the position of corporate manager is *strongly*

---

14.   See, for instance, the texts mentioned in notes 5
and 7. I gather from my business ethics students (at the
University of Ottawa) that the theory of the "social responsible" firm is now widely accepted in management curricula.

15.   Alan Goldman, *The Moral Foundations Of Professional
Ethics* (Totowa, NJ: Rowman & Littlefield, 1980), p. 261.

role-differentiated . . . [16]

(where a social position is strongly role-differentiated if special, and morally justified, professional norms are applicable
to it, and if its occupant is thereby permitted or required to
ignore, or weight less heavily in relation to the professional
norm, considerations that would otherwise be morally crucial.) [17]
Goldman states the case for profit maximization subject
only to legal constraints. [18] From a utilitarian point of view,
with the focus on aggregate social welfare, the position is
found wanting. [19] Although Friedman does not appear to be a
utilitarian, [20] the utilitarian case for profit maximazation subject only to legal constraints may be worth examining and
rebutting, if only to clear the deck. Goldman also considers
the question from the standpoint of "rights". Unfortunately,
no specific theory of moral rights is invoked, and contentious claims about positive or welfare rights are made without
adequate defense. [21] Goldman concludes that

> The profit-maximization principle, then, does not
> appear to be morally justifiable, except within

---

16. Goldman, p. 260, (emphasis added).

17. Goldman, p. 260.

18. Goldman, pp. 262-268. It is not clear whether Goldman believes that Friedman holds such a thesis.

19. Goldman, pp.268-271.

20. See the interview in *Reason* 6 (December 1974), p.
6.

21. Goldman, pp. 276-277. Although the lack of a clear
theory of moral rights is characteristic of much of the literature, it is precisely such positive or welfare rights that
many defenders of the free market reject.

> ordinary   moral   constraints   of   honoring
> rights...(T)he position of business manager does
> not appear to be strongly role-differentiated:
> profits cannot be placed above moral rights that
> impose constraints in all areas of nonprofessional
> behavior as well.[22]

Goldman goes on to press many points against those who
would claim that the law is sufficient to ensure compliance of
business people with social and moral rules.[23]

Goldman's analysis of the issues and his case against the
view that managerial positions are strongly role differentiated
are useful for understanding what might be at stake in the
debate over the social responsibility of business.   If my
account of Friedman is correct, Goldman is merely restating,
albeit in an illuminating manner, the concerns of Friedman's
critics.   He is not, however, directly challenging Friedman's
stated position.   The debate required further clarification.[24]

Friedman's original article appears to have been a
response to some of the then popular proposals that corporations take on a wide variety of social projects.   The disagreement Friedman expresses does not seem to be over the
legitimacy of imposing (some) moral constraints on business
over and above the demands of the law, or so I have
argued.   Friedman and, say, Ralph Nader could both agree
that profit maximization should be permitted only within the
constraints of legal *and* moral norms.   But much disagreement would undoubtedly remain.   The *nature* and *extent* of
these moral (and legal) constraints are matters about which
they would surely disagree.   And this should provide us

---

22.   Goldman, pp. 276-277.

23.   Goldman, pp. 277ff.

24.   After I wrote this essay I read a very interesting
article by Christopher McMahon, entitled "Morality and the
Invisible Hand" in *Philosophy & Public Affairs* 10 (1981),
247-277, which touches on the issues that I am discussing.

with the clue for understanding what is at stake in the debate between Friedman and his critics.

It appears that the debate over the social responsibilities of corporations really concerns the *nature* and *extent* of the moral (and legal) norms that should constrain the pursuit of profit. Although all agree that profit maximization is permissible only if subject to certain constraints, both moral and legal, some believe that the constraints should be of a certain type and very extensive, while other disagree.

I should like to advance the debate further by clarifying the question of the nature of the moral constraints that are to be imposed on corporte pursuit of profit. And I should like to do so in a manner that does justice to what I believe are the concerns of economists such as Friedman. To do this I shall make use of the notion of a Prisoners' Dilemma Norm.

The Prisoners' Dilemma (hereafter a PD) is well-known situation which may be represented by the following matrix (for two person PDs):

		B	
	b1		b2
a1	(3,3)		(1,4)
A			
a2	(4,1)		(2,2)

where a1 and a2, b1 and b2 are actions open to A and B respectively, and where the numbers in parentheses represent the preferences of A and B respectively on a scale of 1 to 4, with 1 being the best and 4 the worst outcome. The problem with a PD is that if A and B are rational (in the utility-maximization sense) and disinterested, they will select a1 and b1 respectively. For a1 *dominates* a2; that is, whatever B does, A is better off choosing a1. The argument is simple: if B does b1, A is better off doing a1, and if B does b2, A is better off doing a1. Since B's reasoning is the same, B chooses b1. The outcome, if both parties reason thus, is the outcome represented by (a1,b1)

The problem here is that (a1,b1) is sub-efficient in the Pareto sense (where an outcome is *efficient*, or "optimal", if and only if no one can do better, given the returns to others). Both could have done better had each acted differently; the outcome represented by (a2,b2) while neither party's first choice, is more advantageous to each than (a1,b1). The latter if Pareto-inferior to (a2,b2) But the more advantageous (a2,b2) is not available if A and B act independently (and rationally). The mutually advantageous (a2,b2), which we may call the "cooperative outcome", is not stable in the absence of constraints on rational, independent choices of A and B (where an outcome is *stable* if and only if no one can do better given the actions of others). The cooperative outcome (a2,b2) is Pareto-efficient but not stable; the "non-cooperative" outcome (a1,b1) is stable but not efficient. Thus the Prisoners' Dilemma.

There are a number of "solutions" to PDs. An "agreement" between A and B would bring about the Pareto-preferred (a2,b2) only if rendered stable. An enforcer, who would prevent either party from defecting from such an "agreement", could solve the problem. Norms internalized or backed up by sanctions would also work. Let us consider this solution.

A norm I shall characterize simply as a general prescription which regulates conduct and obligates all to whom it applies. A norm in this sense should be understood as overruling considerations of immediate interest. Norms, backed up by sanctions or internalized by agents, can provide a way out of PDs. For compliance with the appropriate norm ensures that each party to a dilemma selects that act which jointly secures the desired Pareto-efficient outcome; each party is constrained not to select his/her dominant act.

Let us call a norm which constrains agents to forego their cominant act in a PD a "PD norm".[25] Given general compliance, such a norm allows rational agents to secure the mutually advantageous (a2,b2) outcome of a PD. A general argument for such norms would run as follows: in a PD, the outcome of individual rational actions is sub-efficient, in the

---

25. See Edna Ullmann-Margalit, *The Emergence of Norms* (Oxford, Oxford University Press, 1977), chapter II.

Pareto sense. A Pareto-preferred "cooperative" outcome, while mutually advantageous, is not stable. Rational agents will not constrain their independent choices unless assured that others will do so as well. Each has good reason to believe that the others will not so comply, given than non-compliance dominates compliance. A PD norm, if respected, will constrain agents from defecting from the cooperative outcome. Assuming that the norm has the form, "When in a PD, choose the cooperative action, unless the other defects, in which case defect", each is to comply provided the other complies. By so constraining the actions of each, the PD norm secures the mutually advantageous cooperative outcome[26]

This general argument for PD norms is an argument that can be given for (much of) morality. It can be argued that (most) rational moral rules are in fact PD norms, and that their justification is their role in enabling rational agents to secure pareto-preferred, mutually advantageous outcomes in PD situations.[27] Essentially this is the approach of contractarian moralists beginning with Hobbes and Hume.[28] On this

---

26. See the argument for "constrained maximization" in David P. Gauthier, "Reason and Maximization", *Canadian Journal of Philosophy* 4 (1975), 418-433, partially reprinted in Brian Barry and Russell Hardin, eds., *Rational Man and Irrational Society* (Beverly Hill, CA: Sage Publications, 1982), pp. 85-106.

27. This thesis is a normative one: (most) rational moral norms are of type x. Ullmann-Margalit's concern in her book is explanatory: actual norms are of type x, y, and so on. It should be noted that this account of moral norms is likely to be plausible primarily for rules of justice and mutual aid. Virtues such as courage or charity are probably not explicable in terms of PD norms. On the differences between justice and these virtues see Philippa Foot, *Virtues and Vices* (Berkeley and Los Angeles: University of California Press, 1978).

view, the "theory of justice is a part, perhaps the most significant part, of the theory of rational choice."[29] The contractarian simply identifies (rationally binding) moral norms
with (some) PD norms and invokes the general argument for
the latter in defense of the former. For the contractarian,
PDs are ubiquitous and PD norms conventions necessary to
remedy the problem.

A similar argument for moral constraints on the actions
of profit maximizing corporate managers may be developed.
Simply identify the relevant moral constraints with some PD
norms. But we need not even do this. For there are
already two widely accepted arguments, one for law, the
other for public provision of collective goods, that have the
same form as the general argument for PD norms. And
these widely accepted arguments may simply be extended to
moral constraints. The rationalization of law here is similar
to the general argument for PD norms and thus to the the
contractarian's defense of moral norms.

The general argument for law that I refer to views legal
constraints as conventional devices that (ideally) function to
enable rational agents to overcome what are possibly the
worst of all PDs, those created by the use of force and
fraud. By forbidding or regulating force and fraud, and by
arbitrating disputes, a legal system may serve to enable
rational agents to overcome certain problems of interaction.[30]

---

28. See Thomas Hobbes, *Leviathan* (1651) and David
Hume, *A Treatise of Human Nature* (1739-40), Book III. For
contempory ·contractarians, see especially the writings of
Kurt Baier, James Buchanan, David Gauthier, Gilbert Har-
man, and J. L. Mackie.

29. Rawls, p. 16. Rawls is related to the contractarian
tradition, but his work has many features which make it
hard to classify him as a genuine contractarian. See Jean
Hampton, "Contracts and Choices: Does Rawls Have a Social
Contract Theory?", *Journal of Philosophy LXXVII* (1980),
315-338.

30. James Buchanan, *The Limits of Liberty* (Chicago:

Since the defenders of profit maximization grant the
necessity of legal constraints, insofar as they accept the
above argument for law, they are open to the contractarian's
defense of moral constraints.[31] If moral constraints are more
efficient than the cumbersome arm of the law in certain areas
of business, then it is difficult to see how someone could
accept the general argument for legal constraints but not the
contractarian case for moral constraints.[32]

Such a defense of (some) moral constraints on profit
maximization may, as was mentioned, be reached also by
another route. Most neo-classical economists grant that
where there exits significant collective goods (or collective
"bads"), there is a (defeasible) case for public intervention
in the market. A collective good (or bad) is one which is
"non-rival" in consumption and non-excludable: one person's consumption does not diminish another's, and it is not
feasible to exclude people from its benefits (or costs). We
are all familiar with the discussions of national defense and
lighthouses in micro-economics texts. The problem posed by
collective goods (or bads) is that rational agents interacting
in a competitive market will not produce an efficient quantity
of such goods (or an efficient decrease of collective bads).
Since consumers receive the good whether or not they pay
for it, it can be anticipated that producers will not have a

University of Chicago Press, 1975), especially chapters 4
and 7. Buchanan's account of law is not to be confused
with that associated with the Chicago Law & Economics Program, cf. Richard A. Posner, *Economic Analysis of Law*, 2nd
ed. (Boston: Little, Brown, and Company, 1977).

31. This is not true, of course, of proponents of natural
law or natural rights ethical theories, but then they have
other arguments for imposing moral constraints on business.

32. Goldman mentions many of the standard arguments
for the antecedent; the growth and consequent disadvantages
of government bureaucracy (p. 279), the development of
moral character (p. 279), the limits of the effectiveness of
the law (pp. 279-280).

sufficient incentive to produce Pareto-efficient quantities
(the same for reduction of collective bads, *mutatis mutandis*). Often, economists and public finance theorists conclude that government has a role in the provision of signifi-
cant collective goods (or the abatement of significant
collective bads). The classic statement of this view is provided by Adam Smith:

> According to the system of natural liberty, the
> sovereign has the duty... of erecting and main-
> taining certain public works and certain public
> institutions, which it can never be for the interest
> of any individual, or small number of individuals,
> to erect and maintain; because the profit could
> never repay the expense to any individual or small
> number of individuals, though it may frequently do
> much more than repay it to a great society.[33]

The argument for public provision of significant collective goods is similar to that for PD norms. For the situation
facing individuals seeking to obtain a collective good is a
PD.[34] For any collective good, we may find that individuals
have the following preferences:

(1) the others pay, I do not
(2) we all pay
(3) no one pays
(4) the others do not pay, I do

In the event of (3) or (4), the good is not produced.
Given a sufficiently large number of individuals, the outcome
of individually rational action is (3), or with goods that may
provided in variable quantities the outcome is likely to be

---

33. Adam Smith, *The Wealth of Nations* (1776) (New
York: Modern Library, 1965), p. 651.

34. Ullmann-Margalit, pp. 49-53; Buchanan, pp. 108-110;
Russell Hardin, "Collective Action as an Agreeable n-Prison-
ers' Dilemma", *Behavioral Science* 16 (1971), 472-479,
reprinted in Barry and Hardin, pp. 123-135.

sub-efficient production. The situation is an n-person PD.

Now if one grants this standard argument for the public provision of significant collective goods, and/or if one accepts the PD argument for law and legal constraints (and the empirical claim that moral constraints may be more efficient in certain circumstances), then one has a general (contractarian) argument for moral constraints. Surely most defenders of profit maximization - whomever they may be - must grant the PD argument for moral constraints.

This analysis reveals, I shall now argue, what is ultimately at stake in the debate. Granted that it is not difficult to justify imposing (some) moral constraints on the profit maximizing activities of corporate managers, the real issue is, what is the nature of these constraints? Specifically, are they merely PD norms, or are there some other sorts of moral norms that ought also to be imposed on business? The general argument invoked justifies PD norms but only such norms. We may wish to constrain the activities of business people in other ways as well.

We could probably analyze, for instance, certain proposed constraints on corporate pollution as PD moral norms. After all, pollution is a classical collective bad. Suppose that a number of rational agents have the following preference rankings:

    (1) I pollute, the others cut back
    (2) we all cut back
    (3) no one cuts back
    (4) they pollute, I cut back

Then in the absence of some PD norm, or some system of enforcement, the rational individuals will continue to pollute.

Proposals that corporations generally assist in cleaning up the environment even where they did not contribute much or at all to the original pollution, or proposals that corporations assist in resolving certain other social problems - e.g. devising alternative modes of transportation, solving chronic unemployment - probably could not be analyzed, much less justified, as PD norms.[35] For the relevant norms in these

---

35. Some such proposal might be PD norms, but I am

cases have more to do with redistribution that with resolving PDs.

Sometimes such proposals are better conceived as *goals* for, rather than *constraints* on business. At the extreme, it might be claimed that business (and everyone else) ought to maximize the general welfare of society, or something of the sort. Such proposals ultimately attack the legitimacy of general goal of profit maximization. For unless it can be shown that aggregate welfare maximization and profit maximization always coincide - and I assume that since Bentham there has been universal scepticism on this point - the two will be incompatible goals for business. One cannot *maximize* two values, except insofar as they are identical.

There are no such difficulties with the imposition of *constraints* on profit maximization, since the latter is to be understood in the first place as the maximization of some value subject to certain constraints. One more constraint poses no theoretical difficulty. But the nature of these constraints does raise certain questions.

Let me suggest that the important issue about the "social responsibilities" of corporations concerns the nature of the moral constraints to be legitimately imposed on profit maximization. Specifically, it seems that the important question is whether all legitimate moral constraints on business are PD norms. The defenders of profit maximization thus are actually defending the position that only PD norms may be imposed on business, while the defenders of "responsible" firms seek the imposition of other kinds of norms as well. I would suggest that we should interpret those that share Friedman's concern that we may impose too many constraints on business as arguing that all legitimate moral (and legal?) constraints imposed on business be PD norms. Economists and like-minded social thinkers can easily accept the PD argument for moral norms; indeed, they are committed to it insofar as they accept the parallel arguments for law and for the public provision of significant collective goods. They may argue that *in fact* few such laws, publicly provided collective goods, or moral norms are justified; but they are

---

thinking of cases like the Campaign GM mentioned in note 4.

committed to the claim that at least *some* laws, publicly provided collective goods, and moral constraints are justified
given certain (plausible) empirical assumptions. Thus, it
may be plausible to interpret the position of critics such as
Friedman as defending the view that all legitimate moral (and
legal?) constraints on business be PD norms.

I do not propose to develop a position on this question.
For such a position requires the resolution of certain issues
in contractarian moral theory, especially the problems concerning the determination of the proper baseline for the
contractarian derivation of morality.[36] My analysis of the
debate over the social responsibilites of business does show
how the resolution of the real issue depends in large part on
the resolution of a certain problem in moral theory, namely
whether all legitimate moral constraints - or rather, constraints imposed by justice - are PD norms. Thus, the
question of the social responsibility of corporations turns not
only on certain matters of economic theory (generally ignored
by moral philosophers) but on certain matters of moral
theory (generally ignored by economists).

I shall conclude with some remarks about the significance
of this general issue and of the interpretation I have
offered. Many social commentators worry over what they
perceive as a lack of understanding of the successes and
failures of market economies on the part of reformers seeking
to impose "social responsibilities" on corporations. In recent
years it has often been argued that the success of many
reformers in legislating "progressive" restrictions on business has resulted in decreased economic efficiency and in
benefiting the very interests that were to be constrained.

---

36. Contractarian moral theory seeks to rationalize morality as a mutually advantageous convention constraining the
interactions of rational agents. The need for such a conventional system of norms is the prevalence of PDs. The
major difficulty with such theories has to do with the baseline for determining mutual advantage; it is not yet clear
whether it is necessary to introduce some non-PD norms at
this stage of the theory.

Some legal (and moral) constraints have the effect of
strengthening the position of dominant firms or groups,
often by giving established firms a competitive advantage
over newcomers. We are all familiar with "public interest"
legislation that in effect imposes entry costs on competitors
or which establishes tax or other concessions to established
firms. This worry about apparently progressive legislation
may be clarified by the notion of a PD norm.

It is not obvious that all PD norms are desirable either
from a moral or from some other point of view. When I discussed such norms earlier I did not distinguish between different interests that might be at issue. However, it surely
has already occured to some readers that price-fixing, honor
amongst thieves, and professional prohibitions on advertising
may be PD norms that protect the collective interests of
dominant firms, thieves, and professionals to the detriment
of the rest of the public. Most of us probably would not
want genuine criminals placed in a literal PD by a clever
district attorney to achieve their mutually advantageous
cooperative outcome. Some PDs may, from the point of view
of a larger public, be desirable. A good example of this
may well be market competition itself, which is an n-person
PD for producers.[37] Thus a PD norm may enable certain
competitors to secure an outcome mutually advantageous to
them but disadvantageous to others.

I shall characterize, albeit most inadequately, a
"restricted PD norm" as one which functions to stabilize the
cooperative outcome of a PD to the advantage of the parties
but at the expense of others, where the parties to the PD
are a (proper) subset of the public whose interests we wish
to protect or futher. An adequate account of such norms
depends on·an explication of 'at the expense of others', a
matter that I shall not go into here.

----

37. This point is made by Tal Scriven, "Grovernment
Interference and the Prisoners' Dilemma", this volume, pp.
97-107. See also my review of C. Dyke, *Philosophy of Economics*, in *Dialogue* XXII (1983), p. 182, where I also make
this point.

If in fact many actual social norms are PD norms, it may
be that some are restricted PD norms such as the above.
And it is surely not these that we should wish to impose on
business -- *established* business would only be too glad to
oblige. The danger of much "progressive" legislation is
often exactly of this nature. Witness the now evident
effects of, for instance, professional rules against advertising in law and medicine, "unfair" competition laws, or much
of the post-Watergate legislation on campaign financing. Too
often the main beneficiaries of such legislation are not whom
we might think. What may be justified in the name of the
public interest may too often be a restricted PD norm in the
collective interest of only a small segment of the larger public.

Postscript, 1984

There are two errors in the argument of this essay,
one more significant than the other. First, it is doubtful
that all collective goods problems *are* PDs. For in the former it is *not* always the case that it is rational for an agent
to choose not to contribute *whatever* the others do. Should
my contribution suffice to produce a minimally acceptable
quantity of some collective good once a certain number of
individuals have contributed, then it may not be rational for
me to refrain from contributing. But then I do not have a
dominant strategy, a defining feature of a PD. This is
clearest in the case of what Russell Hardin calls "steps
goods", namely goods that come in steps or lumps. But this
may also be the case of other sorts of goods as well.[38] My

---

38. See Russell Hardin, *Collective Action* (Baltimore:
Johns Hopkins University Press, 1982), pp. 55-61. I am
indebted to my colleague Jean Hampton for the idea that
some collective goods problems are not PDs. See her unpublished monograph, "Solving Free Rider Problems" (UCLA,

argument may not ultimately be affected, as all that I
require is that the "public choice" argument for law, the
economic argument for public provision of collective goods,
and the contractarian argument for moral constraints be
identical in structure. And this may be the case even if the
collective goods problems is not a PD.

  Secondly, it is misleading to say that market competition
is a PD. For the equilibria of interaction in "perfectly competitive" markets are in what game theorists call "the core".
One of the features of the core is that no new coalition can
form that would improve the positions of its members.[39] But
this is to say that there are no PDs in such a market. Market competition can be a PD only if "imperfect."

---

manuscript).

  39. See Michael Bacharach, *Economics and the Theory of
Games* (Boulder, Co: Westview Press, 1977), pp. 9-11, and
Kenneth Arrow and Frank Hahn, *General Competitive Analy-
sis* (San Francisco: Holden-Day, 1971), pp. 183-206.

Corporate Agency and Individual Responsibility

ORGANIZATIONAL REALITY

Michael Keeley

My primary purpose is to raise doubts about widely accepted notions of organizational reality. While my remarks will be directed toward nonphilosophical works in organizational theory, my own specialty, I think philosophers may find them relevant. Some philosophers borrow heavily from organizational theory in analyzing the moral responsibilities of social systems,[1] some adopt the same form of social realism that organizational theorists advocate,[2] and not all seem to be aware of the descriptive and normative shortcomings of our discipline.

Many organizational theorists claim that their subject matter has "objective reality," that organizations possess "an existence independent of their members and...power over peoples' lives."[3] Today, such claims are not generally considered remarkable. But they have historically provoked

---

1. For example, John Ladd, "Morality and the Ideal of Rationality in Formal Organizations," *Monist* 54 (1970), pp. 488-516.

2. For example, Peter French, "The Corporation As a Moral Person," *American Philosophical Quarterly* 16 (1979), pp. 207-215.

3. Howard E. Aldrich, *Organizations and Environments* (Englewood Cliffs: Prentice-Hall, Inc., 1979), p. 2.

controversy,[4] and a few theorists still find it necessary to take up the question, "Are organizations real?"[5] I believe that those who renew past debates over the reality of groups are right in supposing there is more to be said. This essay will contrast two opposing approaches to organizational reality: the dominant "realist" approach, which treats social groups as objects that act like natural entities, and the "interactionist" approach, which treats social groups as processes that consist of the joint acts of individual persons. These views will be further distinguished below. Some presumed theoretical and descriptive merits of the realist approach will then be questioned. And, finally, normative advantages of the interactionist approach will be outlined.

Theoretical Issues

    Richard Hall suggests a major point of dispute between realist and interactionist views in his book, *Organizations: Structure and Process*. Hall states that, at first glance, the question of whether organizations are real seems inane. "Organizations surround us and...we are a part of them most of our lives. But a second look at the question will reveal a very basic issue: whether organizations are anything more than individuals who have come together in an interaction system."[6] If we look even closer, it appears that

----

4. Floyd H. Allport, "The Group Fallacy in Relation to Social Science," *American Journal of Sociology* 29 (1924), pp. 688-703.

5. Richard H. Hall, *Organizations: Structure and Process* (Second Edition) (Englewood Cliffs: Prentice-Hall, Inc., 1977).

6. Hall, p. 23. This book is a useful focus for discussion, since it provides a solid overview of mainstream organ-

this basic issue does not concern whether organizations are
real at all; rather, it concerns whether organizations are one
or another *kind* of reality, one "more than" or not more than
a system of interaction. The basic issue is easily obscured
by the question, "Are organizations real?," which is a red
herring. In addressing this question, in arguing that
organizations *are* real, realists tend to assume that only a
particular (noninteractionist) conception of organization
respects group reality. This assumption is not often chal-
lenged, and it conceals the full extent of the realist proposition. This proposition is that organizations are not just
real, but a specific form of reality -- namely, actors that
have intentional properties we normally attribute to living
organisms:

> When we hear statements such as "It is company
> policy," "Z State University never condones cheat-
> ing," or "Trans-Rhode Island Airline greets you
> with a smile," these are recognizable as being
> about organizations. Organizations do have poli-
> cies, do and do not condone cheating, and may or
> may not greet you with a smile. They also manu-
> facture goods, administer policies, and protect the
> citizenry. These are organizational actions and
> involve properties of organizations, not individu-
> als. They are carried out by individuals, but the
> genesis of the actions remains in the organization.
> The answer to our basic question, then, is:
> Organizations are real. [7]

The attribution of organismic properties to social groups
has long been common in realist theories, at least as

---

izational theory and contains one of the most explicit defen-
ses of the realist approach to appear recently; see Charles
E. Warriner, "Groups are Real: A Reaffirmation," *American
Sociological Review* 21 (1956), pp. 549-554, for an earlier
defense.

7. Hall, p. 27.

advanced in sociological, political, and juristic classics.[8]
Such theories usually imply that other views trivialize organizations by misrepresenting them as social fictions. On this
count, realists have expressed especially sharp opposition to
views depicting organizations as interactions or agreements
among self-interested participants. Gierke, for instance,
opposes the legal view of organizations as contracts and
"treats corporate bodies as real corporate persons...which
are not merely *legally* competent ... but also really capable
of willing and acting."[9] In like manner, Hall opposes the
view of organizations as exchange systems and treats them
as really willing or goal-seeking entities. What interactionist
theories dispute, however, is not the reality of organizations, but the need for anthropomorphic conceptions of
organization. Interactionists simply substitute nonorganic
realities for organic ones as basic models of organizational
processes. One of the more popular strategies has been to
model organizations after games.[10] There is room for argument about the general utility of a game metaphor. But
games are readily understood and they serve to illustrate
how an interactionist model might explain organizational
properties that realists invoke in support of their own view.

---

8.   Emile Durkheim, *The Rules of Sociological Method*
(New York: Free Press, 1938), Otto Gierke, *Political Theories of the Middle Age* (Cambridge: Cambridge University
Press, 1900), and G.W.F. Hegel, *Philosophy of Right* (London: Oxford University Press, translated 1942, first German
edition 1821).

9.   Frederick Hallis, *Corporate Personality* (London:
Oxford University Press, 1930), p.146).

10.   Graham T. Allison, *Essence of Decision* (Boston: Little, Brown and Co., 1971), Erving Goffman, *Strategic Interaction* (Philadelphia: University of Pennsylvania Press,
1969), and David Silverman, *The Theory of Organisations*
(London: Heinemann, 1970).

An Interactionist Response to Evidence for Realism

Realists frequently remind us that organizations remain virtually unchanged despite replacement of individual participants. This fact is taken as evidence that organizations "have an existence of their own, above and beyond the behavior and performance of individuals."[11] The troublesome word here is "existence." One can see that organizations, given their continuity, must have existence in the sense of independent reality. But it is not obvious that they must have existence in the sense of organic being, that in them, for instance, resides the "genesis" of persistent collective action. Imagine that organizations are like games with respect to participant replacement. A game often remains much the same while players change. This fact suggests that the game has an independent existence. Still, it does not suggest that the game has a life of its own, above and beyond those of the participants. Games are stable features of social behavior because some *people* find it worthwhile to perpetuate them. Just as it is unnecessary to attribute organismic properties to games to account for their stability over time, it is unnecesary to attribute these to organizations.

Another fact about organizations that realists submit causes difficulty for interactionist views is this: organizations tend to have much influence over their members, who are not as free to construct lines of behavior as some interactionists suppose. Hall says, "The organization trains, indoctrinates, and persuades its members to respond on the basis of the requirements of their position. This response becomes quite regularized and routinized and does not involve the interaction frame of reference."[12] Realists have traditionally implied that such response involves submission

---

11. Hall, p.26.

12. Hall, pp. 24-25.

to something like the will of a social organism, as manifested
in collective tendencies or goals which direct group activities.[13] But this is not the only possibility. Again, compare
organizations to common games. Normally, a player cannot
change the rules of a game on demand. These rules constrain a player's performance, perhaps even more so than
the rules of most organizations. The game itself, however,
does not will specific performances; it does not itself train,
indoctrinate, or persuade players to behave according to the
requirements of their positions. People can *agree* with one
another to abide by certain rules, both formal and informal,
and no organismic properties need be granted to games--or
organizations--to account for rule-governed behavior.   Of
course, those currently engaged in a social practice (participants in a game, employers in an organization) will frequently have power over newcomers in specifying terms of
agreement, the power to forge "contracts of adhesion."
But, in the game case, we do not confuse this power with
powers *of the game*. Nor do we confuse prudential rule-fol-
lowing in games, wherein participants observe rules to
advance their own interests, with compliance for the sake of
the game's interests, goals or requirements. The avoidance
of this confusion in the case of organizations is characteristic of interactionist models.
        There remains a related issue. We do at times have rea-
son to attribute *acts* to organizations rather than to their
participants.   The statement, "Exxon made a profit last
quarter," probably makes more sense than, "Some named
individuals who associate as Exxon made a profit last quarter." This fact seems to be what realists have in mind in
claiming that the group is "more than" the sum of its parts.
Interactionists, though, do not generally dispute this claim.
Organizations can have many properties that are not simply
aggregates of or reducible to individual properties.   For
instance, an organization may produce consequences, like
profits, that are true properties of the organization and not
just the summed effects of individuals. And it is proper to

---

13.   See, especially, Durkheim on this point.

say that organizations act in the sense of *producing* these
consequences.   But it is a large leap of logic to say that
organizations also act in the sense of *intending* their consequences, that they have, say, goals of their own which
guide their actions.   This is a dubious assertion.

Once more, the game model is useful for purposes of
illustration.   To say that a game, such as football, produces
revenue at many universities is a logical attribution of action
to the game; revenue is a synergistic consequence of the
game as played at the college level.   However, to say that
the game of football intends to generate revenue is inappropriate.   Various people will have intentions or expectations
for the game: university administrators may intend revenue,
players and spectators may intend victory for one team or
the other, and, certainly, the game may have consequences
that are unexpected.   Yet, the game itself intends nothing.
As a real but nonliving system of action, it lacks the capacity to prefer any of its own outcomes.   So too in the case of
organizations, the consequences of action may be properties
of an organization, while the intent of that action may not.

The Challenge to Realism

As mentioned earlier, my aim is not to present a brief
for a game model of organization, but only to demonstrate
how an interactionist approach might handle typical claims of
social realists.   No doubt, organizations are more like contracts than games, the former suggesting a broader type of
interactionist model.[14]   What interactionist views primarily
challenge is the realist implication that pervades organizational theory from introductory through advanced works:

---

14.   Michael Keeley, "Organizational Analogy: A Comparison of Organismic and Social Contract Models," *Administrative Science Quarterly*, 25 (1980), pp. 337-362.

> The primary rationale for the existence of
> organizations is that certain goals can be achieved
> only through the concerted action of groups of
> people. Thus, whether the goal is profit, provid-
> ing education, religion, or health care, ... organi-
> zations are characterized by their *goal directed*
> behavior.[15]
>   The simple but basic fact is that the organiza-
> tion would not exist if it were not for some common
> purpose... The purpose or goal is the basis for
> organizational activities.[16]

> Social scientists have found it useful to distinguish
> formal organizations from ... other forms of social
> organization precisely because formal organizations
> have explicit, specific, and limited goals ... Were
> we to drop goals from consideration, there would
> be no need for special theories or formal organiza-
> tional structure and behavior.[17]

The argument so far is that organizations needs not be goal
directed; they can exist, can have real structure and behavior, and still have no intentional properties. Why does it
matter, though, whether organizations are granted or denied
organismic features? One answer is that realist imagery may
easily distort social description.

---

15. James L. Gibson, John M. Ivancevich, and James H.
Donnelly, Jr, *Organizations* (Dallas: Business Publications,
Third Edition, 1979).

16. Hall, p. 83.

17. Michael T. Hannan and John Freeman, "Obstacles to
Comparative Studies," in Paul S. Goodman and Johannes M.
Pennings, eds., *New Perspectives on Organizational Effec-
tiveness* (San Francisco: Jossey-Bass, 1977), p. 111.

Describing Organizations Realistically

In describing organizational behavior, realist views have historically encountered a serious problem: It is difficult to specify the intentions or goals that social entities are assumed to possess. Ordinary participants may only have a vague notion, if any, of an organization's goals. And organizations are unable to tell us a great deal about their true intentions through official "self" reports (e.g., charters or public communications). To deal with this problem, we are often advised to derive real, *operative* goals from analysis of group policies and procedures.[18] But most organizational operations do not consist of practices whose actual purpose is clear.

Consider a manufacturing operation involving policies and procedures that generate material consequences, such as products, salaries, profits, pollution, etc. Some of these consequences are, presumably, "goals"--reasons for action. Other must be "costs"--expenses of, rather than reasons for, action (unless we are prepared to say that any organizational consequence, even pollution, is a goal). Now, how does one categorize consequences like profits and salaries? Certain participants and observers may regard the manufacturing operation as a profit-maker, whose costs include salaries (e.g., investors). Some may regard this operation as a salary-maker, whose costs include profits (e.g., workers). Still others may consider both profits and salaries to be goals (taxing bodies) or costs (consumers). And there is ordinarily no objective, organizational criterion by which to resolve such disputes. In the final analysis, what are taken to be goals *of* an organization look very much like subjective

---

18. Charles Perrow,"The Analysis of Goals in Complex Organizations," *American Sociological Review*, 26 (1961), pp. 854-886, and Peter French, "The Corporation as a Moral Person," *American Philosophical Quarterly*, 16 (1979), pp. 207-215.

goals *for* an organization, as conceived by someone or other. Frequently, this someone is a top executive in operative-goal accounts.

It is deceptive, I think, to call goals *for* an organization, goals *of* an organization. The latter connotes a degree of unanimity (or at least acceptance) that is rarely evident in complex organizations. In small, cohesive groups with few external dependencies, the same goals *for* an organization may be intended or accepted by all participants. Yet, such cases are of limited interest. In larger organizations, like major corporations, goals *for* the organization are diverse and conflicting. And it is generally important to keep track of *whose* goals one is speaking of -- goals *for* shareholders, managers, other employees, customers, and so on. By obscuring the diversity of participant ends, the collective goal notion precipitates oversimplified analysis of social systems.

The descriptive shortcomings of goal-based theories have been well documented in past studies of organizations. Melville Dalton, for example, reports on inaccuracies of bureaucratic theory, which "assumes that members of the organization are relatively inert and ready to follow the intent of rules. The theory...slights the fact that in the larger organizations, local and personal demands take precedence in most cases."[19] His data suggest that "The typical firm is...a shifting set of constrained disruptions, powered and guided by differentially skilled and commited persons."[20] Conflict and private interest-seeking, therefore, are simply shrouded in a bureaucratic cloak. At another level of analysis, Graham Allison demonstrates how goal-based perspectives promote misleading explanations of international affairs. In his account of the Cuban missile crisis, he shows that a game-like model yields a much richer description of events than models which attribute goals and motives to the governments

---

19.   Melville Dalton, *Men Who Manage* (New York: Wiley, 1959), p. 265.

20.   Dalton, p. 270.

or organizations involved.[21] Anselm Strauss provides other
examples of insights gained by viewing groups as systems of
competitive interaction, wherein order results from agreement
on means, not ends.[22]

While the descriptive aspects of organizational models are
important, the balance of this paper will focus on normative
aspects, which have received less serious study by social
scientists. General social theories do have prescriptive as
well as descriptive implications, and realist theories tend to
oversimplify with respect to both.

Normative Implications

As Anthony Quinton notes, social realism has long
been connected with an ethical position that grants intrinsic
value to associations; groups are seen to have an irreducible
welfare (e.g., "the common good") and come to be valued
for their own sakes.[23] This ethical connection is, perhaps,
not logically necessary but it is compelling. It would seem
strange to attribute goals, needs, interests, and the like to
social entities without also granting them some claim to satisfaction of these things, some right to our respect as autonomous "beings." It is not unusual for this right to over-
whelm similar rights of individuals, as Durkheim implies:

> The interests of others can have...no more intrin-
> sic moral value than our own. In so far, how-
> ever, as another participates in the life of the

---

21.   Allison, *op. cit.*

22.   Anselm Strauss, *Negotiations* (San Francisco: Jossey-
Bass, 1978).

23.   Anthony Quinton, "Social Objects," *Proceedings of
the Aristotelian Society*, 76 (1976), pp. 1-27.

> group and in so far as he is a member of the col-
> lectivity to which we are attached, he tends to
> take on some of its dignity and he becomes an
> object of our affection and interest. ...what
> binds us morally to others is nothing intrinsic in
> their empirical individuality; it is the superior end
> of which they are the servants and instruments.[24]

This end, of course, is the well-being of the group itself.

Few contemporary theorists would express the idea so
strongly, but many popular views incorporate the notion
that, as intentional actors, organizations have a welfare or
good of their own which deserves our respect. This is evidenced in continued use of *organizational* goal attainment as
a standard of system value or "effectiveness" -- it is still
widely believed that organizations should be evaluated on the
basis of success in achieving their own objectives.[25] High
regard for the welfare of social entities is also evidenced in
continued use of *organizational* goals as ultimate values in
the selection of research questions--it is still widely believed
that an administrative science should stress how organizations attain or fail to attain their own ends. These ends
serve as "ethical givens" for focusing inquiry.[26] They indicate which aspects of reality are significant (by virtue of
goal relatedness) and which are not. The goal of organizational survival, for instance, remains an implicit value

---

24.   Emile Durkheim, *Sociology and Philosophy* (New
York: Free Press, 1974), p. 53.

25.   See Robert L. Kahn, "Organizational Effectiveness:
An Overview," in Paul S. Goodman and Johannes M. Pennings, eds., *New Perspectives on Organizational Effectiveness* (San Francisco: Jossey-Bass, 1977) and Richard Steers,
Organizational Effectiveness (Santa Monica, CA: Goodyear,
1977).

26.   Herbert A. Simon, *Administrative Behavior* (New
York: Free Press, Second Edition, 1957).

guiding much research even when attention turns to the
environment,[27] corporate social responsibilities,[28] and other
external matters. Pfeffer and Salancik make the point
explicitly that individuals and their interests have "importance" only in relation to one's power to affect organizational
well-being.[29] This proposition is offered both as a descriptive principle for understanding organizations and a prescriptive principle for managing them. The proposition, on
both interpretations, becomes questionable if organizational
survival is devalued.

Organizational goal attainment *is* regularly devalued in
everyday affairs; this fact casts doubt on the practical relevance of social realist theories. In such theories, the good
of the organization, because of its supposed generality,
tends to assume priority over (or at least parity with) the
good of individuals. But this priority (and even parity) is
contradicted by many well-established customs and well-con-
sidered moral judgments. Many of our laws, for example,
have been established precisely to defend the intrinsic
importance of individual persons against "functional requirements" for organizational goal attainment and welfare. It is
hard to see how the practical concerns that underlie laws
like our Civil Rights Acts can be incorporated in a social
realist model. It might be argued that organizations must
take antagonistic laws and opinions into account to ensure

---

27.   Howard E. Aldrich and Jeffrey Pfeffer, "Environ-
ments of Organizations," in Alex Inkeles, James Coleman and
Neil Smelser, eds., *Annual Review of Sociology*, 2 (1976),
(Palo Alto: Annual Reviews, Inc,), pp. 79-105.

28.   S. Prakash Sethi, "A Conceptual Framework for
Environmental Analysis of Social Issues and Evaluation of
Business Response Patterns," *Academy of Management
Review*, 4 (1979), pp. 63-74.

29.   Jeffrey Pfeffer and Gerald Salancik, *The External
Control of Organizations* (New York: Harper & Row, 1978),
pp. 84-89.

their own survival.[30] But the point is that the very existence of these laws and opinions, which recognize urgent
rights of individuals, calls into question the rights of organizations to pursue their own goals and, indeed, to survive at
all.

Interactionist ideas also call into question organizational
rights. The interactionist approach has historically been
connected with the position of ethical individualism, in which
"social objects, groups or institutions, have no intrinsic
value that is not constitutive of the welfare of individual
people." In contrast to the implication of social realism,
"any value {institutions} possess is purely instrumental."[31]
Again, the ethical implication may not be logically necessary,
but it is hard to escape. In denying that acts of association
create social entities with intentional properties of their own,
an interactionist is consistent in denying that such acts create entities with interests, welfares, and worth of their own.
Entities lacking the latter features are properly denied
rights.[32] Recall the model used earlier for illustration: just
as association in a game does not create intentional properties of the game, it does not create interests or rights of
the game itself. These are all properties of participating
individuals. So it is in the case of organizations.

One might reply that, unlike the game example, we do
often attribute (legal) rights to certain organizations, such
as corporations. From an interactionist standpoint, however,
this represents only the adoption of a simplifying bit of fic-
tion--a shorthand way of referring to the similar rights of
some individuals, which should be (and routinely is) dropped
when it oversimplifies and abridges the rights of other

---

30.   Sethi, *op. cit.*

31.   Quinton, p. 13.

32.   Joel Feinberg, "The Rights of Animals and Unborn
Generations," in W. T. Blackstone, ed., *Philosophy and
Environmental Crisis* (Athens, GA: University of Georgia
Press, 1974), pp. 43-68.

individuals. Robert Hamilton points out that in law, for instance,

> Most business corporation acts provide that a cor-
> poration may sue or be sued in its own name, and
> it is generally accepted that the power to sue or
> be sued in its own name is an attribute of an
> entity. Thus, as a "short and convenient mode"
> of describing the legal relationships surrounding a
> corporation, considering the corporation as a sepa-
> rate entity is undoubtedly useful. It should be
> emphasized, however, that a corporation possesses
> these attributes, not because it is an entity, but
> because the business corporation acts so provide.
> Also, it certainly does not necessarily follow that
> because a corporation possessses certain entity
> attributes under the statutes, it possessses other
> entity attributes as well.[33]

Hamilton concludes,

> Whether or not {a corporation} should be deemed a
> separate "legal entity" or "legal person" should
> depend on the question to be resolved. A corpo-
> ration may be an entity for some purposes and not
> for others. In such circumstances, to argue that
> a corporation is an entity, and therefore that cer-
> tain results follow, is to put the cart before the
> horse.[34]

The central normative weakness of the realist view is that it does not recognize this point. Instead,

> Corporations can be full-fledged moral persons and

---

33. Robert W. Hamilton, "The Corporate Entity," *Texas Law Review*, 49 (1971), p. 98I.

34. Hamilton, p 1009.

have whatever privileges, rights and duties as are
in the normal course of affairs, accorded to moral
persons {like human beings.}[35]

A concrete case concerning "corporate rights" may help to
demonstrate the imprudence of such a view.

Corporate Rights of Speech

Recently the United States Supreme Court, in *First
National Bank v. Bellotti,* invalidated a Massachusetts statute
prohibiting corporate expenditures aimed at "influencing or
affecting the vote on any question submitted to the voters,
other than one materially affecting any of the property,
business or assets of the corporation."[36] The Court held,
five to four, that this statute violated "the corporation's"
rights to free speech. Writing for the majority, Justice
Powell said,

> If the speakers here were not corporations, no one
> would suggest that the State could silence their
> proposed speech. It is the type of speech indis-
> pensable to decision-making in a democracy, and
> this is no less true because the speech comes from
> a corporation rather than an individual.[37]

Concerned with the implication of the statute for media corporations, Chief of Justice Burger added,

---

35.   French, p. 207.

36.   *First National Bank V. Bellotti* 435 U.S. 1978, p.
768.

37.   p. 777.

> The First Amendment does not "belong" to any
> definable category of persons or entities: It
> belongs to all who exercise its freedoms.[38]

Realists would, no doubt, agree. But a more sophisticated
position is outlined in Justice White's dissent.

Justice White argues that corporate communication is not
on a par with individual expression and, thus, may be subject to restrictions that do not apply to individual speech.
He maintains that the First Amendment values self-expres-
sion, self-realization, and self-fulfillment, which are not necessarily furthered by corporate communications: "They do
not represent a manifestation of individual freedom or
choice."[39] Justice White well recognizes that *some* communications of corporations deserve protection as a convenient
means of protecting individual First Amendment rights (e.g.,
in case of the press or common-interest groups like the
NAACP). He explains, however, that profit-making corporations generally have no common political or social goals, that
communications by corporate managers regarding political or
social issues are not ordinarily expressive of the heterogene-
ous beliefs of shareholders, and, therefore, that such communications are not guaranteed full protection as speech *of*
the corporation. The speech in question is, in fact, that of
managers, and it is proper to disallow use of corporate
funds for the propagation of their political opinions (though,
of course, managers may use their own resources for this
purpose). In short, measures designed to prevent dominance of political processes by those who control corporate
wealth are quite consistent with First Amendment guarantees
of a "free marketplace of ideas."[40] An interactionist can find

---

38. p. 802.

39. p. 805.

40. See Gary Hart and William Shore, "Corporate Spend-
ing on State and Local Referendums: *First National Bank of
Boston v. Bellotti,*" *Case Western Reserve Law Review* 29

much to agree with in this analysis.

Charles O'Kelley points out a few relevant errors in Justice White's dissent -- most importantly, his failure to conclude that the Massachusetts statute is overbroad.[41] The statute prohibits corporate expenditures for nonbusiness communications even in situations where unanimity of belief prevails. While these situations may not be the rule, they do arise (e.g., in a corporation sale) and must be exempted from restrictions. In O'Kelley's view, Justice White's error, though major, pales in comparison to mistakes of the majority, whose reasoning confuses corporations with natural persons and ignores principles established in prior cases. O'Kelley shows that, in the past, the Court has consistently granted constitutional rights to corporations only in instances where these organizations are the instruments through which particular individual rights are exercised -- that is, in instances where the denial of legal rights to corporations would deny the constitutional rights of some human beings. The Court has declined to treat corporations as full-fledged persons with independent rights but, rather, has looked to see *whose* rights are being asserted through the corporate device and what constitutional protections are available to these individuals. This precedent was overlooked by the majority in *First National Bank*. The consequence is an opinion that has the earmarks of realist oversimplification. In assuming that corporations have the same rights of speech as natural persons, the Court failed to see that the rights being asserted are mainly those of top managers, who stand to gain unwarranted protection to amplify their speech through the corporate treasury.

The *First National Bank* decision has yet to be reconciled with public·policy in other areas, say campaign financing. Thus, the Court will have future opportunities to reconsider

---

(1979), pp. 808-829.

41. See Charles R. O'Kelley, Jr, "The Constitutional Rights of Corporations Revisited: Social and Political Expression and the Corporation after *First National Bank v. Bellotti,*" *Georgetown Law Journal* 67 (1979), pp. 1347-1383.

the principles abandoned in this case. I would suggest that the Court (and the rest of us) can make sounder judgments about policies toward organizations (including how to evaluate, study, and manage them) by taking more seriously the interactionist point of view. The normative implications of this viewpoint are worth summarizing.

Conclusion

Natural persons, as intentional individuals, are capable of organizing to further their own interests and well-being. The well-being of individuals has intrinsic value and this is expressed in the recognition of individual rights: moral or human rights, such as the right to equal concern and respect,[42] or at least legal rights, such as those specified in our Constitution. Organizations, on the other hand, have no intentions, interests, or well-being of their own, nothing of intrinsic value that deserves respect as a matter of right. They cannot have moral rights (any rights independent of legal rules). And they cannot have legal rights for their own sakes since they have no "sakes." Nevertheless, organizations--governments, corporations, unions, etc.--can acquire legal rights for the benefit of natural persons. It is useful to extend a legal right to organizations when this furthers the enjoyment, *by all participating individuals*, of a prior moral or legal right. Realists are generally not so careful in acknowledging organizational rights. A common mistake is to assume that an activity, which benefits individuals and deserves protection when performed by them, likewise benefits the members of an organization and deserves protection when "performed by" the organization. The problem is that, unlike individual action, action attributed to an organization may be intended by and benefit only

---

42. Ronald Dworkin, *Taking Rights Seriously* (Cambridge, MA: Harvard University Press, 1978).

some influential members of the social "body." In this case, organizational rights to the act may not protect individual *rights* but individual *power*. A main virtue of interactionism is that it reminds us of the difference.

The interactionist approach provides a useful framework for examining other normative issues, such as corporate social performance questions. It can handle the complaint that the concept of "social responsibility" does not make clear sense when applied to organizations[43] yet an interactionist view opens additional possibilities for addressing social performance concerns. To be more specific, a view of organizations as nonorganic systems of interaction suggests that they can have neither moral rights *nor* moral duties, i.e. social responsibilities. Indeed, some writers have argued from an interactionist viewpoint that public interference with organizational affairs in the name of some alleged social responsibility is unjustified.[44] But this is too simplistic.[45] While it may be illogical to expect organizations to behave responsibly, like natural persons, it is not illogical to expect organizations to exhibit those moral or social qualities we find desirable in similar systems, like games. It is certainly odd to ask whether a game is itself behaving responsibly, but it is quite reasonable to ask whether the game is fair, right, harmful, or something of this sort. Most would agree that a potentially violent game, to the extent that it entails penalties for injurious acts, is socially preferable to a comparable game which entails no penalties,

---

43. William Letwin, "Social Responsibility of Business in an Insurance State," in Edwin M. Epstein and Dow Votaw, eds., *Rationality, Legitimacy, Responsibility* (Santa Monica, CA; Goodyear, 1978), pp. 131-155.

44. See Robert Hessen, "A New Concept of Corporations: A Contractual and Private Property Model," *Hastings Law Journal* 30 (1979), pp. 1327-1350.

45. See Robert W. Hamilton, "Response (to Hessen)," *Hastings Law Journal* 30 (1979), pp. 1351-1352.

but allows the participants to inflict unlimited injury on one another to further their own cause. So also in the case of organizations, those minimizing injurious consequences to participants could be considered preferable from an interactionist perspective. In all probability, such a perspective would justify stronger public policies toward organizationally produced harms than an organismic-realist view. The former is more likely than the latter, for instance, to provide a rationale for a strict liability policy, since it denies organizations the kinds of intention-based excuses for their acts that we accept from natural persons.

In sum, an interactionist approach to social performance problems treats these as part of the larger problem of fairly allocating benefits and burdens, rights and duties, among those who participate in organized activities. This larger problem is an important one in the administration of organizations, and it is important in an interactionist research agenda. Realist theories divert attention from allocation questions by emphasizing the overall welfare of social systems. Systems may be indifferent to the fate of particular people. Actual people, of course, are not so indifferent. Interactionist theories respect this fact by acknowledging individual interests and rights as the appropriate "ethical givens" for a science of organization.[46]

---

46. An earlier version of this paper was presented to the Conference on Business and Professional Ethics held at the University of Illinois, Chicago Circle, 1981. This version of the paper is reprinted from my article, "Realism in Organizational Theory: A Reassessment," *Symbolic Interaction*, 6 (1983), pp. 279-200 with the permission of the publisher, JAI Press, Inc.

VICARIOUS AGENCY AND CORPORATE RESPONSIBILITY

Larry May

In this essay I will explore the subject of corporate agency against the backdrop of recent cases of sexual harassment in education and employment. In 1978 a law suit was filed against Yale University charging the university with the sexual harassment of one of its students. On first view the charge was a strange one. Even if corporations could be moral or legal agents, surely in this case the act in question was performed by only one person, a professor, and all other members of the corporation did nothing. There was no decision by the board of directors or stockholders of Yale University to harass the woman student in question. Indeed, there didn't even appear to be a series of actions which would resemble a collective conspiracy. So then, in what sense had Yale University harassed one of its students, and what would one have to show in order to hold Yale University, as a corporation, responsible for the harm done to that student? In what follows I will attempt to set out the theoretical underpinnings of a theory of corporate agency and then briefly discuss some of the conditions necessary for corporate responsibility for harms.

I will contend that corporations have the peculiar property of only being able to act vicariously. In virtue of this fact the fiction that corporations are full-fledged moral or legal agents should not be sustained. Instead corporations should be given a distinct moral or legal status of their own, where they have to satisfy special conditions before they can be held liable or responsible. In the first part of this essay I will set out my reasons for identifying corporate agency with vicarious agency; and in the second part of this essay I will discuss the moral and legal implications of this view by considering one model of corporate responsibility which does justice to the peculiar metaphysical properties of these corporations.

I. Vicarious Agency

In this first section I will consider various ways an entity, such as a corporation, may be an agent and I will show that it is a mistake to view corporations as agents in the standard senses of that term. I will show that corporations should not be treated as persons having the ability to act intentionally, and that they also should not be treated as machines having the ability merely to act (or react) automatically. I will then contend that corporations can only act vicariously, that is, through other persons, and for this reason should be given a unique status as agents. When I say that corporations act vicariously I mean that an action can be attributed to a corporation because of a formal relationship that exists between the corporation and the entity which caused the action. This relationship will be shown to be something like that which exists between a representative and his or her constituents, where the constituents can be said to act through their representative.

P.S. Atiyah has claimed that present English law does allow that corporations can be treated as having personally acted. In tort law, one of the leading cases is *Lennard's Carrying Company, Ltd. v. Asiatic Petroleum Company, Ltd.* (1915). In this case it was recognized that:

> there are some servants or agents of a corporation who can be treated as 'the directing mind and will of the corporation, the very ego and centre of personality of the corporation', whose acts will be attributed to the corporation, not by way of vicarious liability, but on the footing that their acts

are those of the corporation itself.[1]

Peter French has recently argued that corporations can be agents in precisely this sense, thus making corporations "full-fledged moral persons."[2] French tries to sustain this thesis by demonstrating that corporations have distinct intentions and acts of will. The decision structure of the corporation "licenses the descriptive transformation of events seen under another aspect as the acts of biological persons (those who occupy various positions on an organizational chart) as corporate acts by exposing the corporate character of those events."[3]

To show that corporations do not have the intentional ability which French attributes to them, I will try to distinguish between intentions or acts of will and consensual or cooperative decisions. In this section I will be guided by several of Alvin Goldman's contentions about agency. Goldman is willing to allow that collective entities can act as agents. "I contend that in the case of agents, as in the case of other objects, there is no incompatibility between saying that a certain agent was the (object-) cause of a certain event and saying that an event or state involving the agent was the (event-) cause of the same effect."[4] But most philosophers who, like French, claim that corporations are agents do so in the 'object' not the 'event' sense. They agree with Goldman that for objects to be agents they must have properties which incline us to attribute desires and

---

1.   P. S. Atiyah, *Vicarious Liability and the Law of Torts* (London: Butterworths, 1967,) p. 382.

2.   Peter A. French, "Corporate Moral Agency," in Beauchamp and Bowie (eds.): *Ethical Theory and Business* (Englewood Cliffs: Prentice-Hall, Inc., 1979), p. 176.

3.   *Ibid.*, p. 177.

4.   Alvin Goldman, *A Theory of Human Action* (Englewood Cliffs: Prentice-Hall, Inc., 1970), p. 82.

beliefs to them.   Indeed it is for this reason that they try
to show that there are corporate intentions.
    French believes that in the corporate board room "the
intentions and acts of various biological persons" are "subor-
dinated and synthesized" into a "corporate decision."[5] But
does such a synthesis constitute an act of will?   I contend
that this is not an accurate way to characterize what occurs
in these corporate board rooms.   There is no real melding of
wills in the corporate decision process, nor is there a subordination of individual wills to some other will, for indeed
there are only individual wills present.   While no member of
the corporation need hold all of the intentions that are
attributed to the corporation, the corporation cannot hold
any intentions that were not first held by one of the members of the corporation.   The so-called corporate intention is
completely determined by the intentions of the individual
members of the corporation.
    It is true that through the corporate decision-making
process the various members come to vary and even radically
alter their intentions; but this need be seen as nothing different from when any person comes to change his or her
intentions after discussions with another person.   What
French calls subordination and synthesis of wills is nothing
more than the achievement of a type of consensus in which
each board member alters his or her original intentions and
ideas.   But it still remains true that the acts of will are best
described as those of the individual members, and the
changes that occur are described as changes in each of the
individual members' wills.   The vote taken at the board
meeting is no more a collective intentional act than is any
poll conducted by a social science researcher: it merely
describes the current intentions of those board members.
The subsequent acceptance of the majority opinions by the
minority members of the board is not a subordination in any
important sense of that term.   To hold otherwise is to suggest that other types of consensual decisions or compromises
result in the loss of the individual members' wills.   In the

---

5.   French, *op. cit.*

history of philosophy only Rousseau supported the underlying premise of French's argument. Most social philosophers since Rousseau's time have seen the inherent paradox in discussing a 'general will' which is dependent on the wills of the individual members, but which takes on a life of its own independent of those wills.

I have tried to show that French's argument fails in the following respects. First, it does not isolate an act of the corporation which is not initially based on the acts of individual persons, since without the input from these individuals there would be nothing for the corporation to subordinate or synthesize. Secondly, it does not show that the decision-making should be attributed to the corporation due to the subordination and synthesis of wills instead of merely describing it as individual acts of varying and altering intentions in order to achieve consensus and compromise between and among the members. And thirdly, it eventually leads French to the same paradox that plagued Rousseau, where the 'corporate will' takes on a life of its own, but where the path of that life is totally circumscribed by the wills of the individuals. This is seen when it is realized that if a sufficient number of members change their intentions, the supposedly 'independent' corporate will must follow suit.

It has also been contended that the actions of corporations are best described as automatic machine-like responses to external stimuli. John Ladd suggested this line of argumentation in an essay on the morality of formal organizations. He held that formal organizations

> are differentiated and defined by reference to their aims or goals <and> ... any considerations that are not related to the aims or goals of an organization are automatically excluded as irrelevant to the decision-making process .... Again, the point is a logical one, namely, only those actions that are related to the goal of the organization are to be attributed to the organization; those actions that are inconsistent with it are attributed to the individual officers as individu-

als.[6]

The corporation as a formal organization is merely an instrument of the individual persons who compose it. It is best viewed as a machine which cannot properly be described as being morally responsible for what it does.[7]

My view of corporate agency is equally at odds with Ladd's view as it is with French's view. First, it should be noted that Ladd's analysis makes use of a definition which is consistent with legal usage although not, I will argue, with common usage. Ladd claims that formal organizations such as corporations are defined within quite narrow limits and their actions are completely distinguished from the actions of their members. In legal usage this is also true. Black's Law Dictionary defines a corporation as an entity "which is regarded in law as having a personality and an existence distinct from that of its several members, and which is, by the same authority, vested with the capacity ... of acting as a unit or as a single individual in matters relating to the common purpose of the association ...."[8] Yet, in common usage we talk about the excessive profits made by Mobil Oil Co. or the benevolent actions of the Ford Foundation. In Ladd's view these actions are improperly described as the actions of these formal organizations. While I might agree with him that we could, by fiat, confine talk of corporations to a much narrower class of actions than is done in ordinary discourse, I am not sure that this would be a useful strategy.

---

6. John Ladd, "Morality and the Ideal of Rationality in Formal Organizations," reprinted in Donaldson and Werhane (eds.), *Ethical Issues in Business* (Englewood Cliffs: Prentice-Hall, Inc., 1979), p. 105.

7. *Ibid.*, p. 110.

8. For this definition the dictionary cites the cases of *Dartmouth College* v. *Woodward* 17 U.S. (4 Wheat.) 518, 636, 657 and *U.S.* v. *Trinidad Coal Co.* 137 U.S. 160.

Ladd's strategy is especially suspect when the actions attributed to corporations do not resemble automatic behavior patterns. Automatic behavior is purely reactive involving no significant addition from stimulus to response. Most importantly it would make no sense to suggest that there could be a description of Gulf Oil Co. acting beyond its goals and purposes which could not be better described as various individuals, who just happened to be members of this organization, acting. Yet, as I will next show, this is not true of corporate behavior. Some actions performed by individuals can be better described (or re-described) as actions of the corporation even though the actions take place outside of the proper profit-making goals of those organizations.

It seems to me that it is impossible to describe accurately the acts that occur in the corporate setting merely by referring to acts of the individual members of the corporation, and not mentioning in the description a causal role of the corporation itself. Anthony Quinton has claimed that social objects, while composed of individual persons, are as "equally real and objective" as the individual persons who constitute them. Quinton's argument is that "it turns out more often than not that the sense of a statement about a social object cannot be conveyed by a statement which differs from the original only in substituting an explicit if general reference to some collection of individual persons for the name of the social object."[9]

Quinton argued that relationships such as those between a corporation and its members are analogous to the relationship between a forest (a whole) and its trees (its parts). When it is said that Gulf Oil Co. acts it is also true that at least one of the members of that corporate entity acts. But, more often than not, the acts must be described with reference to the corporation, since the acts here are different from the acts of the individual members, just as a whole is different from its parts. Even when the corporate entity acts through its chief executive officers, it is not merely the

----

9.   Anthonly Quinton, "Social Objects," *Proceedings of the Aristotelian Society*, 76, pp. 5 and 10.

case that these officers acted in various ways, one writing a report, a group voting on that report and then delegating one other member to execute the decision. Such a description would fail to capture the fact that Gulf Oil Co. acted, with the various individual acts of the officers being mere parts of that corporate action.

Yet it should be clear that just as the forest is not itself a full-fledged biological entity, so the corporation is not a full-fledged person. Gulf Oil Co. does act in some sense of that term, but its acts are vicarious ones, and its personhood is thus greatly restricted. But, as I will next show, this agency is not restricted to such an extent that moral appraisal of this action is ruled out. There are actions of the corporation which can be morally blameworthy even though the corporation's agency status is much more restricted than full-fledged moral agency.

In most cases the individual persons who are members of the corporation are facilitated in their action by the power which the corporation has delegated to them. If the corporation cannot act on its own, it might be asked, where does this power come from and how is it delegated? The enabling and delegating acts are also performed by persons who are members of the corporation. Could these acts have taken place without the corporate structure which is the defining characteristic of the corporate entity? Perhaps some of them could have taken place, but they would not have been described as acts of the whole group of members of the corporation (those who acted as well as those who did not). Instead, they would be described as acts of individual persons cooperating with each other in various ways. Without the 'incorporating' act whereby the acts of different persons are linked · to one other entity, where the parts come together to form the whole which is different from the mere collection of parts, certain acts could not be described as a single act, the corporate act, by a single entity, the corporation.[10]

'Incorporating acts' are acts which were taken by

10.　French, *op. cit.*, pp. 178-179.

individual persons contemporaneous with the establishment of
a corporation. The institution of the corporation allowed
these individuals to delegate one entity, the corporation, as
that entity which represents them collectively. Thus, the
incorporating act is similar to the act of voting whereby
individual constituents establish the office of congressman
through whose agency the constituents can act collectively.
The original stockholders, for instance, incorporate themselves and can then act through the corporation. But the
stockholders, unlike the voters, cannot truly act through
the corporation without the corporation itself acting through
others, namely its supervisors, employees, etc. The board
of directors, acting as agents for the current stockholders,
acts through the corporation, and the corporation acts
through its employees. The act of incorporation created the
formal structure whereby these vicarious relationships were
henceforth perpetuated. The defining characteristic of the
corporation, because of which it is able to be said to act
when others act for it, is set by the rules and procedures
adopted and formally agreed to by the stockholders. These
incorporating acts also delegate the board of directors as
those individuals whose collective decisions will be called the
corporation's decisions. Before going into these vicarious
relationships in more detail, it should again be emphasized
that the important point here is that the vicarious agency
comes first and the descriptive change comes only after this.
The collection of citizens can act as a group only vicariously; the person who holds the office of representative can
be described as acting for the group because of the vicarious relationships he or she consented to.
   Within corporations two types of vicarious relationships
can be seen, both together contributing to the vicarious
agency which can be described as corporate agency. First,
the stockholders individually initiated a decision-making process which culminates in the formation of a corporate structure, whereby the stockholders can be said to act through
the corporation. Secondly, the corporation itself can only
carry out the decisions of the board acting for the stockholders through its designated agents: managers, supervisors, employees, etc. The corporation is thus a place-
holder, standing in for the stockholders who are the ones,
collectively, who act through the supervisors and employees.
Unlike the legislative representative, through whose agency

the constituents act, the corporation must itself act through someone who has object-agency, since it can neither originate the incorporating process nor the process which results in action. In the case of the legislative representative, the descriptive transformation occurs in that the actions of one person are transformed into the actions of a collectivity. But in the case of corporations, the descriptive transformation (if it is a transformation at all) is merely a short hand way of saying that a collectivity (stockholders or board members) has acted through an individual (a supervisor or employee). It is only because of the vicarious relationship, ultimately between shockholder and employee, that the descriptive transformation makes any sense at all.

Corporate actions can properly be said to occur only where there is a causal nexus between stockholders or board members and supervisors or employees. If the board members, for instance, have collectively decided to create a job with a certain description, then anyone hired for that job who acts in corformity with the job description, and whose actions are not countermanded by a higher employee, acts for the corporate board and hence, in some sense, for the corporation. If the employee acts outside his or her job description or in a way opposed to specific orders from higher employees, his or her actions are not the actions of the corporation, since the causal nexus has been broken. In this case, the employee is solely responsible for the consequences of his or her action.

The biggest problem for a theory of corporate responsibility or liability is to ascertain when an employee, supervisor or manager, etc., is acting on his own and when he is acting for the corporation. Once an employee has been hired and given, say, a wide job description, then actions performed according to that job description are corporate actions unless or until an appropriate party gives a countermanding order to that employee. But it seems hard to see in what sense the corporation is responsible for, say, the harmful actions of its employees when it does not know about or intend that those actions occur, as seems to be most often the case in employee wrongdoing. In such cases, I will argue, the corporation may be responsible and blameworthy because of the causal nexus that exists and because of its negligence. While this is surely not the only way that corporations can be responsible and blameworthy, an analysis of this particular case of corporate responsibility, that is, responsibility for the wrongdoings of its employees, will shed considerable light on the nature of corporate responsibility itself. I have chosen the example of responsibility for harmful conduct so as to sidestep the difficult question of what counts as morally blameworthy conduct which is deserving of ascriptions of responsibility. It is assumed that most, if not all, theories of morality would allow that harmful actions are ones for which responsibility should be assigned.

II. ONE MODEL OF CORPORATE RESPONSIBILITY

It has seemed to some that we have only two theoretical models open to us for assigning corporate responsibility. Either we can treat corporations the same way we treat individual persons in criminal law, by looking to the corporation's state of mind, conduct and the consequences of its acts. Or we can treat corporations as strictly liable for whatever results from their 'actions' regardless of the state of mind or faultiness of conduct, as is sometimes done in tort law. The first strategy is attractive because it calls for no major change in our general view of moral or legal responsibility and comports well with the long tradition of speaking of corporate persons. The second strategy is attractive because it avoids considerable evidentiary problems of the first strategy, namely, finding the corporate mind and will and separating it from the minds, wills and conduct of the individual members of the corporation. We are faced though with a severe problem with each alternative. The first strategy seems inappropriate in most corporate cases since it rests on an analogy which fails to distinguish solitary actions from collective actions, that is, actions involving only one person from actions involving a group of persons (partially independent and partially dependent on the group). The second strategy seems inappropriate as a way of determining responsibility since it fails to distinguish between the types of case where conduct is blameworthy and where conduct is blameless.

Clearly there is no reason to think that these are the only models of responsibility open to us, nor even that these are the models best suited to the peculiar characteristics of the corporation. The two models discussed so far show us, though, what is needed in another model. What we need are models of responsibility aimed at collectivities but where the blame or fault condition is preserved as a condition of responsibility. I shall contend that one such model can be found by combining the concepts of vicarious agency with negligent fault.

Corporate vicarious negligence is that category of responsibility or liability which seems to me in cases of employee wrongdoing to best function as a mean between these two extremes of strict liability and individual intentional wrong-doing. The causal condition of corporate responsibility is that of vicarious agency. I shall define vicarious action to be action *'a'* done by *'y'* but attributable to *'x'* due to a fact such as that *'y' has been delegated to do 'a'* as a substitute for *'x'*. Negligent fault is the fault condition most appropriate to the majority of cases a theory of corporate responsibility would have to deal with. If a collectivity is said to act the question always remains: was not that merely an act of an individual person who only happened to be a member of that collectivity? With negligence, though, if it is said that the collectivity failed to perform an action (which was required by a duty it had), the question does not arise. Since the corporation can only act through one of its members, a failure of every one of the members to act will become a failure of the corporation to act; whereas, an action of a member of a corporation does not necessarily become that corporation's action.

Here is one model of corporate vicarious negligence which sets the conditions which must be met for the harmful conduct of a member of the corporation to become the responsibility of the corporation.

A corporation is vicariously negligent for the harmful acts of one of its members if:

(a) *causal factor* --the member of the corporation was enabled or facilitated in his or her harmful conduct by the general grant of authority given to him or her by corporate decision; and

(b) *fault factor* --appropriate members of the corporation failed to take preventative measures to thwart the
potential harm by those who could harm due to the
above general grant of authority, even though:

1. the appropriate members could have taken such
precautions, and 2. these appropriate members could
reasonably have predicted that the harm would occur.

The major advantage of the type of model I am proposing is
that the corporation is treated not as a single entity but as
a collection of entities or persons, some of whom grant
authority to others, some of whom might harm others and
some of whom might act to minimize the potential of harm.
Most, if not all, cases of supposedly harmful corporate conduct involve some sort of collective action, resembling a conspiracy of individual persons with more than one person acting on his or her own. The link between these persons is
often hard to establish, but in most cases the definitive link
between the individual and the corporate representative
occurs due to an omission rather than a commission. That
is, the person who is designated by the group to be the
supervisor of the actions of an employee of the corporation
fails to take action to thwart the harmful acts of that
employee. This failure to act links the corporation to the
harmful practice of the employee. If this is true then a
model of corporate responsibility and liability directed at
vicarious negligence would be best suited to the realities of
corporate life.
    The second general advantage of the type of model I am
proposing is that it is likely to be more effective than other
models of corporate liability, especially strict liability. Corporate officers will see that there is a clear way to rebut the
charge that the corporation is liable for a particular harm.
It can be shown that (1) either the corporation did not
authorize its member to engage in the type of conduct that
produced the harm, or (2) even though its member was generally authorized to so act, the corporation took reasonable
measures to prevent the occurrence of that harm. This
knowledge would tend to deter future harms since the corporate officers will not feel as powerless (as they do under
standards of strict liability) to affect the future liability of
the corporation.

One might think that the main disadvantage of this compromise between intentional wrongdoing and strict liability is that it shifts the legal burden away from the corporation by increasing the number of excuses that corporation has open to it. I cannot deny that this model of corporate liability would add several special excuses to those presently open to the corporation, namely, excuses which show that due care was exercised by the corporation, say, in a hiring policy or supervisory policy, and thus whatever harm resulted is the responsibility of the individual not the corporation of which that individual is a member. The opening of these special excuses though can not help but make corporations more careful in the establishment of their policies, especially where potentially harmful conduct is concerned.

Finally, it might be objected that what I have been calling vicarious negligence is not vicarious liability at all, as presently conceived in legal circles. Again, I must plead guilty to this charge. It has become quite commonplace to define vicarious liability as a form of strict liability, hence ruling out any negligence, or any other fault condition, by definition. The notion of vicarious liability, or perhaps more properly vicarious agency, I have employed differs significantly from that which is presently employed in legal theory. But I think that the kind of vicarious action I have in mind here is not out of keeping with the commonsense understanding of what vicarious means. Perhaps my thesis here is even more radical than one would otherwise think, for I have been contending that *all* corporate conduct is vicarious, and this claim flies in the face of the fiction in legal theory of speaking of corporations as full-fledged legal persons. I think this fiction should be dispensed with, so that a conceptually clear understanding of corporate conduct and then of corporate liability can be achieved. What we should be concerned with is the nexus of actions taken by the members of a corporation. Liability should be assigned to a corporation when that nexus of actions which cause a harm can be properly described as that corporation's action.

I agree whole-heartedly with Irving Thalberg and others who have contended that it would be absurd to say that corporations could act even though all human beings have perished. This indeed is the central insight that caused me to look for a way of describing corporate agency which was dependent on the acts of individual human beings.

Corporations are not independent agents because unlike
human beings they could not act without other human beings
acting. The concept of acting through another or vicariously acting is meant to capture this insight. As I said earlier this type of agency is similar to what occurs in the legislative process where the acts of one or a number of
individuals is re-described as the act of a collectivity. What
is the causal nexus that warrants one to re-describe an act
of a human being as an act of a corporation? Perhaps the
best I can do here is to give a description of a case which I
hope illustrates the difference between acts of human beings
simply and acts of human beings which, for the purpose of
assigning responsibility, can be described as corporate acts.
     Let me return now to the case of sexual harassment I
mentioned earlier. Professor Smith calls in one of his graduate students, Ms. Jones, and says "I'd like you to sleep
with me. If you won't I'll make sure you lose your assis-
tantship." Now, can this personal encounter between two
human beings be re-described as Y University harassing one
of its students? Here is one set of facts for which it could
plausibly be held that Y University acted through Professor
Smith. The Board of Trustees of Y University voted favora-
bly on a bill creating the office of university professor of
philosophy. The job description said that anyone holding
this office could teach as a university professor and advise
and evaluate graduate students in philosophy. Anyone holding the office of philosophy professor was to be supervised
respectively by the Chairman of Philosophy, the Dean of
Humanities and the Vice President for Academic Affairs.
Those supervising the holder of this office could further sti-
pulate appropriate conduct on the part of the office-holder,
in this case Professor Smith. Let's assume that in this
instance Professor Smith had threatened graduate students
before and word of this travelled to the Chairman, the Dean
and the Vice President, yet they had said nothing to Professor Smith or to any of his graduate students.
     It seems clear to me that *Mr.* Smith could have made
similar threats to graduate students attending Y University.
But those threats would not be described as the threats of a
professor of Y University if certain necessary conditions had
not been met by the Board of Trustees, the Vice President,
the Dean and the Chairman. (I leave aside the point that
the threat would probably have little effect without these

conditions being met.) If Mr. Smith weren't employed by Y
University, the event in question could not be described as
Professor Smith harassing one of his students, and then as
Y University harassing one of its students through Professor
Smith.

It is true, notice, that no one told Smith to harass student Jones and importantly, no one member of the corporate
entity Y University straightforwardly caused Smith to harass
Jones.   In fact, Smith could have tried to harass Jones
whether Y University existed or not.   But the redescription
of the event required an action by the Board of Trustees
and several acts of omission, negligent omissions at that. [11]

What might have broken the 'causal nexus' such that the
re-description could not take place?   Professor Smith's
Chairman could have forbidden Smith to threaten his students, the Dean could have threatened to dismiss Smith from
the graduate faculty, the Vice President could have threatened to dismiss Smith from the University if he didn't stop
harassing his students.   Any of these acts would disassociate the University from these actions of Smith, something
like a recall petition would disassociate a constituency from
the acts of a congressman.   What is being caused by the
commissions and omissions of the Trustees, the Vice President, the Dean and the Chairman is the re-description of
Smith's act as an act of the corporation, Y University,
where the corporation can be said to act through Smith.
The acts of these people are the necessary conditions for
this re-description and thus for the ascription of the vicarious agency and liability to the corporation.   I hope this
example helps to explain how the connections between members of a corporation warrant the re-description of these
acts as corporate acts.   Liability should only be assigned
when it is proper to describe these acts as corporate acts.
But contrary to the contention of John Ladd and others,
there is nothing in principle which limits these descriptions

---

11.   For further discussion of this subject see John C.
Hughes and Larry May, "Sexual Harrassment," *Social Theory
and Practice*, 6 (1980), pp. 249-280.

to actions for which moral or legal responsibility would be
inappropriate. [12]

---

12.   An earlier version of this paper was presented to
the Conference on Business and Professional Ethics held at
the University of Illinois, Chicago Circle, May 1981.   My
commentator at that conference, Irving Thalberg, has been
quite helpful in getting this paper into its present form.   I
also gratefully acknowledge help that I received from Lilly
Russow and Rod Bertolet.   This present essay is reprinted
from *Philosophical Studies*, vol. 43 (1983), pp. 69-82, with
the permission of the publisher.

Ethics and Bribery

ETHICS AND THE FOREIGN CORRUPT PRACTICES ACT

Mark Pastin and Michael Hooker

Not long ago it was feared that as a fallout of Watergate, government officials would be hamstrung by artificially inflated moral standards. Recent events, however, suggest that the scapegoat of post-Watergate morality may have become American business rather than government officials.

The focus of this article is on one aspect of recent attention to corporate morality--the controversy surrounding payments made by American corporations to foreign officials for the purpose of securing business abroad. In particular we discuss the Foreign Corrupt Practices Act (FCPA) and the question whether it should be repealed. Since any law or system of laws should be grounded in morality, the Foreign Corrupt Practices Act should be judged from an ethical perspective. Unfortunately it has not been adequately addressed heretofore from that perspective. We do so.

Background of the FCPA

On December 20, 1977 President Carter signed into law S.305, the Foreign Corrupt Practices Act, which makes it a crime for American corporations to offer or provide payments to officials of foreign governments for the purpose of obtaining or retaining business. The FCPA also establishes record keeping requirements for publicly held corporations to make it difficult for them to conceal political payments proscribed by the Act. Violators of the FCPA, both corporations and managers within the corporation, face severe penalties. A company may be fined up to $1 million, while its officers who directly participated in violations of the Act or had reason to know of such violations, face up to five years in prison and/or $10,000 in fines. The Act also prohibits corporations from indemnifying fines imposed on their directors, officers, employees, or agents. The Act does not prohibit "grease" payments to foreign government employees whose duties are primarily ministerial or clerical. Such payments are sometimes required to persuade the recipients to perform their normal duties.

At the time of this writing the precise consequences of the FCPA for American business are unclear, mainly because of confusion surrounding the government's enforcement intentions. Vigorous objections have been raised against the Act by corporation attorneys and recently by a few officials of the government. Among the latter is Frank A. Weil, former Assistant Secretary of Commerce, who has stated that "the questionable payments problem may turn out to be one of the most serious impediments to doing business in the rest of the world."[1]

The potentially severe economic impact of the FCPA was highlighted by the Fall 1978 report of the Export Disincentives Task Force, which was created by the White House to recommend ways of improving our balance of trade.

The Task Force identified the FCPA as contributing significantly to economic and political losses in the United States. Economic losses come from constricting the ability of American corporations to do business abroad, and political losses come from the creation of a holier-than-thou image.

The Task Force made three recommendations in regard to the FCPA:

> 1) The Justice Department should issue guidelines on its enforcement policies and establish procedures by which corporations could get advance Government reaction to anticipated payments to foreign officials.

---

1. *National Journal*, June 3, 1978, p. 880.

2) The FCPA should be amended to remove enforcement from the SEC, which now shares enforcement
responsibility with Justice. 3) The Administration
should periodically report to Congress and the public
on export losses caused by the FCPA.

In response to the Task Force's report, Justice, over
SEC objections, drew up guidelines to enable corporations to
check any proposed action possibly in violation of the FCPA.
In response to such an inquiry the Justice Department would
inform the corporation of its enforcement intentions. The
purpose of such an arrangement is in part to circumvent the
intent of the law. As of this writing, the SEC appears to
have been successful in blocking publication of the guidelines, although Justice recently reaffirmed its intention to
publish guidelines. Justice, being more responsive to political winds, may be less inclined than the SEC to rigidly
enforce the Act.

Particular concern has been expressed about the way in
which bookkeeping requirements of the Act will be enforced
by the SEC. The Act requires that company records will
"accurately and fairly reflect the transactions and dispositions of the assets of the issuer." What is at question is
the interpretation SEC will give to the requirement and the
degree of accuracy and detail it will demand. The SEC's
post-Watergate behavior suggests that it will be rigid in
requiring the disclosure of all information that bears on
financial relationships between the company and any foreign
or domestic public official. This level of accountability in
record keeping, to which auditors and corporate attorneys
have strongly objected, goes far beyond previous SEC
requirements that records display only facts material to the
financial position of the company.

Since the potential consequences of the FCPA for American businesses and businessmen are very serious, it is
important that the Act have a rationale capable of bearing
close scrutiny. In looking at the foundation of the FCPA, it
should be noted that passage followed in the wake of intense
newspaper coverage of the financial dealings of corporations.
Such media attention was engendered by the dramatic disclosure of corporate slush funds during the Watergate hearings
and by a voluntary disclosure program established shortly
thereafter by the SEC. As a result of the SEC program,

over 400 corporations, including 117 of the *Fortune* 500, admitted to making over $300 million in foreign political payments during a period of less than 10 years.

Throughout the period of media coverage leading up to passage of the FCPA, and especially during the hearings on the Act, there was in all public discussions of the issue a tone of righteous moral indignation at the idea of American companies making foreign political payments. Such payments were ubiquitously termed "bribes," although many of them more accurately would be said to have been extorted, and some were more akin to brokers' fees or sales commissions.

American business is to be faulted for its reluctance during this period to bring to public attention the fact that in a very large number of countries, payments to foreign officials are virtually required for doing business. Part of that reluctance, no doubt, comes from the awkwardly difficult position one is in when he attempts to excuse bribery or what looks at first very much like it. There is a popular abhorrence in this country of bribery directed at domestic government officials, and that abhorrence transfers to payments directed toward foreign officials as well.

Since its passage, the FCPA has been subjected to considerable critical analysis, and many practical arguments have been advanced in favor of its repeal.[2] However, there is always lurking in the background of such analyses the uneasy feeling that no matter how strongly considerations of practicality and economics may count against this law, one always comes back to face the fact that the law protects morality in forbidding bribery. For example, Gerald McLaughlin, Professor of Law at Fordham, has shown persuasively that where the legal system of a foreign country affords inadequate protection against the arbitrary exercise

---

2.   David C. Gustman, "The Foreign Corrupt Practices Act of 1977," *The Journal of International Law and Economics*, Vol. 13, 1979, p. 367-401, and Walter S. Surrey, "The Foreign Corrupt Practices Act: Let the Punishment Fit the Crime," *Harvard International Law Journal*, Spring 1979, p. 203-303.

of power to the disadvantage of American corporations, payments to foreign officials may be required to provide a compensating mechanism against the use of such arbitrary
power. McLaughlin observes, however, that "this does not
mean that taking advantage of the compensating mechanism
would necessarily make the payment moral."[3]

The FCPA and questions regarding its enforcement or
repeal will not be addressed adequately until an effort has
been made to come to terms with the Act's foundation in
morality. While it may be very difficult, or even impossible,
to legislate morality--that is, to change the moral character
and sentiments of people by passing laws that regulate their
behavior--still the laws that we do have undoubtedly reflect
the moral beliefs that we hold. Passage of the FCPA in
Congress was made easy by the simple connection most Con-
gressmen made between bribery, which they see to be morally repugnant, and the Act, which is designed to prevent
bribery.

Given the importance of the FCPA to American business
and labor, it is imperative that attention be given to the
question whether there is adequate moral justification for the
law.

Ethical Analysis of the FCPA

The question we will address is not whether each payment prohibited by the FCPA is moral or immoral, but
whether the FCPA, given all of its consequences and ramifi-
cations, is itself moral. It is well known that morally sound
laws and institutions may tolerate some immoral acts. The
First Amendment guarantee of freedom of speech allows individuals to utter racial slurs. And immoral laws and

---

3. Gerald T. McLaughlin, "The Criminalization of Questionable Foreign Payments by Corporations," *Fordham Law
Review*, Vol. 46, p. 1095.

institutions may have some beneficial consequences, for
example, segregationist legislation brought deep-seated
racism into the national limelight. Our concern is with the
overall morality of the FCPA.

The ethical tradition has two distinct methods of assessing social institutions, laws and individual behavior. These
methods may be called *End-Point Assessment* and *Rule
Assessment*. Since there is no consensus as to which
approach is correct, we will apply both types of assessment
to the FCPA.

The End-Point approach assesses a law in terms of the
contribution to general social well-being the law makes. The
ethical theory underlying End-Point Assessment is Utilitarianism. According to Utilitarianism

> A law is morally sound if and only if the law promotes
> the well-being of those affected by the law to the
> greatest extent practically achievable.

To satisfy the Utilitarian principle, a law must promote the
well-being of those affected by it at least as well as any
alternative law that we might propose, and better than no
law at all. A conclusive End-Point Assessment of a law
requires specification of what constitutes the welfare of those
affected by the law. The liberal tradition generally sides-
teps this problem by identifying an individual's welfare with
what he or she takes to be in his or her interests.

Considerations raised earlier in the paper suggest that
the FCPA does not pass the End-Point test. The argument
is not the too-facile argument that we could propose a better
law. (Amendments to the FCPA are now being considered.)[4]
The argument is that it may be better to have no such law
than to have the FCPA. The main domestic consequences of
the FCPA seem to include an adverse effect on the balance
of payments, a loss of business and jobs, and another
opportunity for the SEC and Justice to compete. These

---

4. "Foreign Bribery Law Amendments Drafted," *American
Bar Association Journal*, February 1980, p. 135.

negative effects must be weighed against possible gains in
the conduct of American business within the United States.
From the perspective of foreign countries in which American
firms do business, the main consequence of the FCPA seems
to be that certain officials now accept bribes and influence
from non-American businesses. It is hard to see that who
pays the bribes makes much difference to these nations.

Rule Assessment of the morality of laws is often favored
by those who find that End-Point Assessment is too lax in
supporting their moral codes. According to the Rule
Assessment approach

> A law is morally sound if and only if the law accords
> with a code embodying correct ethical rules.

This approach has no content until the rules are stated, and
different rules will lead to different ethical assessments.
Fortunately, what we have to say about Rule Assessment of
the FCPA does not depend on the details of a particular ethical code.

Those who regard the FCPA as a worthwhile expression
of morality, despite the adverse effects on American business
and labor, clearly subscribe to a rule stating that it is
unethical to bribe. Even if it is conceded that the payments
proscribed by the FCPA warrant classification as bribes, cit-
ing a rule prohibiting bribery does not suffice to justify the
FCPA.

Most of the rules in an ethical code are not *categorical*
rules; they are *prima facie* rules. A categorical rule does
not allow exceptions, whereas a prima facie rule does. The
ethical rule that one ought to keep promises is an example of
a *prima facie* rule. If I promise to loan you a book on
nuclear energy and later find out that you are a terrorist
building a private atomic bomb, I am ethically obligated not
to keep my promise. The rule that one ought to keep promises is "overridden" by the rule that one ought to prevent
harm to others.

A rule prohibiting bribery is a *prima facie* rule. There
are cases in which morality *requires* that a bribe be paid.
If the only way to get essential medical care for a dying
child is to bribe a doctor, morality requires one to bribe the
doctor. So adopting an ethical code which includes a rule
prohibiting the payment of bribes does not guarantee that a

Rule Assessment of the FCPA will be favorable to it.

The fact that the FCPA imposes a cost on American business and labor weighs against the *prima facie* obligation not to bribe. If we suppose that American corporations have obligations, tantamount to promises, to promote the job security of their employees and the investments of shareholders, these obligations will also weigh against the obligation not to bribe. Again, if government legislative and enforcement bodies have an obligation to secure the welfare of American business and workers, the FCPA may force them to violate their public obligations.

The FCPA's moral status appears even more dubious if we note that many of the payments prohibited by the Act are either not bribes at all, or do not share the features that make bribes morally reprehensible. Bribes are generally held to be malefic if they persuade one to act against his good judgment, and consequently purchase an inferior product. But the payments at issue in the FCPA are usually extorted *from the seller*. Further, it is arguable that *not* paying the bribe is more likely to lead to purchase of an inferior product than paying the bribe. Finally, bribes paid to foreign officials may not involve deception when they accord with recognized local practices.

In conclusion, neither End-Point nor Rule Assessment uncovers a sound moral basis for the FCPA. It is shocking to find that a law prohibiting bribery has no clear moral basis, and may even be an immoral law. However, this is precisely what examination of the FCPA from a moral perspective reveals. This is symptomatic of the fact that the moral conceptions which were appropriate to a simpler world are not adequate to the complex world in which contemporary business functions. Failure to appreciate this point often leads to righteous condemnation of business, when it should lead to careful reflection on one's own moral preconceptions.[5]

---

5.   This article was originally published in *Business Horizons* 23, December, 1980. It is reprinted by permission of the publisher and the authors.

Addendum to "Ethics and the Foreign Corrupt Practices
Act,"
August 1981

There has been an increasing outcry against the FCPA
since this article originally appeared. The Reagan administration has called for weakening of the law, especially the
burdensome accounting provisions. While we view such
weakening of the law as commendable, on the ground that it
decreases the cost of the law to business and the American
public, the key issue has not been joined. That issue is
whether the payments proscribed by the law,
heavy-handedly or otherwise, are in fact unethical. There
is no doubt that many executives and government officials
hold the view that these payments are not unethical. But it
is unacceptable to publicly argue that bribes to foreign officials are ethical. Thus it will take considerable audacity to
argue for total repeal of the FCPA. Only an increasing
appreciation of the barriers to international trade attributable to the law, and of the ethical pointlessness of the law,
can be effective.

MORAL DIMENSIONS OF THE

FOREIGN CORRUPT PRACTICES ACT

Kenneth D. Alpern

I

A number of considerations must be taken into account in order to determine whether a given law ought to be enacted or maintained. These considerations include the implications of the law for social welfare; its constitutionality; its efficacy, enforceability, and cost; its compatibility with personal rights; and the evenhandedness of the law compared with that of other laws governing similar activities. Usually no single factor is by itself dispositive. However, in the case of the Foreign Corrupt Practices Act (FCPA), one consideration, the morality of the law, has been crucial to its support. It is widely, if not universally, held that this law *is* supported by morality. In a recent essay, "Ethics and the Foreign Corrupt Practices Act,"[1] Mark Pastin and Michael Hooker dispute this belief. They evaluate the

---

1. Reprinted in this volume, immediately preceding this essay, pp. 169-77.

FCPA from the perspectives of the two presently dominant
theories of morality, end-point or utilitarian assessment and
rule or deontological assessment, and conclude that neither
theory provides a sound moral basis for this law.

This conclusion is mistaken. The FCPA is, in fact, supported by morality. I will show this by examining the deontological support for the Act. I will not address utilitarian
arguments directly, since an analysis of costs and benefits is
likely to be inconclusive even if all the relevant empirical
data could somehow be collected. Some of what I say, however, can be used to challenge, on conceptual grounds,
much utilitarian criticism of the Act.

II

Pastin and Hooker offer two argument sketches
intended to show that the Act does not receive support from
deontological considerations. The key to the first argument
is the claim that corporations have particularly weighty moral
obligations to their investors and employees which override
the moral obligation not to bribe. The key to the second
argument is the claim that many of the activities made unlawful by the act are, in fact, of a type that is not morally
objectionable. I will consider each argument in turn.

The first argument is roughly this:

1. The FCPA is essentially a prohibition of bribery. Pastin and Hooker allow this for the sake of
argument. Actually, more than just bribery is
unlawful under the Act, and this fact is used in
their second argument discussed in Section III
below.

2. Bribery is morally wrong--in the sense that
there exists a prima facie moral obligation not to
engage in bribery. This is to say that the prohibition of bribery is not absolute. It can be
overridden by other considerations.

3. Corporations have moral obligations, again,

merely prima facie, to protect the investments of
their shareholders and the jobs of their employees.
The federal government may also be under a prima
facie moral obligation to secure the welfare of
American business and workers.

Pastin and Hooker leave the argument hanging at this point.
But from these premises all that follows is that the moral
rule against bribery is not the only deontological consideration that may be relevant. Something like the following must
be added in order to complete their argument.

4. There are situations governed by the FCPA in which
the prima facie moral obligations of corporations and government override the prima facie moral obligation not to bribe.
That is, in some cases, considered individually and other
things being equal, corporations *morally ought to bribe* and
the government *morally ought not to punish* corporations for
bribing. Thus, as the law now stands, some actions are
required legally that are contrary to morality.

5. Cases in which the FCPA requires actions that are
contrary to morality are numerous or are of great moral
moment.

From this the conclusion is to be drawn that the FCPA does
not have the support of morality from a deontological perspective on bribery and is therefore unacceptable.
There is much to agree with in this argument. Its pattern of reasoning is good; the premises do license the conclusion. It is certainly the case that any moral rule prohibiting bribery cannot be absolute. And it is surely true that
corporations have some sort of obligation to pursue profit. I
am even prepared to allow that there could conceivably be
situations in which the prohibition of bribery is overridden
by other obligations that corporations are under. Nonetheless, the conclusion is still false.
What gives the argument a large part of its appeal is its
apparent discovery of a second moral principle, the principle
that promises should be kept, which, in situations covered
by the FCPA, weighs against the moral principle prohibiting
bribery. If this second moral principle is recognized, the
moral predicament of corporations would appear to involve

being forced to choose between which of two conflicting
moral principles to satisfy: keep promises or do not bribe.
    But these principles appear to be of the same moral sta-
tus: both are basic principles of deontological moral theories.   Given this equality of status, there would seem to be
no a priori reason for favoring the principle prohibiting
bribery over the principle requiring promise-keeping.
Pastin and Hooker do not go far enough into the argument to
indicate what sorts of considerations are supposed to tip the
scales in favor of promise-keeping.   Perhaps they have in
mind some further deontological principles; or maybe at this
point they would fall back on utilitarian considerations.   In
any case, they want us to believe that in situations governed by the Act, the bribery rule conflicts with a rule for
keeping promises, and that the promise-keeping rule is generally to be favored.
    In order to show that this position is mistaken, I will
argue that the supposed conflict is only apparent and that
the introduction of the rule of promise-keeping at this place
in the argument is irrelevant and misleading.   Furthermore,
I will argue that the moral considerations which do properly
stand in the place thought to be held by the obligation to
keep promises can be demoted, on the basis of conceptual
considerations, to where it will be clear that the prohibition
of bribery generally takes precedence in a determination of
the morally acceptable action.   In order to make this case,
we must look more closely at the way obligations to keep
promises are supposed to enter the picture.
    Pastin and Hooker mention three specific obligations
deriving from the principle of promise-keeping:

      (1) an obligation of corporations to promote the
   investments of their shareholders;
      (2) an obligation of corporations to protect the
   security of their employees' jobs; and
      (3) an obligation which the federal government may
   possibly be under to protect the welfare of American
   business and workers.

I do not have enough space to examine all three of these
obligations in detail, so I will concentrate on the one that I
take to be most important, the obligation of corporations to
their investors.   At the end of this section I will offer a

brief remark about each of the other two obligations.

How does the obligation of corporations to their investors come about? The essence seems to be this. Corporations are *agents* for their investors. In effect a corporation says: "If you allow us the use of your capital, we promise in return to work to increase the value of your investment."[2] Having made the promise to act as agents, corporations are morally obligated, by virtue of the moral rule that promises be kept, to promote the financial interests of their principals.

So corporations promise to promote their investors' financial interests and are morally obligated to them. What difference does this make to the morality of international corporate bribery? My answer is: None. The promise merely *transfers* the responsibility for looking after the investors' interests. It does nothing to affect the type or weight of the claim that can be made in behalf of those interests against other moral considerations. In the situations with which we are concerned, who the guardian is and how that guardianship comes about make no difference outside the relationship between the agent and the principal. If this were not the case, one could indefinitely increase the moral righteousness of one's causes merely by enlisting a series of agents, each promising the other to pursue one's ends. But this is ridiculous; moral weight does not accrue like the return due on a chain letter.[3]

Thus, any talk of the solemn promises or sacred trusts of corporations, while it may refer to actual obligations, is irrelevant to the issue at hand, which is the weight of

---

2. This promise must be understood as a promise to endeavor to a reasonable extent to increase investment value, not to maximize it at all costs.

3. The general moral principle here is, very roughly, that a promise to pursue the interests of another cannot increase the moral weight of those interests against moral considerations external to the relationship of promiser to promisee.

investor interests against moral rules. There is no conflict here between a moral principle requiring that promises be kept and a moral principle prohibiting bribery. What stands in opposition to the moral rule prohibiting bribery is not a moral principle at all, but is, at best, merely the *self-interest* of the investors.

This, I think, considerably deflates the original argument against the FCPA. However, the attack could be relaunched with the observation that even unadorned self-interest has moral status and that even if this moral status is not, like the bribery rule, based on deontological considerations, it may nonetheless carry substantial moral weight. After all, the idea that satisfying interests is *morally* good is fundamental to all forms of utilitarianism and recognized as well in most other moral theories. Thus, the realigned attack would conclude, the interests of investors have moral weight in themselves and these interests may oppose and override the principle prohibiting bribery.

What is to be said of this argument? I think it must be admitted that investors' interests do have moral weight. However, I also think that it is quite unlikely that this weight will often be great enough to render international corporate bribery moral. First of all, what we have before us now is the opposition of *self-interest* and a moral rule. And within the deontological perspective, which we are being asked to take, moral rules are just the sort of things that override claims of self-interest. So, as long as we take the deontological perspective, there is strong a priori reason to hold that the rule prohibiting bribery controls.

A second line of defense against this argument can be developed out of the example Pastin and Hooker use to show that personal interests may sometimes override moral rules. It would in some circumstances be moral, they point out, to bribe a doctor--say if that were the only way in which to get essential medical treatment for a dying child. This example contains what I think are two characteristic, if not quite absolutely essential, features of such cases: (1) the personal interest at issue is not a mere desire, but a *dire need*, and (2) the rule is broken on a special occasion; it is

PROFIT AND RESPONSIBILITY
                                    The Ethics of Sensitive Payments

not to be a continuing general policy to break the rule.[4] In
contrast, when we are asked to reject the FCPA, we are
asked to endorse a *policy* of bribery, and this for the pro-
motion of interests that are not matters of life and death.

Yet it still might be objected that in cases of corporate
investment the moral claim of the investors' interests is *considerable* and that it may well outweigh the bribery rule.
There can be little justification for this objection. Indeed,
the opposite is almost certainly true. The reason is that not
all interests are of equal moral weight. Classical utilitarianism is mistaken in holding that equal additions to the sum
total happiness or well-being are morally indifferent.

For example, an increase in happiness which satisfies a
need is of greater moral moment than the same increment
added to the total happiness by way of providing someone
with adventitious pleasure. It is morally better to raise a
person from poverty to security than to add an equal amount
to the total happiness in contributing to a person's rise from
ease to opulence. (Better a few more mouthfuls of rice for a
starving Sudanese than a monthful of feasts for Bunky
Hunt.) Thus, when it comes to comparing personal interests
against moral rules, interests which rest in the satisfaction
of mere desires which are not needs have little moral weight.

This point applies to the FCPA in two ways. First,
although American investors include pension plans, philan-
thropic organizations and people of modest income, the average American investor is still quite comfortable by world
standards and return on investment is not a matter of survival. Second, even if return on investment were a matter
of survival, the fact is that corporations can and do derive

---

4. For continuing treatment of the child or when there is
continuing and widespread corruption among doctors, it
would be necessary to endorse bribery as a temporary policy. However, one's obligation in such a case would not be
merely to engage in bribery, but rather to engage in
bribery while doing what one can to rectify the situation.
Regardless of the precise way this is to be worked out, a
simple endorsement of bribery is not justified in such cases.

substantial profits from activities that do not call for bribery, and most American corporations have dealt successfully
in international trade without having to resort to payments
the FCPA makes unlawful.

One misunderstanding of the preceding argument must be
forestalled. At issue is not a comparison of the degree of
need of American investors and the degree of need of citizens of the country in which the bribery takes place.
Rather, the point is that because American investors on the
whole are not in dire need, the moral weight of their financial interests is small compared with the moral weight of
moral principles.

It remains to say something, necessarily very brief,
about the obligation of corporations to their employees and
the obligation of the federal government to American business and workers. First, corporations are not morally obligated to secure profits by whatever means it takes in order
to fulfill their responsibilities to their employees (cf note 3).
There are restrictions, such as those imposed by law. If a
corporation fails to meet its obligations because of the costs
and effects of adhering to the law, then, other things being
equal, the employees can have no *moral* complaint against the
corporation.

In addition to the restrictions imposed on profit-seeking
activities by the law, I submit that there are also moral
restrictions. For example, corporations are not morally culpable for financial losses incurred by a failure to be ruth-
less, even when ruthlessness is within the limits set by the
law. Employees (and other interested parties) cannot complain on *moral* grounds that they have suffered because the
corporation failed to cheat, lie, deceive, bribe, or pay
extortion.

Finally, consider the obligation of the federal government
to promote and protect the welfare of American business and
workers. Pastin and Hooker are not sure whether such an
obligation actually exists, but assuming that it does, the
argument against the FCPA would presumably go something
like this:

1. Government is created to serve the citizens' interests.

2. Greater corporate profit is in the citizens' interest.

(And therefore government should promote greater corporate profit.)

3. International corporate bribery secures greater corporate profit.

Conclusion: Government should promote (or at least not prohibit) international corporate bribery, and so the FCPA should not be law.

This argument is open to criticism on a number of grounds, but I will comment only on the nature of the con-clusion. The "should" in "Government should promote greater corporate profit" and in "Government should promote international corporate bribery" state *legal* or *political* obli-gations, but not always *moral* ones, for if what is in the cit-izens' interest or the means to satisfying it is *immoral*, the government cannot have a *moral* obligation to promote that interest by that means. That is, any *moral* obligation of the government's to promote a certain end or means extends only to those ends and means that can be determined antecedently to be moral. If acts of bribery are, all things considered, generally immoral-- as I have been arguing--the government can have no *moral* obligation to condone activities calling for bribery. Thus, the question of whether or not the FCPA is moral is to be determined independently of any obligation of the government to protect business and worker welfare.

This concludes my comments on Pastin and Hooker's first argument. I now turn to their second argument.

III

In their second argument Pastin and Hooker marshal three distinct considerations behind the idea that "many of the payments prohibited by the Act are neither bribes nor share features that make bribes morally reprehensible." My general observation on this claim is that even if it is true, each of the three points falls before the fact that bribery is not the only morally objectionable form of behavior; an activ-ity can be morally reprehensible even if it does not exhibit

the morally reprehensible features peculiar to bribery.   Let
us take up each of the three considerations in turn.

1. Pastin and Hooker point out that quite often the payments in question are not bribes at all, but are *extorted*
from corporations.   Thus, the morally objectionable coercion
of foreign officials characteristic of bribery is absent.[5]
This may be true.   Nonetheless, caving in to an extortion demand is morally objectionable in its own right.   For
one thing, to pay extortion is to participate in and foster
the expansion of corruption in the country in which the payment is made.   This naturally leads to the unjust concentration of power in the hands of the people who receive the
payments and thereby contributes to the oppression of the
people the recipients of the payments are supposed to serve.
In addition, if the extortion payments are concealed, competition will be unfair and shareholders and the public at large
will be deceived about the operations of a public corporation,
while if the extortion is open and common knowledge, there
will be an even more rapid disintegration of free bargaining
and a return to the state of nature in which any form of
influence and coercion is deemed acceptable.
Some businesspeople may feel that the condition of international corporate competition is in fact that of the state of
nature.   However, this is hyperbole: murder is still a fairly
rare tactic in the competition for contracts; not everyone in
the business community behaves like the Mafia.   But even if
this were not hyperbole, it still would not make such practices *moral*.   It is also worth pointing out that the state of
nature is not a condition we *want* to be in: Few of us *want*
to deal with a government like that of Idi Amin's Uganda;
still fewer of us would want to live in a world in which that

---

5.   In practice it may be difficult to distinguish between
bribery and extortion on the one hand, and goodwill gestures (such as gifts) and facilitating payments (so-called
grease) on the other.   However, the conceptual issue of the
wrongness of extortion does not turn on how the practical
problem is solved.

was the norm.

2. Pastin and Hooker's second observation is that whereas bribery is objectionable, in part, because it tends to result in the purchase of inferior products for the parties represented by the recipients of a bribe, the fact is that in many cases *failure* to make a so-called bribe or extortion payment may be what leads to the purchase of inferior products.

This, too, may be true, as, for example, where the corporation with the best product can secure a market only by making such a payment. However, this is not enough to justify the payment. To consider only the quality of the goods and services provided is to take too narrow a view. Rather, the *overall* result must be considered. This overall result will almost certainly include a more costly product, for the cost of the questionable payment must be made up somewhere, probably out of the foreign consumer's pocket, and perhaps the American's as well. But much more importantly, the effect of fostering corruption and injustice must also be included.

3. The final consideration raised by Pastin and Hooker is that the payments in question may be in accordance with local practice and thus may lack the morally objectionable feature of deceptiveness which is exhibited by bribery proper.

Once again, the observation may be true, but all it shows is that such payments need not exhibit every evil known to man. The other evils already mentioned still remain. That one's contribution to corruption, injustice, oppression, the disintegration of fair bargaining, and a return to the state of nature is acknowledged openly hardly does much to excuse it.

It might still be objected that if the society in which the business is being conducted engages in such practices, it would be wrong for us to try to impose our standards in dealings with them in their country.

This line of argument raises important conceptual issues about intercultural social, legal, and moral standards which are too complex to do justice to here. However, I can offer a few comments which I think considerably reduce the problems about how one ought to act. First, it is absolutely essential to distinguish between practices that are engaged in, recognized, and even tolerated, and those that are condoned and held to be moral. To say simply that in many countries bribery is the norm disguises the fact that what is regularly done may not be what is held to be proper or moral even in the countries where that is the practice. A rough indicator of international moral judgment is the illegality of bribery in every part of the world.[6] Second, to require American corporations to adhere to "our" moral standards with respect to such activities as bribery and extortion is hardly to *impose* our standards on the rest of the world: for a Muslim to refrain from eating pork in England is not for him to impose Muslim standards on the British. Finally, there is some reason for us to refrain from a practice which *we* judge to be wrong and harmful to others even if we do not receive agreement: that settlers in the upper Amazon hunt native Indians for sport does not give us good reason to conform to that practice when in their company. Obviously, more needs to be said on these issues, but I hope that it has been made clear that a passing reference to moral relativism establishes nothing and that there are a number of lines of defense which can be taken against more serious relativistic criticisms.

My conclusion concerning Pastin and Hooker's second argument is that though all the practices prohibited by the act are not bribes and though some of the practices may not exhibit all the same morally objectionable features as bribery, these practices still exhibit morally objectionable features of their own, and so the law that prohibits them is on solid moral ground.

---

6. Judson J. Wambold, "Prohibiting Foreign Bribes: Criminal Sanctions for Corporate Payments Abroad" (*Cornell International Law Journal* 10 (1977), pp. 235-237. Wambold also found that though bribery generally is illegal, corporate contributions to political parties are acceptable in many countries. This complicates the moral evaluation of the FCPA. The next two points in my text suggest directions in which to go to defend the Act in this connection.

In closing, I want to add a few short remarks. First, in asserting that the FCPA is supported by morality, I am not claiming that the act prescribes the morally best behavior in every single case. All laws can be improved. Furthermore, I think that it is *conceptually* impossible for any general rule to classify all cases to which it may be applied properly and unambiguously. But admitting these problems, we should recognize that an imperfect law can still be moral and just.

Second, it should be noted that if Pastin and Hooker were correct, their arguments would go a long way toward justifying bribery and extortion *within* the United States by both foreign and domestic companies--unless we are to believe that a return to the state of nature is morally acceptable in one place (someone else's country), but not in another.

Finally, I think that I have shown that the FCPA is supported by considerations of morality. This should weigh heavily in favor of retaining the law. However, I do not claim to have necessarily provided *motivation* for supporting or adhering to the stipulations of this law. Morality may require sacrifice; in this case, at least, sacrifice of financial gain. For those who care more for financial gain and for the ruthlessness through which it can be obtained than for the moral values of justice and integrity, I cannot claim to have provided motivation.

A BUSINESS VIEW OF THE

FOREIGN CORRUPT PRACTICES ACT

Thomas M. Calero

In their discussions of the Foreign Corrupt Practices Act (FCPA), the business and political press have stayed very largely on the level of normative advising and pay little or no attention to moral theory in contrast to philosophers (e.g., Mark Pastin and Michael Hooker) who argue forcibly for moral assessment in both End-Point and Rule Forms. If critics are proven right in concluding that "it is shocking to find that a law prohibiting bribery has no clear moral basis", they force a shift from moral defense of the Act to other grounds. It is the intent of these comments to make such a shift, leaving others to critique the adequacy of moral assessment, but keeping in mind their belief that "moral conceptions appropriate to a simple world ...are not adequate for the complex world in which contemporary business functions."

The Mood of Congress in passing the FCPA

The mood and collective intent of Congress in debating and passing a statute takes on considerable significance when held up against later events. Recall, for example, the stunned reactions of the (particularly) conservative press when the Supreme Court issued its ruling in *Weber vs Kaiser Aluminum and Chemical* (June, 1979). The majority opinion

in this 5 to 2 decision (two other Justices did not take part)
focused on the *spirit* and *intent* of Congress in passing the
Civil Rights Act of 1964 and not on the literal language of
that Act as it pertains to employment discrimination. The
Court was accused of seeing provisions of the Act which
were simply not there.

What appeared to motivate Congress relative to the
FCPA? The record contains considerable citation of the various social and economic ills presumably caused by U.S.
business participation in corrupt foreign dealings. Congress
appeared strongly convinced that acts of bribery, and
closely similar behaviors, are reprehensible as such and produce most, or all, of the following negative outcomes:

- Depressing of stockholders' earnings
- Driving up consumer prices
- Selling a country what it doesn't need
- Distorting the nature of competition
- Damaging U.S. foreign relations
- Undermining foreign governments
- Eroding the quality of U.S. moral leadership
- And, promoting generalized disrespect for law

No doubt some members of Congress believed the FCPA was
drafted in haste and would prove unworkable, but the majority appeared to take comfort in the Act's tough stand against
corruption and its consequences. What emerged from Congress was essentially a law in two distinct parts: a relatively
limited part enumerating proscribed actions related to bribery and the accompanying criminal penalities, and a relatively demanding part specifying the record keeping and
internal controls aimed at preventing "creative accounting."
Both parts of the FCPA have drawn widespread criticism.
Business people often describe themselves as caught between
foreign customs encouraging or even requiring bribery and
the Act's prohibitions and record-keeping requirements.
The business press has been sprinkled with corporate references to significant overseas business lost to unrestrained
foreign competitors, to ambiguities in the Act as to what
constitutes a bribe (when does "grease" stop and "real"
bribery begin?), to uncertainties over a U.S. management's
responsibilities for actions of its foreign subsidiaries or foreign agents, and to the allegedly burdensome, costly, and

unproductive nature of the Act's internal controls.

Impact of the FCPA on U.S. Export Trade

What can be said about the relationship between the
Act and export volume? A 1981 survey of major U.S. corporations by the Government Account Office showed that top
officials of 76% of these firms thought the law had been
effective in deterring bribery and in cleaning up corporate
record keeping. But rather than making plain the magnitude
of U.S. export business loss, the survey results concentrate upon the substantive and procedural ambiguities of the
FCPA, what should be done about them and how the criminal
penalities should be modified.

The nature of the information most readily available is
perhaps the most troublesome problem in getting a grip on
the export impact of the Act. In most cases it is anecdotal
or, on occasion, of the case study variety. As examples:

- Representatives of Dow Chemical and Union Carbide
in 1977 went to the Philippines to discuss a potential
one billion dollar petrochemical complex. An in-law of
President Marcos wanted a three million dollar "fee"
for his help. After some soul searching, the offer
was rejected.

- In South Korea, it is reported U.S. companies have
had to greatly increase the salaries of their Korean
executives rather than follow the former practice of
not fully disclosing their local managers incomes for
tax purposes. Thus, operating costs rose.

- Lockheed Corporation, a name closely associated
with foreign bribery in the early 1970's, now is said
to not even pay hotel bills for customers visiting its
California headquarters.

- In Xerox Corporation's Cairo office, the local manager has now to get permission from a senior official
in the United States in order to pay eight dollars a

month in tips to Egyptian telephone repairmen.

Just these few instances illustrate both the scattered nature
of the data and the range of its significance, from major to
trivial. Very likely numbers of other relevant instances simply go unreported by the firms involved. What *does* seem
plain is that no systematic evidence has been assembled
which shows that the U.S. export trade has been seriously
damaged by the workings of the FCPA. Department of Commerce figures show that non- agricultural exports have
almost doubled to $179.8 billion in 1981 from $96.5 billion in
1977. The latest data available, January through May of
1982, shows export volume continuing at about the '81 level,
despite depressed worldwide economic conditions. Other
forces which impact U.S. foreign trade would appear far
stronger than any influence traceable to the FCPA.
These include:

> - The dollar's strength abroad. The Wall Street
> Journal recently declared (October 18, 1982) that the
> dollar's rise against major foreign currencies "has
> made U.S. exports the least competitive of the eleven
> major industrialized nations."

> - Reagan administration policy initiatives regarding
> such matters as the Soviet Union's natural gas pipe-
> line to Western Europe, grain sales to the Soviets,
> and heavily stepped up arms and military supplies to
> a number of countries.

> - The continued gain in the ability of other nations to
> compete with the U.S. and in so doing to restructure
> the nature of trading relations in a number of signifi-
> cant ways. And this restructuring seems to have
> taken place quite aside from any role played by busi-
> ness bribes and related dealings.

What Should Be Done?

Some thinkers conclude that the FCPA has no firm moral basis and is really worse than no law at all. Some Reagan administration insiders are in favor of substantially limiting the scope and meaning of the Act or in favor of allowing it to languish through non-enforcement. Presumably, the many corporate critics would be quite happy with any of these choices. Viewed from a somewhat different perspective, is it accurate to say interest in the FCPA and its objectives has waned? Comparatively little current attention is being paid to it in the business press. The attempt by I.I.T.'s Center for the Study of Ethics in the Professions to convene a conference (during 1981) on the Act, its nature and future, drew very limited corporate audience response and was dropped. Has Congress lost interest as well? Would it vote for repeal?

Two formidable consequences seem quite likely if the FCPA dies through inaction or is repealed. One is the implicit endorsement of business misconduct through the removal of threat, and the other additional public questioning if corporate managerial integrity is no longer subject to the Act's specific restraints. Since convincing evidence is still lacking relative to the FCPA's damage to U.S. export trade, neither unenforcement nor repeal are justified.

BRIBERY

Michael Philips

Although disclosures of bribery have elicited considerable public indignation over the last decade, popular discussions of the morality of bribery have tended largely to be
unilluminating. One reason for this is that little care has
been taken to distinguish bribes from an assortment of
related practices with which they are easily confused.
Before we can be in a position to determine what to do about
the problem of bribery, we need to be clearer about what
count and ought to count as bribes. Unfortunately, there is
as yet no philosophical literature on this topic.[1] In this

---

1. At the time the first version of this paper was
written there were no references to bribes or bribery in the
Philosopher's Index. Since that time one paper has been
indexed -- Arnold Berleant's "Multinationals, Local Practice,
and The Problem of Ethical Consistency," (*Journal of Business Ethics*, 1 (1982), pp. 185-193) - but as the title of that
short paper suggests, Berleant is not primarily concerned to
provide an analysis of the concept of bribery. However,
three presentations on the topic of bribery were made at the
1983 Conference for Business Ethics (organized by the Society for Business Ethics, DePaul University, July 25-26).
And papers based on these presentations will soon be published. These are Kendall D'Andrade's, "Bribery," *Journal
of Business Ethics*, forthcoming, Tom Carson's "What's Wrong
with Bribery?" *Philosophy and Public Affairs*, forthcoming,

paper I shall remedy this defect by presenting an account of
the concept of bribery and by employing that account to
clarify matters in three areas in which there is public controversy and confusion.

At least some confusion in discussions of bribery arises
from a failure adequately to appreciate the distinction
between bribery and extortion. This is true, for example,
of accounts of the notorious case of Lockheed in Japan. I
shall attempt to show that the morality of this and similar
transactions are better assessed if we are clear on that distinction.

A second problem area arises out of the fact of cultural
variability. As is generally recognized, the conduct of business, government and the professions differs from culture to
culture. In some places transactions that many Americans
would consider bribes are not only expected behavior but
accepted practice as well. That is, they are condoned by
the system of rule governing the conduct of the relevant
parties. Are they bribes? Are only some of them bribes?
If so, which?

A third problem arises out of the general difficulty of
distinguishing between bribes, on the one hand, and gifts
and rewards on the other. Suppose that a manufacturer of
dresses keeps a buyer for a catalogue company happy by
supplying him with any tickets to expensive shows and athletic events that he requests. Are these bribes? Or suppose that a special interest group rewards public administrators who rule in its favor with vacations, automobiles, and
jewelry. May we correctly speak of bribery here?

---

and John Danley's "Toward a Theory of Bribery," *Journal of
Business and Professional Ethics*, 2 (*1983*), pp. 19-40.
Since these papers were not in print at the time this paper
came out, I did not refer to them in the body of the text.
Where my account differs significantly from D'Andrade's,
Carson's or Danley's, I discuss this in footnotes.

I

To answer such questions we need to say, more precisely, what bribes are. A bribe is a payment (or promise
of payment) for a service. Typically, this payment is made
to an official in exchange for her violating some official duty
or responsibility. And typically she does this by failing
deliberately to make a decision on its merits. This does not
necessarily mean that a bribed official will make an improper
decision; a judge who is paid to show favoritism may do so
and yet, coincidentally, make the correct legal decision
(i.e., the bribed party may in fact have the law on her
side). The violation of duty consists in deciding a case for
the wrong sorts of reasons.

Although the most typical and important cases of bribery
concern political officials and civil servants, one need not be
a political official or a civil servant to be bribed. Indeed,
one need not be an official of any sort. Thus, a mortician
may be bribed to bury a bodyless casket and a baseball
player may be bribed to strike out each time he bats. Still,
baseball players and morticians are members of organizations
and have duties and responsibilities by virtue of the positions they occupy in these organizations. It is tempting,
then, to define a bribe as a payment made to a member of an
organization in exchange for the violation of some positional
duty or responsibility. This temptation is strengthened by
our recognition that we cannot be bribed to violate a duty
we have simply by virtue of being a moral agent (hired kill-
ers, for example, are not bribed to violate their duty not to
kill). And it is further strengthened when we recognize
that we may be paid to violate duties we have by virtue of a
non-organizationally based status without being bribed
(e.g., I am not bribed if--as a non-handicapped person--I
accept payment to park in a space reserved for the handi-
capped; nor am I bribed if--as a pet owner--I accept payment illegally to allow my dog to run free on the city
streets).

Still, it is too strong to say that occupying a position in
an organization is a necessary condition of being bribed. We
may also speak of bribing a boxer to throw a fight or of
bribing a runner to lose a race. These cases, however, are

importantly like the cases already described. Roughly, both
the boxer and the runner are paid to do something they
ought not to do *given* what they are. What they are, in
these cases, are participants in certain practices. What they
are paid to do is to act in a manner dictated by some person
or organization rather than to act according to the understandings constitutive of their practices. Civil servants,
business executives, morticians and baseball players, of
course, are also participants in practices. And their
responsibilities, as such, are defined by the rules and
understandings governing the organizations to which they
belong. At this point, then, we are in a position to state a
provisional definition of bribery. Thus, P accepts a bribe
from R if and only if P agrees for payment to act in a manner dictated by R rather than doing what is required of him
as a participant in his practice.[2]

----

2. Danley defines "bribing" as "offering or giving something of value with a corrupt intent to induce or influence
an action of someone in a public or official capacity." Carson defines a bribe as a payment to someone in exchange for
"special consideration incompatible with the duties of his
position." Both go on to discuss bribery as if it were
restricted to officials of organizations. Since these are the
most typical and important cases of bribery, their focus is
understandable. But it does have at least one unfortunate
consequence. For it leads both Danley and Carson to think
that the question of whether it is *prima facie* wrong to offer
or accept bribes reduces to the question of whether officials
have obligations to satisfy their positional duties. Danley
argues that they do not, if the institutions they serve are
illegitimate. Carson argues that they do on the ground that
they have made a tacit agreement with their institution to
discharge those duties (accepting a bribe, for Carson, is an
instance of promise breaking). Whatever the merits of their
arguments concerning the responsibilities of officials, both
approach the question of the *prima facie* morality of bribery
too narrowly. For different issues seem to arise when we
consider bribery outside the realm of officialdom. Clearly it

One advantage of this account is that it enables us to deal with certain difficult cases. Suppose that a high-ranking officer at the Pentagon is paid by a Soviet agent to pass on defense secrets. The first few times he does this we would not hesitate to say that he is bribed. But suppose that he is paid a *salary* to do this and that the arrangement lasts for a number of years. At this point talk of bribery appears less appropriate. But why should something that has the character of a bribe if done once or twice (or, perhaps, on a piecework basis) cease to have that character if done more often (or, perhaps, on a salaried basis)? On my account the explanation is that the frequency or basis of payment may incline us differently to identify the practice in question. Thus, if an American officer works for the Soviet Union long enough we begin to think of him as a Soviet spy. In any case, to the extent to which we regard his practice as spying we are inclined to think of the payments in question as payments of a salary as opposed to so many bribes. A similar analysis holds in the case of industrial spies, undercover agents recruited from within organizatins, and so forth.[3] We do not think of them as bribed because we do not think of them as full-fledged practitioners of the practices in which they appear to engage.

---

is more difficult for Carson to make his tacit consent argument in relation to the bribed athlete. For it is not clear that a runner who enters a race tacitly agrees to win it (if so, he would be breaking a promise by running to prepare for future races or by entering to set the pace for someone else). Nor is it clear that a boxer who accepts payment not to knockout his opponent in the early rounds violates a tacit agreement to attempt a knockout at his earliest convenience.

Danley must expand his account to accommodate such cases as well. For it is not clear what it means to say that a practice such as running or boxing is legitimate.

3. Such cases present some difficulty for the definitions of both Danley and Carson. Each needs to expand his account to enable him to distinguish, e.g., between a bribe and a salary paid to a spy.

202 PROFIT AND RESPONSIBILITY

This practice conception is further supported by the fact that a person may satisfy my account of bribery on a long term and regularized basis and still be said to be a recipient of bribes. This is so where his continued and regularized acceptance of payments does not warrant any change in our understanding of the practices in which he participates. Thus, we do not think of a judge who routinely accepts payments for favors from organized crime as participating in some practice other than judging, even if he sits almost exclusively on such cases. This may be arbitrary: perhaps we ought rather think of him as an agent of a criminal organization (a paid saboteur of the legal system), and treat him accordingly. My point, however, is that because we do not think of him in this way--because we continue to think of him as a judge--we regard each fresh occurrence as an instance of bribery.

The present account, however, is not entirely adequate as it stands. Consider the following counter-examples: (a) an artist is offered $5,000 by an eccentric to ruin a half-completed canvas by employing an unsuitable color; and (b) a parent is paid $500 for the use of his eight year old son in a pornographic film.

It might be argued in relation to (a) that it is consistent with the practice of being an artist that one accept payment to produce whatever the client is willing to pay for. However, the conception of a practice that underlies this response seems to me questionable. What seems to me counter-intuitive about speaking of bribery in (a) is that the act in question is private. By this I mean, roughly, that it affects no one who is not a party to the transaction. If I pay an artist to ruin a painting that has been commissioned by a museum, the oddity of speaking of bribery disappears. In general, where there is no violation of an organizational duty, we might say that a payment is a bribe only if it affects the interests of persons or organizations who are not parties to the transaction. To forestall counter-examples based on remote or indirect consequences, we must add that the parties affected must be parties whose interests are normally affected by the conduct of the practice in question, and that they must be affected in the manner in which they are normally affected.

It is tempting to go further than this and claim that a bribe occurs only when the act agreed to by the bribed

party violates the moral rights of some third party or organization. But this seems to me mistaken. We may speak of
bribing officers of terribly corrupt institutions (e.g., concentration camps) but it is not at all clear that these office
holders necessarily violate the rights of any person or
organization by violating their institutional duties (e.g., by
allowing prisoners to escape). Or consider a society in
which slaves are used as boxers and masters wager on the
bouts. It seems clear that one can bribe a slave to lose a
fight here, but it is not at all clear that a slave violates
anyone's rights by accepting payment for so doing. (To say
this would be to imply that a slave boxer has a *prima facie*
duty to try to win his fight, and this seems to me untena-
ble).

What, then, of the second counter-example? Why are we
reluctant to speak of bribery in the case of parents? One
way to deal with this case is to attribute this reluctance to
an anachronistic linguistic habit developed and sustained by
centuries of thinking according to which children are the
property of parents. According to this outmoded way of
thinking, either there is no such thing as the practice of
parenting, or that practice far more resembles an account
that Thrasymachus might offer of it than an account most of
us would now accept. It sounds odd to speak of bribing
parents, then, because our linguistic habits have not caught
up with our new vision of parenting. But this is something
we should change, i.e., we ought to allow that parents may
be bribed.

But I am uncomfortable with this reply. Most of us now
agree that children have rights which ought to be protected
by law and/or community pressure and that parents have
duties not to violate these rights. To this extent, we are
coming to understand families as organizations. Thus, if we
allow that parents are bribed, we will almost certainly hold
that they are bribed in the way that members of organizations are typically bribed, viz., they are paid to violate
their positional duties. But there is something disturbing
about this. For despite our conviction that children have
rights, many of us are uncomfortable thinking of the family
as just another organization, and thinking of a parent as
just another functionary. Our reluctance to maintain that
parents may be bribed, then, may express a healthy resis-
tance to thinking of a parent on the model of an official.

Just how we ought to think of the family, I cannot say; the challenge is to arrive at a conception that acknowledges that children have legally enforceable rights without reducing the family to just another institution.

If we exempt the family from consideration and we build in the condition required by the second counter-example, we are now in a position to present a tentative definition of bribery. Thus, P is bribed by R if and only if: (1) P accepts payment from R to act on R's behalf[4] (2) P's act on R's behalf consists in violationg some rule or understanding constitutive of a practice in which P is engaged; and (3) P's violation is either a violation of some official duty P has by

---

4. Thus D'Andrade defines bribery as "an alienation of agency." On his account bribery occurs when someone is seduced into abandoning his role as an agent of one person or organization and, for a price, becomes the agent of another. This highlights an important feature of bribery that is ignored by Carson and Danley and that was neglected in my own earlier thinking on this subject, viz. that a bribe taker acts on behalf of someone. But D'Andrade's claim that agency is alienated when one accepts a bribe implies that the bribe taker necessarily is committed to act on behalf of some person or organization before he is in a position to accept a bribe. And it is difficult to see what helpful truth this might express in relation to the runner or boxer of my examples. Surely it is not helpful to say that a bribe taker begins as his *own* agent in these cases and, for pay, alienates that agency to another. This applies to anyone who takes a job. Nor is it helpful to say--as D'Andrade did say at one point--that he may begin as an agent of some abstraction (e.g., in the case of an independent scientist paid to falsify a result, truth). Surely the point behind this obscure claim is better made by speaking of what is expected of someone as a participant in a practice. It is also worth noting that D'Andrade's alienation of agency account offers no basis for distinguishing between bribed officials, on the one hand, and undercover agents and spies, on the other. For these too alienate agency.

virtue of his participation in that practice or P's violation significantly affects the interests of persons or organizations whose interests are typically connected to that practice.

At least two additional important features of bribery deserve mention. The first is a consequence of the fact that bribes are payments. For, like other kinds of payments (e.g., rent), bribes presuppose agreements of a certain kind.[5] That is, it must be understood by both parties that the payment in question is exchanged, or is to be exchanged, for the relevant conduct. In the most typical and important cases, the bribed party is an official and the conduct in question is the violation of some official duty. In these cases we may say simply that an official P is bribed by R when she accepts payment or the promise of payment for *agreeing* to violate a positional duty to act on R's behalf. This agreement requirement is of great importance. As I shall argue in Section IV, without it we cannot properly distinguish between bribes and gifts or rewards.

Such agreements need not be explicit. If I am stopped by a policeman for speeding and hand him a fifty dollar bill along with my driver's license, and he accepts the fifty dollar bill, it is arguable that we have entered into such an agreement despite what we might say about contributions to the Police Benevolence Association. As I shall argue, some of the difficulties we have in determining what transactions to count as bribes may stem from unclarity concerning the conditions under which we are entitled to say an agreement has been made.

It is a consequence of this account that someone may be bribed despite the fact that she subsequently decides not to perform the service she has agreed to perform. Indeed, we must say this even if she has never been paid, but has been

---

5. This feature of bribery is insufficiently attended to by Carson and is inconsistent with Danley's account. Danley understands a bribe as an attempt to induce or influence someone. In this matter he appears to have most dictionaries on his side (including the *O.E.D.*). However, as I argue in more detail in Section IV, he is mistaken.

only promised payment, or even if she has been paid but returns this payment after she decides not to abide by her part of the agreement. I see nothing strange about this. After all, if one accepts a bribe it seems natural to say that one has been bribed. Still, I have no strong objection to distinguishing between accepting a bribe and being bribed, where a necessary condition of the latter is that one carries out one's part of the bribery agreement. As far as I can see, no important moral question turns on this choice of language.

A final interesting feature of bribery emerges when we reflect on the claim that offering and accepting bribes is *prima facie* wrong. I will begin with the case of officials. The claim that it is *prima facie* wrong for someone in an official position to accept a bribe is plausible only if persons in official capacities have *prima facie obligations to discharge their official duties*. The most plausible argument for this claim is grounded in a social contract model of organizations. By accepting a position in an organization, it might be argued, one tacitly agrees to abide by the rules of that organization. To be bribed is to violate that agreement, i.e., to break a promise, and is, therefore *prima facie* wrong.[6] While I concede that this argument has merit in a context of just and voluntary institutions, it seems questionable in a context of morally corrupt institutions (e.g., Nazi Germany or contemporary El Salvador). And even were it technically valid for those contexts, its conclusion would nonetheless be a misleading half-truth.

It is beyond the scope of this paper to discuss, in detail, the problems with the tacit consent argument in a context of corrupt institutions. In brief, my position is that actions which create *prima facie* moral obligations in just or ideal contexts do not necessarily create comparable obligations in unjust or corrupt contexts. Thus, for example, it does not seem to me that if I join the Mafia with the intention of subverting its operations and bringing its members to justice, I have thereby undertaken a *prima facie* obligation

---

6. This is Carson's argument.

to abide by the code of that organization. Of course, one could say this and add that the obligation in question is typically overridden by other moral considerations. But this seems to me an *ad hoc* move to defend a position. We use the expression "prima facie duty" to point to a moral presumption for or against a certain type of action. And surely it is strange to insist that there is a moral presumption, in the present case, in favor of carrying out the commands of one's Don.

But even if we grant that there is a *prima facie* duty here, we must be careful to qualify this assertion. For it is also clear that participants in unjust institutions have a *prima facie* right to interfere with the normal functioning of those institutions (at least where these functionings can be reasonably expected to produce unjust outcomes). Indeed, where the injustice is great enough they have a *prima facie* duty to interfere. And in some contexts, the strength of that duty typically will exceed the strength of any promise-keeping obligation generated by tacit consent. Thus we may say, other things equal, that the commandant of a concentration camp ought to act in a manner that frustrates the genocidal purpose of that institution. And, assuming that that institution is "rationally" designed to serve its purpose, there will be a strong moral presumption in favor of the violation of his positional duty.

What, then, of the morality of accepting bribes in such cases? If an official has no *prima facie* duty to satisfy her positional duties--or if the presumption in favor of satisfying them is outweighed by the presumption against so doing---then, other things equal, it is difficult to see why it is *prima facie* wrong to accept payment for violating them. After all, there may be serious risks involved. This at least is so where the case *against* carrying out the purposes of one's organization is strong enough to *permit* one to violate one's positional duty but is not so strong that one has a *prima facie* obligation to do this. For it does seem *prima facie* wrong to make compliance with a *prima facie* duty contingent upon payment (it ought rather to be contingent upon an assessment of what one ought to do, all things considered). And it certainly seems wrong to demand payment for doing what is one's duty, all things considered.

Still, this may be too quick. Consider a concentration camp guard who lacks the courage to help inmates escape

but who would be courageous enough to undertake the risks
involved were he assured of sufficient funds to transport his
family to another country and comfortably to begin a new
life.   If he is *in fact* reasonably certain that he would be
brave enough to do what is required of him were he paid, it
seems not improper of him to demand payment.   In general,
if the wrong of demanding payment for doing one's duty is
outweighted by the importance of doing it and if demanding
payment for doing it is causally necessary for doing it,
then, all things considered, it is not wrong to demand payment.

If it is not wrong for an official to accept a bribe, one
does not induce him to do something wrong by offering him
one.   Thus, we cannot say in all contexts that it is *prima
facie* wrong to offer someone a bribe *because* this is an
attempt to induce him to do something wrong or to corrupt
him.[7] On the other hand, there may be cases in which it is

---

7.   Nor can we say that it is *prima facie* wrong because
it is an attempt to get someone to do something that is *prima
facie* wrong.   This argument is flawed in two ways.   To
begin with, as we have seen, the premise expresses what is
at best a dangerous half-truth.   Were we to reason from the
whole truth we must conclude that there are some contexts
in which the presumption in favor of violating one's official
duties is stronger than the presumption against it.   In the
second place, moreover, the inference is invalid: it is not
necessarily *prima facie* wrong to induce someone to do something that is *prima facie* wrong.   Rather, it is *prima facie*
wrong to induce someone to do something that is wrong, all
things considered.   Thus, if it is *prima facie* wrong for P to
do A, but P ought to do A, all things considered, there is
no presumption against my inducing P to do A; I do not
need to justify this by appealing to countervailing moral considerations.   I require such justification only when it *is*
wrong for P to do so.   Cases of this latter sort are interesting, but typically neglected by philosophers.   (The following
are examples: (a) P is a soldier in a war in which each side
has equal claim to justice; R is a guard on the opposite

prima facie wrong to offer a bribe despite the fact that it is perfectly acceptable for the bribed party to accept one. Recall the case of the boxer slave. Despite the fact that the slave has no obligation to try to win, a wagering master may have a *prima facie* obligation not to pay him to lose. For by so doing the master may gain an unfair advantage over other wagerers. It might be objected that the master's obligation in this other case is misleadingly described as an obligation not to bribe. He is obligated, rather, not to fix fights; or, more generally, not to take unfair advantage of his fellow wagerers. This objection raises issues we need not consider here. It is enough to point out that the purpose of offering a bribe is very often to seek some unfair or undeserved benefit or advantage, and that this is one reason we are rightly suspicious of the morality of bribe offers.

We are now in a position to state a fifth interesting feature of bribery. Even if it is not *prima facie* wrong to offer and to accept bribes in all contexts, it is *prima facie* wrong to do so in morally uncorrupted contexts. Accordingly, a bribe offerer or a bribe taker must defend the morality of his act either by showing that there are countervailing moral considerations in its favor *or* by showing that the moral context is so corrupt that the factors that generate *prima facie* duties in uncorrupted contexts do no apply here. This strategy of moral justifications, of course, is not unique to bribery. It may hold in relation to a wide range of what are ordinarily taken to be *prima facie duties*. In case of bribery, however, arguments to the effect that the moral context

---

side. Though it might be wrong for R to accept a bribe from P, it is not wrong for P to offer R a bribe; and (b) P's father is certain to be convicted of a crime he did not commit because the evidence is overwhelmingly against him. It is permissible for P to offer a bribe to R, an Assistant District Attorney, to "lose" some evidence; but it is wrong for R to accept the bribe).

In any case, the upshot of this is that even if there were a general moral presumption against accepting bribes it would not follow that there is a comparable presumption against offering bribes.

is corrupted will have a certain characteristic form. Thus, in the most important case--the case of officials--they will be arguments that challenge the legitimacy of an institution.

II

I now turn to the first of three problem areas I shall address in this paper. Compare the following cases:

> (a) Executive P hopes to sell an airplane to the national airline of Country C. The deal requires the approval of Minister R. P knows that R can make a better deal elsewhere and that R has a reputation for honesty but that R is in serious financial difficulties. Accordingly P offers R a large sum of money to buy from him. R accepts and abides by the agreement.

> (b) The same as (a) except that P knows that he is offering the best deal R can get and R knows this too. Nonetheless, P is informed by reliable sources that R will not deal with P unless P offers to pay him a considerable sum of money. P complies and R completes the deal.

According to my analysis (a) is a clear case of bribery; and (b) is not bribery at all.

The difference between (a) and (b) is clear enough. In (a) P pays R to violate R's duty (in this case, to make the best deal that R can). In (b) P does no such thing. Instead, he pays R to do what is required of R by his institutional commitments in any case. Moreover, he does so in response to R's threat to violate those commitments in a manner that jeopardizes P's interests. Accordingly, (b) more resembles extortion than bribery. For, roughtly speaking, R extorts P if R threatens P with a penalty in case P fails to give R something to which R has no rightful claims.

If this is true it may be that American corporate executives accused of bribing foreign officials are sometimes more like victims of extortion than offerers of bribes. For in at

least some cases they are required to make payments to
assure that an official does what she is supposed to do in
any case.   This is especially true in the case of inspectors
of various kinds, and in relation to government officials who
must approve transactions between American and local companies.   An inspector who refuses to approve a shipment that
is up to standards unless he is paid off is like a bandit who
demands tribute on all goods passing through his territory.

It does not follow that it is morally correct for American
companies to pay off such corrupt officials.   There are cases
in which it is morally wrong to surrender to the demands of
bandits, and other extortionists.   But it is clear that the
moral questions that arise here are different sorts of questions than those that arise in relation to bribery.   The moral
relations between the relevant parties differ.   The bribery
agreement is not by its nature an agreement between victims
and victimizers.   The extortion agreement is.   Moral justifications and excuses for complying with the demands of an
extortionist are easier to come by than moral justifications
and excuses for offering bribes.

Of course the distinction in question is often easier to
draw in theory than in practice.   An inspector who demands
a payoff to authorize a shipment is likely to fortify his
demand by insisting that the product does not meet standards.   In some cases it may be difficult to know whether or
not he is lying (e.g., whether the shipment has been con-
taminated in transit).   And given the high cost of delays, a
company may decide that it is too expensive to take the time
to find out.   In this case, a company may decide to pay off
without knowing whether it is agreeing to pay a bribe or to
surrender to extortion.   Since the morality of its decisions
may well turn on what it is in fact doing in such cases, a
company that does not take the time to find out acts in a
morally irresponsible manner.   (Unless, of course, it is in a
position to defend both courses of action).

What sorts of justifications can a company present for
offering bribes?   It is beyond the scope of this paper to
provide a detailed discussion of this question.   However, I
have already mentioned a number of considerations that
count as moral reasons *against* bribery in a variety of contexts.   To begin with, in reasonably just contexts, officials
ordinarily are obligated to discharge the duties of their
offices.   In these cases bribe offers are noramlly attempts to

induce officials to violate duties. Moreover, if accepted, a bribe offer may make it more likely that that official will violate future duties. Accordingly, it may contribute to the corruption of an official. In addition, the intent of a bribe offer is often to secure an unfair advantage or an undeserved privilege. Where this is the case, it too counts as a reason against bribery. To determine whether a bribe offer is wrong in any particular case, then, we must decide: (1) whether these reasons obtain in that case; (2) if they obtain how much weight we ought to attach to them; and (3) how much weight we ought to attach to countervailing considerations (e.g., suppose that we must bribe an official in order to meet an important contractual obligation). It is worth remarking in this regard that where officials routinely take bribes, the presumption against corrupting officials normally will not apply. Similarly, to the extent that bribery is an accepted weapon in the arsenal of all competitors, bribe offers cannot be construed as attempts to achieve an unfair advantage over one's competitors.

III

It is sometimes suggested that an environment may be so corrupt that no payments count as bribes. These are circumstances in which the level of official compliance to duty is very low, and payoffs are so widespread that they are virtually institutionalized. Suppose, for example, that the laws of country N impose very high duties on a variety of products but that it is common practice in N for importers and exporters to pay customes officials to overlook certain goods and/or to underestimate their number or value. Suppose, moreover, that the existence of this practice is common knowledge but that no effort is made to stop it by law enforcement officials at any level.[8] Indeed, that any attempts

---

8.   On D'Andrade's account bribes are necessarily secret

to stop it would be met by widespread social disapproval. One might even imagine that customs officials receive no salary in N, but earn their entire livelihood in this way. One might further imagine that customs officials are expected to return a certain amount of money to the government every month and are fired from their jobs for failure to do so. Finally, one might suppose that the cumulative advantages and disadvantages of this way of doing things is such that the economy of N is about as strong as it would be under a more rule-bound alternative. Are these officials bribed?

On my analysis, the answer to this question depends on how we understand the duties of the customs officer. If the official job description for the customs officer in N (and the written laws of N) are like those of most countries the customs officer violates his official duties *according to these codes*, by allowing goods to leave the country without collecting the full duty. The question, however, is how seriously we are to take these written codes. Where social and political practice routinely violates them, and nothing is done about it, and few members of the legal and non-legal community believe that anything ought to be done about it, it is arguable that these codes are dead letters. If we find this to be true of the codes governing the duties of the customs officials in country N, we have good reason for saying that the real obligations of these officials do not require that they impose the duties described in those written codes. (But only that they return a certain sum of the money they collect to the central government each month). Anything collected in excess of that amount they are entitled to keep as salary (recall that they are officially unpaid). In reality we might say that duties on exports in country N are not fixed, but negotiable.

Of course if we decide that e.g., the written law of N is the law of N we must describe the situation otherwise. In that case, the official obligations of the customs officials are as they are described, and the system in N must be characterized as one of rampant bribery condoned both by government and by popular opinion. It seems to me that the

---

so these could not count as bribes.

philosophy of law on which this account rests is implausible. However, there is no need to argue this to defend my analysis of this case. My position is simply that whether or not we describe what goes on here as bribery depends on what we take the real legal responsibilities of the customs official to be. To the extent that we are inclined to identify his duties with the written law we will be inclined to speak of bribery here. To the extent that we are unwilling so to identify his duties we will not.[9]

IV

Let us now consider the problem of distinguishing bribes from rewards and gifts. The problem arises because gifts are often used in business and government to facilitate transactions. And to the degree to which a business person, professional person or government official is influenced in her decision by gifts, it is tempting to conclude that she is violating her duties. In such cases we are tempted to

---

9. A corresponding point holds in relation to bribery outside the realm of officialdom. Consider the case of professional wrestling. Most of us believe that the outcome of professional wrestling matches is determined in advance. Are the losers bribed? (To simplify matters let us assume that they are paid a bit of extra money for losing). The answer here depends on how we understand their practice. If we take them to be participating in a wrestling competition, we must say that they bribed. In that case, by failing to compete they violate an understanding constitutive of their practice. It is reasonably clear, however, that professional wrestlers are not engaged in an athletic competition. Rather, they are engaged in a dramatic performance. This being the case the losers are not bribed. They are merely doing what professional wrestlers are ordinarily paid to do, viz. to play out their part of an informal script.

speak of these gifts as bribes.

If I am correct, however, this temptation should be resisted. A bribe, after all, presupposes an agreement. A gift may be made with the intention of inducing an official to show favoritism to the giver, but unless acceptance of what is transferred can be construed as an agreement to show favoritism, what is transferred is not a bribe.

In some case, of course, the acceptance of what is offered can be so construed. Again, if I offer $50 to a policeman who has stopped me for speeding, he has a right to construe my act as one of offering a bribe and I have a right to to contrue his acceptance in the corresponding manner. If I regularly treat the neighborhood policeman to a free lunch at my diner and he regularly neglects to ticket my illegally parked car we have reason to say the same. Agreements need not be explicit. My point is just that to the degree that it is inappropriate to speak of agreements, it is also inappropriate to speak of bribes.

It follows from this that if I present an official with an expensive item to induce him to show favoritism on my behalf, in violation of his duty, I have not necessarily bribed him. It does not follow from this, however, that I have done nothing wrong. So long as you are morally obligated to perform your official duty, normally it will be wrong of me to induce you to do otherwise by presenting you with some expensive item. Moreover, if you have any reason to believe that accepting what I offer *will* induce you not to do your duty you have done something wrong by accepting my gift. To prevent such wrongs we have laws prohibiting persons whose interests are closely tied to the decisions of public officials from offering gifts to these officials. And we have laws forbidding officials to accept such gifts.

It might be objected that this account is too lenient. Specifically, it might be argued that wherever P presents Q with something of value to induce Q to violate Q's official duties P has offered a bribe.

But this is a mistake. It suggests, among other things, that an official is bribed so long as he accepts what is offered with this intent. Yet an official may accept such a gift innocently, believing that it is what it purports to be, viz. a token of friendship or goodwill. And she may do so with justifiable confidence that doing so will not in any way affect the discharge of her duty.

It may be replied that officials are bribed by such inducements only when they are in fact induced to do what is desired of them. But again, it may be the case that an official accepts what is offered innocently, believing it to be a gift, and that she believes falsely that it will not affect her conduct. In this case she has exercised bad judgment, but she has not been bribed. Indeed, it seems to me that it is improper to say that she accepts a bribe even when she recognizes the intent of the inducement and believes that accepting it *is* likely to influence her. There is a distinction between accepting a drink with the understanding that one is agreeing to be seduced and accepting a drink with the knowledge that so doing will make one's seduction more likely. To be bribed is to bought, not merely to be influenced to something.

From a moral point of view, wherever failure to perform one's official duties is wrong, it may be as bad to accept a gift that one knows will influence one in the conduct of one's duty as it is to accept a bribe. And clearly we are entitlted morally to criticze those who offer and accept such inducements. Moreover, we are right to attempt to prevent this sort of thing by legally restricting the conditions under which persons may offer gifts to officials and the conditions under which officials may accept such gifts. Nonetheless, such gifts ought not to be confused with bribes. If P accepts a gift from R and does not show the desired favoritism, R may complain of P's ingratitude but not of P's dishonesty (unless, of course, P lead him on in some way). If P accepts a bribe from R and does not show the desired favoritism P has been dishonest (perhaps twice).

·   This point is now without practical importance. People who work in the same organization or in the same profession often form friendships despite the fact that some of them are in a position to make decisions that affect the interests of others. Here, as everywhere, friendships are developed and maintained in part by exchanges of favors, gifts, meals, and forth. Were we to take *seriously* the inducement theory of bribery, however, this dimension of collegial and organizational existence would be threatened. In that case, if P's position is such that he must make decisions affecting R, any gifts, favors, etc., from R to P should be regarded with at least some suspicion. To guard against the

accusation that he has been bribed by R, P must be in a
position of offer reasons for believing that R's intent in
inviting him to dinner was *not* to induce him to show favoritism.   And for R to be certain that he is not offering P a
bribe in this case, R must be certain that his intentions are
pure.   All of this would require such vigilance in relation to
one's own motives and the motives of others, that friendships in collegial and organizational settings would be more
difficult than present to sustain.

Since decision-makers are required to show impartiality
they must in any case be careful not to accept gifts and
favors that will influence them to show favoritism.   Moreover, if they are required by their position to assess the
moral character of those affected by their decisions they may
be required to assess the intent with which such gifts or
favors are offered.   Most officials, however, are not
required to assess character in this way.   In order to avoid
doing wrong by accepting gifts and favors they need only be
justly confident of their own continued impartiality.   Thus,
they are ordinarily entitled to ignore questions of *intent*
unless there is some special reason to do otherwise.   If the
intent to influence were sufficient for a bribe, however,
they would not be at liberty to bestow the benefit of the
doubt in this way.

Again, there are cases in which impartiality is so important that decision-makers should be prohibited both from
accepting gifts or favors from any persons likely to be
directly affected by their decisions and from forming friendships with such persons.   And they should disqualify themselves when they are asked to make a decision that affects
either a friend or someone from whom they have accepted
gifts or favors in the reasonably recent past.   Judges are a
case in point.   In other cases, however, institutions and
professions should be willing to risk some loss in impartiality
in order to enjoy the benefits of friendship and mutual aid.
For these are essential to the functioning of some organizations and to the well-being of people within them.   Consider,
e.g. universities.   The practical disadvantage of the inducement account is that it may require us to be unnecessarily
suspicious of certain exchanges consituitive of mutual aid
and friendship (at least if we take it seriously).

V

An interesting related problem arises in cultures in which a more formal exchange of gifts may be partly constituitive of a special relationship between person, viz. something like friendship. In such cultures, so long as certain other conditions are satisfied, to make such exchanges is to enter into a system of reciprocal rights and duties. Among these duties may be the duty to show favoritism toward "friends," even when one acts in an official capacity. Moreover, the giver may be expected to show gratitude for each occasion of favoritism by further gift giving. On the face of it, this certainly looks like bribery. Is that description warranted?

To begin with, we need to distinguish between cases in which the special relationships in question are genuine and cases in which they are not. In the latter case certain ritual or ceremonial forms may be used to dress up what each party regards as business transaction of the standard Western variety in a manner that provides an excuse for bribery. I shall say more about this presently. But let me begin with the first case.

Where the relationships in question are genuine and the laws of the relevant society are such that the official duties of the relevant official do not prohibit "favoritism", this practice of gift-giving cannot be called bribery. For in this case there is no question of the violation of duty. All that can be said here is that such societies condone different ways of doing business than we do. Specifically, they did not mark off a sphere of business and/or bureaucratic activity in which persons are supposed to meet as "abstract individuals," i.e. in which they are required to ignore their social and familiar ties. Their obligations, rather, are importantly determined by such ties even in the conduct of business and governmental affairs. "Favoritism" is shown, then, not in order to carry out one's part of a bargain, but rather to discharge an obligation of kinship or loyalty. Failure to show "favoritism" would not entitle one's kinsman or "friend" to complain that one reneged on an agreement, but rather that one had wronged him as an ally or a kinsman.

This is not to say that one cannot bribe an official in

such a society. One does this here, as elsewhere, by
entering into an agreement with him such that he violates his
official duties for payment. The point is just that "favoritism" shown to friends and kinsmen is not necessarily a violation of duty in such societies. Indeed, one might be bribed
not to show "favoritism."

The official duties of an official, of course, may not be
clear. Thus, the written law may prohibit "favoritism" to
kin an ally though this is widely practiced and condoned and
infrequently prosecuted. This may occur when a society is
in a transitional state from feudalism or tribalism to a West-
ern-style industrial society but it may also occur in an
industrial society with different traditions than our own. To
the extent that it is unclear what the official duties of officials are in such cases it will also be difficult to say what
count as bribes. Indeed, even if we decide that an official
does violate his duty by showing "favoritism" to kin and ally
who reciprocate with gifts, we may not be justified in speaking of bribery here. For the official may not be acting as
he does *in order* to fulfill his part of an agreement.
Rather, he may be acting to fulfill some obligation of kinship
or loyalty. Again, his failure so to act may not entitle his
kinsmen or allies to complain that he has welched on a deal;
rather, it would entitle them to complain that he has
wronged them as kinsmen or allies.

Of course, all this is so only when the relationships in
question are genuine. In some case, however, the rhetoric
and ceremonial forms of a traditional culture may be used to
camouflage what are in fact business relations of the standard Western variety. To the extent that this is so, the
favoritism in question may in fact be bribery in ethnic
dress. The relationships in question are not genuine when
they are not entered into in good faith. It is clear, moreover, that when American executives present expensive gifts
to foreign businessmen or foreign government officials they
do so for business reason. That is, they have no intention
of entering into a system of reciporocal rights and duties
that may obligate them in the future to act contrary to their
long-term interest. Rather, they perform the required cere-
monies knowing that they will continue to base their decisions on business reasons. Their intentions is to buy favoritism. And the foreign officials and companies with whom
they do business are typically aware of this. This being the

case, invitations of the form "First we become friends, then we do business" cannot plausibly be construed as invitations to participate in some traditional way of life. Typically, both parties recognize that what is requested here is a bribe made in an appropriate ceremonial way.

VI

On the basis of this analysis it seems clear that American officials are not always guilty of bribery when they payoff foreign officals. In some cases they are victims of extortion; in other case, the context may be such that the action purchased from the relevant official does not count as a violation of his duty. The fact that American executives engaged in international commerce are innocent of some of the charges that have been made against them, however, does not imply that those who have made them are mistaken in their assessment of the character of these executives. One's character, after all, is a matter of what one is disposed to do. If these executives are willing to engage in bribery *whenever* this is necessary to promote their perceived long-term business interests, whatever the morality of the situation, it follows (at the very least) that they are amoral.[10]

---

10. This essay is reprinted from *Ethics*, 94 (1984), with the permission of editor and the publisher, the University of Chicago Press.

Practical Problems…
and Solutions

TWIN-PLANTS AND CORPORATE RESPONSIBILITIES

John Haddox

It is startling and instructive to read such statements as the inspiring proclamation by Ruth Nada Anshen:

> There is in mankind today a counterforce to the sterility and danger of a quantitative mass culture; a new, if sometimes imperceptible, spiritual sense of convergence toward human and world unity on the basis of the sacredness of each human person. [1]

Then look at the reality here on the U.S.-Mexico border. How beautiful the ideality; how harsh the reality; and how great the distance between!

Now, in order to examine some questions of corporate ethical responsibilities in relation to multinational operations, specifically as regards the "twin-plants" or maquiladoras in cities of Mexico bordering on the United States, first a brief presentation of certain basic ethical assumptions, then an examination of the history and present status of multinational corporations (with a close look at the maquiladoras), and finally an analysis of the ethical implications of such operations will be undertaken.

---

1. Ruth Nanda Ashnen, "World Perspectives, What This Series Means," in Milton Mayeroff's *On Caring* (New York: Harper and Row Publishers, 1972), p. 98.

Ethical Assumptions

        Corporate/business ethics must be concerned with the
development and maintenance of significant relationships
among employers, employees, and customers; these include
job security, a safe working atmosphere, appropriate wages,
fair prices, and profits that are not excessive. Concerning
the last of these, if there is no moral responsibility present
then anything is allowable that will increase profits--and the
public be damned.
        However, it seems clear that some policies and practices
productive of greater profits may be morally wrong and thus
should be shunned. This view is, of course, vigorously
opposed by Milton Friedman and his followers who insist that
there is "one and only one social responsibility of business--
-to use its resources and engage in activities designed to
increase profits" (so long as there is no fraud or deception). The idea that corporate officials have any social
responsibility other than to make as much money for stockholders as possible is, from this viewpoint, fundamentally
subversive."[2] (Owners and operators of multinational corporations quite obviously agree as will be shown later.)
        To counter this position it may merely be noted that cor-
porations are often provided special rights and privileges
(like favorable tax rates) by states or nations, so they have
a responsibility, an obligation, not to harm the communities
in which they are situated. In his book *Liberty, Justice
and Morals*, Burton Leiser puts it well: "No corporation is
exempt from the principles of fairness and decency that
apply to all ·human affairs."[3]
        A further assumption here is that these "principles of

_____

        2. Milton Friedman, *Capitalism and Freedom*. (Chicago:
University Press, 1962), p. 133.

        3. Burton M. Leiser, *Liberty, Justice and Morals*. (New
York: Macmillan Publishing Co., 1979), p. 300.

fairness and decency" are not restricted or limited in their application by national borders. Now, a fundamental need for the nations in which the multinational twin plants are located is economic development, and, while these plants undoubtedly contribute to the economic growth of the city/ state/nation in which they are located (in terms of employ-ment, capital, and industrialization), there is some question as to what extent this kind of growth merits the designation "development".

Raul Prebish, distinguished economist from Argentina and former General Director of the Latin American Institute for Economic and Social Planning, has argued that a primary purpose of development is "to integrate socially (the) large masses of the population that have been left behind in the process of economic development. If this is not done, devel-opment is incomplete and unjust."[4] He thus insists that if so-called "development" leads to increased dependence it is harmful for the locale in which it takes place. Prebish fur-ther argues that decisions concerning economic matters should be made by persons within the nations involved; oth-erwise, policies of "international cooperation" would actually be policies employed to subordinate developing countries politically while creating new forms of dependence.[5]

Now, how do multinational corporations measure up using such ethical/economic criteria? Was Pope Paul VI justified in warning in his encyclical *Octogesima Adveniens* that the "multinational enterprises...largely independent of the national political powers and therefore not subject to control from the viewpoint of the common good...can lead to a new and abusive form of economic domination on the social, cul-tural, and even political level?"

---

4.   Raul Prebish, *Latin American: a Problem in Develop-ment*. (Austin: Institute of Latin American Studies, 1971).

5.   Prebish, p. 12.

The Status of Multinationals

Corporations in their present form are only 150-200 years old, and huge multinational conglomerate firms have only been in existence as a major world economic factor for a generation or two. The ethical status of such corporations is intriguingly ambiguous in that in the process of incorporation a group of persons acquires a charter giving it as a body a number of legal rights, powers, and privileges over and above ones they have as individual persons within the group. The corporation thus becomes a separate legal entity, a "legal person" that shields its members from financial, legal or moral responsibility for what the corporation does. Generally the owners control decisions concerning profit goals and the means to be utilized to achieve them so most other persons involved with corporations (middle management, workers, stockholders) have no real voice in these areas. (This seems to be especially true as regards those involved in the multinational plants themselves.)

It must be emphasized that corporations and, again, especially multinational corporations, possess a tremendous amount of power. In fact, of the top one hundred financial powers in the world, fifty-one are multinational corporations, while only forty-nine are nations. Eighteen multinational corporations earned more than $10 billion each in 1978--with Exxon alone making $60 billion. It is estimated that by 1985, three hundred world firms will produce one-half of the globe's goods and services. Of the world's five hundred largest corporations, two hundred and nineteen are U.S. based. Further, United States-based multinational corporations (with government, political, and military backing, and with billions of dollars in foreign investment tax credits) increasingly depend on foreign locations, foreign production, and foreign profits.

Finally, it should be noted that corporations earn their greatest profits from Third World investments because a profit differential results from inexpensive natural resources and low wages. Thus the income gap between rich and poor nations continues to widen.

The importance of multinational corporations is well summarized by Richard Barnet in his challenging study, *The*

Lean Years: *Politics in an Age of Scarcity*:

> Increasingly, global resource systems are being
> managed by multinational corporations. The min-
> ing, melting, refining, and mixing of animal, vege-
> table, mineral, and human resources into products
> for sale is an integrated operation on a planetary
> scale, and more goods are now made in the poor
> countries of the southern periphery under direc-
> tions from the headquarters in the North, and
> most are destined to be consumed in the industrial
> heartland.[6]

These corporations' very size makes them almost impervi-
ous to any antitrust legislation or to international investigation. Nestle, Exxon, and similar corporations can even have
their own independent foreign policy. (Max Gloor, a director of Nestle Corporation, once commented that Nestle is neither exactly a Swiss Corporation nor a multinational; it has,
he avers, a special nationality--"a Nestle nationality.")

Twin-Plant or Maquiladoras on the U.S.-Mexico Border

Let us look at a few items of (estimated) data concerning the employment situation in Mexico and the origins of
the maquiladoras. With millions unemployed and huge numbers of young people entering the job market each year,
about 900,000 new jobs are needed each year.[7] With the end
of the bracero program (which provided temporary legal

---

6. Richard J. Barnet, *The Lean Years*: *Politics in an
Age of Scarcity*. (New York: Simon and Shuster, 1980), p.
239.

7. This data was provided me by the Mexican economist
V. G. Moreno.

entry of workers, mostly farm workers, from Mexico to the
U.S) in 1964, unemployment in border cities mushroomed to
40 or 50%. Then on May 20, 1965 the Mexican government
initiated the Border Industrialization Program in an effort to
improve conditions in these cities. As part of this program
the maquiladoras were established, taking advantage of items
806.30 and 807.00 of the U.S. Tariff Act of 1930 that allows
the export of materials for assembly from the United States
with import duties imposed only on the "value-added" on the
basis of the cost of production outside of the U.S. when the
products were assembled in Mexican plants.

The purported goals of these plants (from the Mexican
viewpoint) were the providing of jobs, job training, and
income. (Some have argued that these plants were set up
by U.S. companies *not* to solve the unemployment problem
along the Mexican border but *because* such large numbers of
the unemployed provided a huge reserve of workers from
which to choose in hiring.)

In any event these plants, the maquiladoras, are labor
intensive, the wages paid are five or six times less than
those for comparable work in the U.S., and the the proxim-
ity of Mexico to the U.S. allows substantial savings in transportation compared to Far Eastern plant sites.

Richard Barnet, in the work cited earlier, points out
that production in developing countries takes place for the
most part in "free production zones." These zones are
enclaves established to attract foreign capital by offering a
range of commercial and financial incentives such as exemp-
tion from taxes and duties on machinery and raw materials,
often a five-to-ten year income tax "holiday", freedom in
many cases from foreign exchange controls, preferential
financing, preferential tariffs, and finally, a furnishing by
the local or regional government of factory and office build-
ings, and a variety of supporting services.[8]

The maquiladoras are often electronics or garment
plants, though a wide variety of other industries are present. Represented are many major corporations like RCA,

---

8.   Barnet, *op. cit*, p. 246.

NCR, IBM, 3M, XEROX, Pepsi, Dupont, General Electric, Rockwell, Samsonite, and their subsidiaries. Components are shipped for assembly from the U.S. to Mexico where workers assemble them for re-shipment to the U.S.

Machinery, equipment, parts, and raw materials are allowed to be imported temporarily into Mexico and exported free from the usual duties. The items produced cannot be sold in Mexico and the plants must (in principle, if not always in practice) comply with such Mexican laws as the Law of Social Security, the Labor Laws, and the Law of Mexican Mercantiles.

The number of persons working in the maquiladoras has grown rapidly, from around 10,000 in 1966 up to 131,300 (in 598 plants) in 1980. They pay over seven billion pesos in salaries; 80-95% of the workers are women with ages ranging from 16 to 25 years (with a *few* older workers, but not many). These workers, who are managed 98% of the time by American administrators, have achieved production rates 25-40% higher than their U.S. counterparts. The work is extremely tedious. Tom Miller, in an article for *New West* gives this example:

> One group of six workers sits on stools dabbing glue in four spots on the inside of each cassette casing to hold the plastic window. Each worker puts in 12,000 windows per eight-hour shift, meaning 48,000 dabs of glue--enough to get the most sober workers stoned from the fumes, if they aren't already deaf from the noise.[9]

---

9.   Tom West, "Baja's Blues," *New West*, 1978.

Positive Features of Maquiladoras

Robert Heilbronner in his *The Great Ascent, The Struggle for Economic Development in Our Time*, after discussing the exploitive features of colonialism, points out that the impact of foreign economic intervention was not all negative. Equipment, roads, factories, railroads, docks, certain skills and techniques were often provided by the colonial powers. They often were more an extension of the colonizer's economy than an integral part of the colonies and were largely managed by a relatively isolated management clique from the colonizing country--but they did provide the beginnings of industrial development.[10]

Concerning the maquiladoras, the benefits to Mexicans and to Mexico are obvious; a great deal of employment is provided in areas where unemployment is endemic, significant foreign exchange earnings result for Mexico and wages are made available for Mexican workers, job skills training is supplied to unskilled workers and employment opportunities are there for women on a scale hitherto unheard of in Mexico. Taking just one city in Mexico, Cd. Juarez, Chihuahua, as an example, the maquiladoras started there in a limited way in 1965. In 1969 there were only 11 companies with 250 workers but by 1981, just 12 years later, there were approximately 45,000 workers employed by 124 companies. The 1980 payroll was $111,000,000, with an estimated $33,000,000 of this spent in El Paso, Texas directly across from Juarez. Further benefits to the local economy result from the employment of almost 5000 persons from the United States earning close to $28,000,000. In the year 1980 alone over 500 managment and technical personnel for the twin plants in Juarez moved to El Paso, paying city and county taxes of approximately $2,000,000.

---

10. Robert L. Heilbronner, *The Great Ascent, The Struggle for Economic Development in Our Time*. (New York: Harper Torchbooks, 1963), pp. 63 and 64.

Benefits to the U.S. corporations involved are also substantial. Electricity and natural gas are quite inexpensive. Unemployment rates of 24% and more in Juarez provides a readily available labor pool and labor costs average $1.58 per hour. As noted before, workers are 25 to 40% more productive than their counterparts in the United States (partly because "there's not that many jobs and they're hungry" according to Carlos Riquelme, general director of the Juarez Industrial Park). Bill Mitchell, marketing manager for Juarez' Bermudez Industrial Park, recently told a group of U.S. corporation executives that with proper management the plants in Mexico could increase their profits by 20 to 47%.

Materially, the above elements apparently are significant positive factors for the Mexican economy, for the U.S. border cities involved, and for the U.S. corporations.

Negative Features of Maquiladoras

First of all, it seems clear (and later attempts will be made to substantiate this) that a special kind of exploitation is present in this situation, and the words of Lawrence Hinman, Professor of Philosophy at the University of San Diego, (that he applied to the question of undocumented Mexican workers) seem particularly appropriate here: "From a moral point of view, I think we have to be aware of the injustice being done to those who are being exploited. There is a diminishing of ourselves as moral agents insofar as we condone or participate in procedures of exploitation."[11] If we claim to believe in human rights, these rights do not change or disappear when we cross national borders.

---

11. Lawrence Hinman, "Working Conditions of Undocumented Workers", *Undocumented Workers in the U.S. Labor Market*. (Pasadena: American Friends Service Committee, 1980), p. 30.

On the part of those favoring the maquiladoras, a
common attitude seems to be: well, they are better than
nothing; but is this true? Might these twin-plants as a partial cure for Mexico's economic ills be rather like an aspirin
intended to cure a cancer. The cancer might well *not* be
fatal but the aspirin might just mask or otherwise cover the
symptoms lulling the patient into a false sense of security.

A primary question here would seem to be: Do multinationals contribute to the genuine development of the communities in which they are located? Employing the criteria for
development presented by Raul Prebish (and mentioned earlier) the answer would evidently be "no".

Alejandro Portas, in an article titled "Modernity and
Development: A Critique" expresses even more inclusive
criteria for national development: a complex of three factors, economic, social, and cultural. The first requires
sharp and sustained increases in production and the creation
of self-sustained industrial growth; the second requires a
relative redistribution of national income and the incorporation of the marginal masses into the economy; the third
requires the emergence of a new national self-image with
confidence in the future and a willingness to make sacrifices
leading to economic and social improvements.[12]

It is revealing to compare these criteria with how multinationals do operate. They are virtually responsible to no
one but themselves, being minimally restrained by government regulations, labor unions, or competition; they generally operate outside the laws of individual nations; and if a
labor union seeks to gain such things as increased wages or
improved working conditions in a multinational plant, it can
simply cease operations in that locale and move to another
(like Taiwan where there are no strikes).

In the field of agriculture, multinational corporations
promote cash crops, exportable luxuries like beef in Guate-
mala and carnations in Colombia, rather than grains that

----

12.   Alejandro Portes, "Modernity and Development: a
Critique", in *Studies in Comparative International Development*, IX, 2(1974), p. 253.

could be a staple needed to overcome malnutrition.

A new book by John Coatsworth, *Growth Against Development: The Economic Impact of Railroads in Porfirian Mexico* shows how the construction of railroads in Mexico increased productivity and *growth* but did not provide a stimulus for *development* because it fostered a dependence on foreign manufactured goods and capital, tied Mexico more securely to raw materials exportation than ever before, and did not stimulate real industrial development.[13] The analogy to a growth instead of development syndrome of modern twin plants seems very close.

Turning to specific problems relating to the maquiladoras, first there are the low wages for the type of work performed and the often unhealthy, poorly ventilated working conditions that prevail due to a lack of regulations or a failure to enforce existing regulations. In a report published in the *Boletin Informativo* Jorge Carillo notes:

> The vast majority of the workers in Juarez earn only the minimum wage, independent of the number of years that they have been working and the level of skill they have reached. They regularly work forty hours a week with an additional percentage of extra hours. After years of working with exaggerated production quotas, their high productivity is reduced and they find themselves in a grave state of physical and psychological exhaustion. And in terms of the companies' optimal selection possibilities, we note that in Juarez, with a female reserve labor force which is more than twice as large as the number of women employed by the maquiladoras and which tends to grow due to immigration to the cities provoked by said plants, the companies can use single women with an average age of twenty years old, who end

---

13.   John H. Coatsworth, *Growth Against Development: The Economic Impact of Railroads in Porfirian Mexico.* (DeKalb, Illinois: Northern Illinois Press, 1981).

up staying with the company an average of 2 1/2 years.[14]

Furthermore, when it comes to the claim that these jobs in the twin-plants provide the workers with useful technical skills, in most cases this is simply not true. The jobs tend to be simple, boring, and routine, involving, it is true, a degree of manual dexterity but little else. The skills achieved can only rarely be applied to other types of work. Even in a publication of Banamex (the Banco Nacional de Mexico) generally extolling the virtues of the maquiladoras it is admitted that the skills and the ability to use the proper tools in these plants require a short time to learn and "a certain physical skill and a high level of perceptiveness and concentration, faculties most frequently found in young female members of the labor force."[15]

Other serious problems result from the fact that only a small percentage of the many thousands of Mexican workers who come to the border seeking employment find work, so unemployment has increased dramatically in the Mexican border cities. As was noted earlier, about 90% of the workers are women on the average (with the percentage fluctuating with different types of plants). This leaves large numbers of men unemployed who then see as their only recourse emmigration to the United States without obtaining (or being able to obtain) the proper documents.

Anthropologist Patricia Fernandez Kelly, who has studied intensively the social impact of the maquiladoras, discovered that an average of five relatives (and sometimes friends) come to Cd. Juarez for every migrating maquila worker. Because of the large labor supply, workers, knowing they can be easily replaced, become, and tend to remain, very docile.

---

14. *Boletin Informativo* No. 9, Nov.-Jan., 1979-80) of the Mexican Quakers (El Comite de Servicio de los Amigos),

15. *Review of the Economic Situation of Mexico.* (Mexico: Banamex), LVII, 669 (August 1981), p. 285.

The management of the twin-plants explains that they hire mostly women because they have greater patience (and thus can do the boring, repetitive work better than men) and also because they have small fingers and delicate muscle coordination so they can handle the intricate machinery better. However, it seems just as likely, often more likely, that it is because men being the traditional head of the home in Mexico want more steady and better paying work than the women. Another reason was explained by Donald Baerreson in a 1971 primer for businesses planning to set up maquilas:

> From their earlier conditioning, (women) show respect and obedience to persons in authority, especially men. The women follow orders willingly, accept changes and adjustments easily, and are considered less demanding... Thus a steady flow of passive workers, not seeking unionization or better wages and working conditions, continues -- and the U.S.-based corporations achieve greater productivity and higher profits.[16]

There are also such devious practices as the laying-off of workers to avoid paying seniority benefits, blacklisting workers who attempt to organize others, and employing persons on a temporary basis with the overt or, at times implied, threat of easy termination.

As noted before, twin-plants clearly create an economic enclave that increases unemployment. Almost 70% of the

---

16. Attendant problems related to the imbalances of female employment under these conditions include many children being left uncared for, many children being born to unmarried women, the family disintegrating, continual sexual harrassment of the young women by their male supervisors, and attempts on the part of the company to manipulate them by words and gestures that are supposed to touch their so-called feminine sensibility. Any one of these topics would of course, be deserving of a major study, but they should at least be noted here.

work force had never worked before outside the home before
entering the maquila and they probably would not otherwise
have formed part of the economically active population; also
the large numbers of employees losing jobs at an early age
contributes to the jobless rolls.

Looking at the situation in broader terms, the twin-
plants in Mexico seem to be a clear example of a colonial
power, the U.S., with (economic) imperialistic designs.
Robert Heilbroner, in the work cited earlier, has commented
cogently:

> Colonialism and imperalism are the schools in which
> most of the underdeveloped nations learned their
> lessons in economic development, and although the
> schooling was very different from colony to colony,
> a common distaste for their instructors is all too
> clearly apparent among all of the ex-students. [17]

Do these maquiladoras genuinely benefit Mexico in an
enduring fashion, or is this a case where an aspirin is supposed to remedy a (curable) cancer? Do these twin-plants
provide a stable basis for future development -- development
so terribly needed -- in Mexico? Possibly in a very limited
sense mentioned earlier -- but for the most part, certainly
not! Another concise answer to this question is:

> The real problem lies in the heart of the corporate
> system and the structure of its institutions, in the
> control of resources and human labor, in its
> unchecked power and ability to manipulate the
> political process, in its subtle influence on human
> values ·and culture, and in its embracing of an
> ideology which places it in direct opposition to
> political and social needs in the global commu-
> nity. [18]

---

17.   Heilbronner, pp. 63-64.

18.   *Corporate Action Guide* (Washington, D.C.: Corpo-

What the maquiladoras do is increase the dependency relationship of Mexico on the United States because, among other things, the component parts are not produced in Mexico and by prohibiting countries from using the technology involved, the twin-plants perpetuate a situation of technological dependence.

Even in the favorable Banamex report on the maquiladoras cited earlier there are complaints that development is hindered by the absence of a true transfer of technology, its dependence on U.S. economic cycles, and the fact that integration of domestic input is almost nil despite Mexico's relatively diversified manufacturing base."[19]

As regards solutions to these problems, much can be done, but that would be another article. It is hoped that here the problems themselves are articulated clearly. For the present, the suggestion of the American Catholic Appalachian Bishops will have to suffice as a starting point in a movement toward justice:

> As a counter-force to the unaccountable power of these multinational corporations, there must arise a corresponging multinational labor movement, rooted in a vision of justice, rising above corruption and narrowness, with a universal concern
> -for all workers
> -for all consumers
> -for all people.

rate Action Project, 1974), p. 7.

19. *Review of the Economic Situation of Mexico.* p. 289.

NURSING HOMES: WHY ARE THERE SO MANY SCANDALS?

Barry R. Chiswick

Introduction

One of the striking features of the nursing home sector of the economy, compared with other sectors, is that nursing homes frequently make the front page of the daily newspapers. Every few months, in one major metropolitan area newspaper or another, there is a nursing home scandal. Some nursing home or another is providing grossly substandard care for its residents, feeding them inappropriate food, giving residents the wrong medicines, or engaging in gross neglect of the physical or emotional needs of the residents. Another characteristic of nursing homes is the phenomenal growth in this industry in the past few decades. Why are there so many scandals and what can be done to improve conditions? Why has there been this growth, and what are the prospects for the future?

This essay begins by describing the nursing home sector and how it has changed over time. It then discusses an econometric (statistical) analysis of the supply and demand for nursing home care. This analysis is in part concerned with the question: Does this sector behave in a way that is different from other sectors of the economy? This very important question needs to be answered before appropriate public policies can be developed and implemented regarding the nursing home sector. The paper closes with a return to the question raised in the subtitle, "Why are there so many

scandals?"   It ends   with   a   discussion   of   alternative   solutions.

The Background[1]

In 1960, about $0.5 billion per year was spent on nurs-
ing home care, and by 1979, the figure was $20.7 billion.
This is approximately a 40-fold increase in expenditures at a
time when prices in general were 2.8 times the 1960 level.
In real dollars, therefore, there was a 15-fold increase in
expenditures on nursing home care.   In part this reflects a
rapid increase in the cost of medical care, as all aspects of
medical care have become relatively more expensive.   The
index of the medical care component of the Consumer Price
Index in 1979 was 3.4 times the 1960 level.   But this is a
small part of the story.   The share of nursing home expenditures in the national health expenditures increased from
1.9 percent in 1960 to 8.4 percent in 1979.   Thus, in a
period of twenty years the share of nursing homes in the
national expenditures on medical care increased to 4.4 times
the previous level.
      The nursing home sector has experienced very rapid
growth in the number of residents and expenditures per resident.   The number of residents in nursing homes increased
from less than a 0.5 million in 1963 to about 1.2 million in
1978.   This 2.4-fold increase represents a 6.0 percent
annual rate of increase.   Employment in nursing home facilities grew somewhat more rapidly than the number of residents, from 0.49 employees per resident in 1965 to 0.54 in
1978.
      Nursing homes are primarily relatively small enterprises.
Of all nursing home beds (1976), 78 percent are in facilities
that have less than 100 beds, 21 percent are in facilities

---

1.   The data in this section are drawn largely from U.S.
Bureau of the Census, *Statistical Abstract of the United
States*, 1981, Washington, D.C.: 1981, pp. 100-115.

with 100 to 349 beds and only one-half of one percent of all
nursing home beds are in facilities with more than 350 beds.
Most nursing home facilities and most beds are in proprietary institutions.[2] Proprietary institutions own 61 percent of the facilities, and 66 percent of the beds. Government facilities are a little less than 5 percent of all nursing
home facilities but they tend to be large and are responsible
for 20 percent of the beds. Nonprofit institutions (e.g.,
churches and civic organizations) operate about 33 percent
of all nursing home facilities, but have only 14 percent of all
nursing home beds. Nonprofit institutions, on the average,
have very small facilities.

Thus, nursing homes tend to be small institutions that
are predominantly owned and operated by profit-making individuals or corporations.[3] There has been a trend toward
proprietary institutions, and chains of nursing homes are
becoming more common.

The average size of nursing home facilities has been
increasing; in the early 1960's there were about 35 residents
per facility, now it is over 70 residents per facility. This
increase in the average size is an interesting development,
and an important one, because there do seem to be economies
of scale in nursing home care. Very small facilities are
becoming increasingly expensive to operate, particularly with
the growth of regulations regarding kitchen facilities, recreation facilities, nursing care, and physical therapy. These
regulations tend to add fixed costs to maintaining a facility,
thereby increasing the competitive advantage of larger nursing homes and nursing home chains.

---

2. A proprietary institution is owned by an individual, a
partnership or a corporation, with the profit motive as its
objective. Profits are retained by the owners. The distribution of "profits" in "nonprofit" institutions is more ambiguous.

3. This can be contrasted with hospitals (short-term
care institutions) in which less than 5 percent of the facilities and a smaller proportion of the beds are proprietary.

Nursing home beds are almost always occupied. The occupancy rate in recent years has averaged 92 percent. This high an occupancy rate is feasible in long-term care institutions.

Who are the residents of nursing homes? Seventy percent of the residents are at least 75 years old, and half of these are 85 or over. Another 16 percent are between the ages of 65 to 74. The remaining 14 percent are less than age 65. These younger residents are either severely physically disabled, mentally retarded or mentally ill. In recent years there has been a tendency to put psychiatric hospital patients on drug therapy and, if they cannot live in the general community, place them in a nursing home. Nursing homes are a less expensive substitute for psychiatric hospitals. Two thirds of the residents of nursing homes are women and 8 percent are non-white. These proportions closely match the proportion of women and non-whites in the aged population.

There is a relationship between one's ability to manage outside an institutional framework, that is, to cope within one's own residence or with relatives, and moving into a nursing home. Those who have a spouse or who have children are more likely to be able to manage outside a nursing home, even if they have several disabilities or chronic conditions. Those that do not have this outside family support tend to enter nursing homes at a younger age and with fewer chronic conditions. For example, data on the health status of people entering a nursing home indicate that those who are married or recently widowed tend to be in poorer health than those who have never been married. It is not because marriage reduces health status, indeed it probably has an opposite effect. Rather, those who are married are more likely to have the family support that enables them to delay institutionalization. Those without family support are more likely to enter nursing homes even if they only have one or two minor disabilities or limitations.

How do people leave a nursing home? By far the most frequent way of leaving a nursing home is through death. The second most frequent is through transfer to another nursing home. The least frequent is returning to one's own residence or living outside an institution.

A Model of Supply and Demand

Is behavior in the nursing home sector comparable to that of other sectors of the economy, or is there something special about nursing homes? This question was addressed indirectly in my study of the supply and demand for nursing home care.[4] I used residents of nursing homes per thousand aged population in the metropolitan area (SMSA) as my quantity variable, and estimated a demand equation and a supply equation.

The explanatory variables in the demand equation include price, that is, the cost of nursing home care in that area, and average family income in the area. It is expected that when nursing home care becomes more expensive, fewer people are placed in nursing homes. Income is also important. A nursing home can provide a more comfortable residence for the aged with given levels of disability than living in their own residence or with their adult children. Many move their aged or infirm relatives not into their own house, but into a nursing home facility near where they live. This is likely to be more common the higher the level of income in the area.

One important aspect of the institutionalization decision is who is going to provide non-institutional care. It is not costless for the adult daughter (or daughter-in-law) to stay home to provide care for aged parents. The cost is what the adult daughter could otherwise earn in the labor market or in some other activity that is the alternative use of her time. Thus a dimension of the cost of providing non-institutional care for the aged is the value of time of relatives who would be providing the care. The labor force participation rate of adult women can serve as a proxy for this variable. In cities in which women have good job opportunities, it is

---

4. See my "The Demand for Nursing Home Care: An Analysis of the Substitution Between Institutional and Non-Institutional Care," *Journal of Human Resources*, Summer 1976, pp. 295-316.

more expensive for them to stay home and care for aged relatives and so the aged relatives are more likely to be sent to
a nursing home. It may seem cruel and heartless but it is
not. It is a comparison of the cost of providing care in an
institutional setting versus a non-institutional setting.

One would expect that the health of the aged would also
be important. The age-specific death rate of the aged was
used as a measure of their health status. Of course, the
most important variable for understanding differences in utilization of nursing homes is the age-sex structure of the
aged population. The older the average age of the aged
population, the larger the proportion of the aged with disabilities. Because of their greater prior experience in providing home care (cooking, cleaning, shopping, personal
care, etc.) aged women may be better able to live more
independently than aged men. The age-sex distribution of
the aged was explicitly included in the analysis.

A demand equation without a supply equation is like one
half of a pair of scissors--you cannot cut anything with it.
In the supply equation, the price of nursing home care in
the area is related to the cost of inputs in the production of
nursing home care (that is, the wages of nurses, nurses'
aides, and cleaning service workers), and the number of
physicians per capita, among other variables.

This analysis indicates that the extent of institutionalization is very sensitive to the price variables. The price
elasticity of demand is very high, -2.3; the institutionalization of the aged population is very sensitive to the market
price of nursing home care.[5] It is also very sensitive to the
other dimension of price: the labor market opportunities of
adult women who would otherwise provide care at home for
the aged. In cities in which women have good labor market
opportunities, a larger proportion of the aged are in nursing
homes.

The proportion of the aged who are women is also an
interesting and important variable. Women have had much

---

5. The price elasticity of demand is the percent decrease
in quantity demanded for a one percent increase in price.

more experience than men at providing home care. In particular, the current cohort of aged women have had very little experience working in the labor market, and have had
decades of experience working at home--cooking, cleaning,
caring for children, sewing, and the like. They are better
able to cook for themselves, clean for themselves, and do a
little sewing for themselves, than are men of the same age
and health status. The data show that in areas in which the
aged population is disproportionately female, there is less
institutionalization--aged women are less likely to be institutionalized than are aged men. This suggests that as
younger cohorts of women work more in the labor market and
spend less time at home, when they are aged they may not
be as able to provide their own care as were their grandmothers, because their grandmothers had six or seven decades of working in the home!

Changes Over Time

    The supply and demand model can answer an important
policy question. Why has there been such a phenomenal
increase in the utilization of nursing homes by the aged population? The parameters estimated in the cross-sectional
data (different metropolitan areas at a point in time) can be
used to predict time series values of the extent to which the
aged are in nursing homes. These predicted values can be
compared with the observed values. From 1963 to 1973 there
was a 67 percent increase in the number of residents per
thousand population. About 64 percentage points (or 95
percent) of this increase is explainable by three variables:
family income, labor market opportunities for women and the
age-sex composition of the aged population. The anticipated
changes over time in these variables are likely to continue
increasing the proportion of the aged living in nursing
homes.
    If real incomes resume their historic increase more of the
aged will be institutionalized. If the labor force
participation rate of adult women continues to increase (and
all forecasts suggest it will), institutionalization of the aged
will increase. The age structure of the population is

changing in such a way as to increase institutionalization. The aged population is getting older, death rates among older people have been declining. The reasons for this declining death rate are not fully understood, but the trend is expected to continue.

Medicaid, created by the 1964 Amendments to the Social Security Act, provides medical and nursing home care for the aged poor.[6] It has impacted the system but not in a way that most people think. Medicaid apparently is not responsible for the big increase in institutionalization, but it has changed the sources of funding.[7] State and local government funding and charity funding of nursing homes have gone down. Medicaid funding has gone up, and the quality of care in nursing homes (as measured by employees per residents) has increased. Much of the Medicaid funds has been used as a substitute for other funds, rather than as a cause of increased admissions.

Is the Nursing Home Sector Unique?

Thus far, the discussion suggests that the nursing home sector behaves as one would expect from economic theory. When the price goes up, people use it less. When the price of substitutes (e.g., home care) goes up, people use more nursing home care. When incomes go up, more is purchased. The supply equation behaves like a normal supply

---

6. Medicare, the federalized health insurance program for recipients of social security, provides only short-term nursing home care following hospitalization.

7. The spread of Medicaid among the states is estimated to be responsible for an additional 7 percentage points increase in utilization. That is, Medicaid may be responsible for only 10 percent of the 67 percent increase in utilization from 1963 to 1973.

equation.   Prices are higher in an area where factor inputs are more expensive.

Why are nursing homes different from, say, resort hotels? Why resort hotels? They provide beds, food, and recreation, as do nursing homes. Why do we not have reports every few months of scandals regarding resort hotels as we do regarding nursing homes? The difference relates to the demographic characteristics of the "guests" or "residents." The residents of nursing homes are by and large not able to monitor their own care and, if dissatisfied with their own care, they have limited capability for altering the situation. A guest in a resort hotel who does not like it, say because the room is dirty or the food is spoiled, can "vote with his feet." This is very difficult for residents in nursing homes. Many of the residents are not capable of monitoring their own care or evaluating the quality of care. Even if they are capable, many do not have readily available alternative places to live. In addition, even if an aged person has an alternative residence, it is often-times traumatic for people who are very old and frail to be abruptly changed from one institution to another. It is not something you do casually. This makes the nursing home sector different from most other sectors of the economy.

We generally assume that a dissatisfied customer will switch to another firm or product, especially when there are no monopolies. There is no monopoly, in the usual sense of the term, in nursing homes. They are mainly small institutions privately owned or government owned and there are a large number of such facilities in any major metropolitan area. The problem arises in the limited capabilities of the "consumer."

"Consumer" is in quotes because in this instance the consumer may not be an effective decision maker. The aged person is being acted upon. The aged person is often-times not capable of being the rational decision-maker assumed in models of competitive or lassiez-faire markets.

Who Are the Decision Makers?

It has been suggested that there are three solutions to the problem of the decision maker. One is professionalization, the second is government regulation, and the third is family involvement.

Professionalization refers to the type and extent of training of employees and managers of nursing homes. It is alleged that with higher standards, that is, greater professionalization, conditions will improve. Mandatory courses for administrators and other employees designed by states to increase the quality of nursing home care have been described as "Mickey Mouse" courses. Even if they were redesigned to improve the quality of instruction, the problem is not the degree of professionalization. The problem is many professionals do not have the appropriate ethical standards for running a clean home, and they close their eyes when they see a roach running across the table, or a patient restrained because of inadequate staffing. The fundamental issue is not really whether they have a college degree or took correspondence courses. Most professional training does not focus on improving one's ethical standards and it is probably too late for schooling to influence ethical standards for all but pre-teens. Ethical standards are ingrained in a person's personality from early childhood experiences. Up to a point, making managers and employees of nursing homes satisfy more burdensome standards may improve the quality of care through reducing ignorance, but it will not solve the problem of scandals. It will raise the cost of nursing home care by making entry into the sector more expensive. I am highly skeptical about professionalization as a solution to the continuous problem of the quality of care.

Government regulation is often suggested as a solution. Government regulators can come in and check on care. Are people being restrained who should not be restrained? Are patients actually being given the medicine that they are supposed to be given, when they are supposed to be given it? Is the food nutritious? Is the food of adequate quantity? Who has the patient's interest at heart? The more regulation, the greater the temptation for corruption. What is then required is not just regulators of nursing homes, but

regulators of regulators and they in turn eventually need
regulators. It is difficult, if not impossible, to design regulations appropriate for the variety of circumstances and conditions in the nursing home sector. Inefficiency arises to
the extent that the regulations are inappropriate for the
particular circumstances. What is missing from government
regulation is somebody who has an overriding long-run
interest in the resident's well-being and who can perceive
needs relevant for that particular individual.

That is where the family enters as the third aspect of
how to improve the quality of nursing home care. Family
participation has two important dimensions. The first dimension is in choosing a nursing home. Decisions regarding the
initial selection are usually made, not by professionals, not
by government regulators, but by members of the family,
oftentimes without authentic participation by the aged person. It is typically family members who are the primary
decision makers. Family members have to be careful to
select homes that are of better quality and to avoid homes
that are of poorer quality. Once the marketplace is aware
that a "good" home will always have its beds filled and a
"low quality" home will have difficulty getting residents,
there is an economic incentive to provide "good" service.

Second is the monitoring of care. There is a difference
between institutions in which the aged are deposited
("warehoused") and the relatives send a Christmas card once
a year, and institutions in which the aged receive periodic
visits from family members. According to the regulations,
nursing homes have to be open to visitors about twelve
hours a day seven days a week. One of the most effective
policing mechanisms is spontaneous visits to observe what is
really going on. If relatives only come on Sunday between
three and five, an unscrupulous nursing home operator may
spruce up the residents on Sunday at noon so that at three
to five, they look nice, and the Sunday meal is always a
well-balanced, nutritious meal. But what are the meals like
on Monday through Saturday?

Suppose family members discover that the home is not
what they thought it would be. They may have made an
error or the management may have changed. They can help
move the aged persons from the institution into another.
That is easier to do if there is family support. The aged
generally cannot do this by themselves and the move may be

traumatic. Family support is needed to decrease the trauma.
Of these three potential solutions to the problem of the quality of care, two may have marginal benefits, professionalization and government regulation. The third is overriding, and that is the family recognizing its responsibility. The family needs to view itself as the active decision maker. The kind of care that the aged in nursing homes will receive will be a function of the extent to which they and their families participate in the decision-making process. Greater family involvement may be the most effective weapon against nursing home scandals.

THE COMMONWEAL AND FINANCIAL ACCOUNTING

DISCLOSURE PRACTICES

Michael J. Barrett and Leticia Verastegui

Introduction

Why should anyone be concerned about what organizational accounting information is reported to the public? The
following brief but true story shows the impact an accountant's report can have on organizations and individuals.
The financial accounting disclosure policy of large U.S.
based corporations is then considered along several dimensions to indicate its nature and flaws, and to specify several
changes which might make it more relevant.

> During the 1950's, the CIA secretly funded Italy's
> Christian Democratic Party as part of U.S. Foreign
> policy to check Communism's growth in Western
> Europe. But changes in the preparation and pres-
> entation of U.S. federal budgets in the 1960's
> would have made these and other secret payments
> obvious by reading the Federal Budgets. In order
> to continue its funding and to keep it hidden, the
> CIA asked certain U.S. based companies to funnel
> money to selected political parties in various coun-
> tries, including Italy. Exxon, over a period of
> eight   years,   made   political   contributions

approximating 50 million dollars to the Italian
Christian Democratic party. In return, legislation
was specifically enacted to provide certain business
benefits to Exxon in Italy. Exxon also reportedly
received benefits from the U.S. State Department.
ITT's payments in Chile are another example. But
in the 1970's, financial accounting disclosure policy
changed and these payments were revealed in corporate financial statements.

These foreign payments were deemed 'illegal
political contributions.' The administration in power
at that time felt that if information concerning
these 'contributions' were released publicly, foreign political parties and governments might fall
and foreign officials and innocent people jailed or
even executed. And American companies stood to
lose established business relations as well as facilities in these foreign nations. The Justice Department and the Securities and Exchange Commission
(SEC) decided that 'telling all' was simply too dangerous even though these companies were engaged
in illegal activities. So, a decision was made to
require only a general type of disclosure decision
rule, such as:

Payment = X dollars.
Payments generated N dollars of sales.
Payments took place outside of the United
States.
Payments have been stopped.

Obviously, the disclosure of financial information to the general public can, at times, have far-reaching and even disas-
trous consequences.

Perhaps we should try to define commonweal disclosures
by asking, "What is a secret? and What is not a secret?"
"Can we get more information about secrets out to the public
for their consideration?" Implicit in this perspective is that
some information may be too dangerous for the common welfare, or "*I* know what is good and bad, so *I am* going to
decide what organizational information can and cannot be disclosed." But, it is difficult to decide what should or should
not be published and to develop criteria which can be

applied to the phenomena moving through various financial
accounting systems.

Moving this issue of proper disclosure into a more positive vein, we can say, "What should individuals know about
organizations on a routine or recurring basis?" or "What
financial accounting information will inform and help the commonweal?" To talk in this vein, a few definitions are necessary:

> The commonweal is the common good of society, the
> social welfare, the good of the nation, the greatest
> good for the largest number or the good of indi-
> viduals impacted by large organizations.

> Financial accounting records organizational
> performance by measuring enterprise revenues and
> expenses during a fixed period of time (income
> statement) and stating the condition or health of
> an enterprise by measuring assets and liabilities as
> of a point in time (balance sheet).

> To disclose is to reveal, make available, to
> publish.

> Disclosure policy is a function of the types
> and amounts of information made available or pub-
> lished.

What is financial accounting disclosure policy? First, let
us think about the nature of accounting. Accounting is
composed of two activities: measurement and reporting.
Accountants measure objects: revenues, expenses, assets
and liabilities, and report their measurements to shareholders
and creditors. This is done in two primary financial statements: the balance sheet, a statement of condition or health
which displays assets and liabilities, and a statement of performance which displays the magnitude of income or loss.
Given these measurements, what should be disclosed in
accounting reports? Today, accountants think too much
about *how much must* or *how little can* be disclosed, and not
enough about *what should* be disclosed. This follows from
assuming that the more information, the less comprehension
because of the volume and complexity.

The accountant takes pride in being able to measure net
assets and income and aggregate them into concise summaries
of the detailed and lengthy measurement process of individual sales and purchases. But are these summarizations useful? *Useful* information should be reported to investors and
the general public.

The Existing Financial Statement Disclosure Policy

What is the prevailing financial statement disclosure
policy in the United States? Most commentators on accounting disclosure policies say the U.S. has the world's best
financial accounting disclosure system. Therefore, U.S.
corporations are not hiding things to the extent of organizations headquartered in other countries. But is this a proper
comparison?

Is it not more accurate to state that the largest, strong-
est capitalist country in the world has and must have the
best disclosure system relative to other poorer and in many
cases underdeveloped countries? It probably is not relevant
to compare the U.S. with countries having few individual
investors. It is more relevant to ask "Can the 'best' be
'bettered'?"

U.S. corporate financial accounting disclosure policies
have been articulated by the SEC since 1934, yet its
accounting oversight role is now under investigation. The
Oversight and Investigations arm of the House of Representatives Commerce Committee alleges that the SEC has not
been tough enough on establishers of accounting standards
or moved quickly enough in studying debt-hiding tactics.
According to present SEC policy, financial statements are
considered adequate when enough is disclosed so the financials are not false and misleading. But the only way to
decide is to ask whether or not anyone is severely injured
as a direct result of relying on them. This may not be
known for several years--if ever.

Currently, what accountants and auditors disclose to
investors is based on two assumptions.

1. A reasonably informed investor exists.

(Typically this investor is considered to be a shareholder, not a creditor, who understands both
accounting and financial statements. However, one
can thoroughly understand accounting and still seldom fully understand published financial statements.)

2. Enough disclosure is not full or fair disclosure but *adequate* disclosure. (When considering
adequate disclosure, accountants often do not think
about what should be disclosed but rather the
amount to be disclosed about assets, liabilities, revenues and expenses.)

These are not trivial matters when considering the complexity of the large conglomerate, whose ratio of common
stock market price relative to the expected annual net income
is almost always lower than for organizations not having
highly diversified lines. Perhaps the generally lower market
prices of conglomerates reflect investors' difficulty in understanding what makes these organizations tick. More extensive disclosure of different attributes (not more detail about
presently measured attributes) may be necessary to justify
paying higher security prices for conglomerates. But since
disclosure is presently considered to be inadequate, lower
stock prices are justified.

Problems with the Existing Disclosure Policy:
Two-Tiered Communication

What are some of the problems with our existing
financial accounting disclosure policies? Today, we have a
two-tiered communication system. Accountants argue that
there are two kinds of investors, the reasonably informed
investor and the uninformed. The informed investor is generally thought to be a financial analyst or advisor to individuals, pension funds, and other types of insitutional investors. The uninformed investor is not considered to know
very much about accounting or how to interpret and understand financial statements or both.
Reasonably informed investors should receive very

detailed financials and uninformed investors should receive
highly summarized, easy-to-read comments about the reporting organization.

Presumably accountants produce financial data for the
reasonably informed--the analyst. Analysts then break down
this complex data and convey it in a simplified and understandable form so others can make informed investment decisions.

Thus, the purpose of accounting disclosure has changed
from providing information useful for investment decision-
making to presenting:

1. Information useful for financial analysts in making
investment decisions about stocks, *and*

2. Information the uninformed investor can use to
exercise control over management in the form of voting
for management through proxies.

Users' Expanding Information Needs

Creditors

Today a more forceful class of financial statements users
is emerging. Its been assumed, that since the early 1930's,
the principal user of corporate financial information is the
shareholder. But in the last five years, creditors have
emerged as very interested readers. Their information
needs are being provided for by the financial accounting
community to a greater extent now than any time in, at
least, the last two generations. For example, a concerted
amount of practical and theoretical research is being directed
at the nature of liabilities. Some new liabilities entered as
line items in the balance sheet include leases and pension-
fund obligations. These usually large items were not even
shown in the conventional financials published ten years ago,
but today they are now major liabilities for most large organizations.

Leases traditionally were never shown in published
financial statements because they were though of as

executionary contracts which were not fulfilled until certain future events occurred. Yet most items included in the financial statements usually are based on the results of completed contracts. Creditors also have demanded additional measurements of assets. Organizations are disclosing additional data about cash and its elements, such as compensating balance requirements.

Concerned Citizens

Socially conscious and concerned individuals have become vocally unhappy about American based corporations making investments in South Africa. The Sisters of Mercy are attending a number of shareholder meetings to protest U.S. corporate investments in racist foreign nations. There is also concern about environmental pollution, including the safe disposal of nuclear and hazardous wastes.

Other individuals are disturbed about companies who have made illegal domestic or foreign payments to curry political favor and/or to generate sales. Widespread general concern arose about management improprieties in the early 1970's when it was reported that more than half of the *Fortune* list of the 500 largest companies had engaged in paying bribes, receiving kickbacks, and making illegal or improper political contributions. And there is concern about the size of management compensation, and the poor performance of some corporations who are paying high management compensation. There is also continuing concern about 'cooking the books', where for example, a subsidiary or division falsifies its revenues to qualify for bonuses.

Reconsideration of Disclosure Policy

Financial statement disclosure policy is discussed here in terms of two questions:

"Who is the audience?" or "To whom is the information directed?" and

"What are the appropriate objects to be measured?"

The Audience Reconsidered

Who should be the audience for corporate financial accounting disclosures in this country? Should the audience be composed of:

> -Shareholders,
> -Shareholders and creditors,
> -Financial analysts and creditors
> -Only financial analysts
> -Only creditors,
> -Or some other group such as government, or
> -Simply citizens?

But where an audience is specified, the problem of determining what constitutes a "non-legitimate" group arises. Financial information will be directed only to those groups that have asserted their legitimate interests in the affairs of a corporation.

This question usually is resolved by preparers of corporate financial statements by resorting to a philosophical statement describing the legitimate rights of certain claimants.

In a capitalist society both shareholders and creditors are granted full legitimacy. Organized labor and government also are legitimate, but to a lesser extent. But what about the ordinary citizen?

Today, many individuals who are not shareholders, creditors, employees or governmental regulators are directly affected by the actions of large corporations operating in their midst. The announcement of a large steel mill closing or a manufacturing plant shutting its doors directly affects nearby institutions such as schools and individuals including shopkeepers as well as the soon-to-be-unemployed. Should these parties be a part of the legitimate audience, at least while significant corporate changes are being considered and major decisions are being implemented? Again, one has a difficult time deciding the proper limits of financial accounting disclosure in terms of what constitutes the "legitimate" audience.

The Commonwealth is the Audience

Perhaps the financial statements of major corporations should be directed at those parties having the greatest recurring need for financial accounting information. If so, then government would become the chief claimant since its regulatory needs are varied and many, and financial information is useful in demonstrating compliance with government laws and regulations. It is government, after all, in the form of such agencies as the Environmental Protection Agency, the Securities and Exchange Commission and so forth that routinely require large amounts of financial accounting information from corporations. As long as laws and regulations remain on the books and are enforced, it will be easy to state that government has the largest continuing need for the corporate financial accounting information now disclosed.

So which parties should constitute the proper audience for corporate financial accounting disclosures? Obviously this is not a question which can be resolved easily or neatly. Its resolution is not likely to appear anytime soon for several reasons.

First, we continue to witness mergers between publicly held companies at an increasing rate even during periods of high interest rates and even recession. This means that more and more productive corporate assets are coming under the unified direction of fewer and fewer persons since managements are being brushed aside as one or two companies come to dominate. Consider, for example, the shake-out occurring among producers of home computers and micro computers for business use.

Second and tied to the first, citizens are demanding greater governmental regulation of industries characterized by few producers or distributors of products and services, especially as offerings to consumers become defined as "necessaries" like shelter, food, television, health care and so forth.

Third, dominant corporations operating in one or more industries often encourage governmental agencies to develop additional legislative requests or additional regulations to create imposing barriers of entry which companies not currently operating in the affected industrial sectors will have to contend with should they seek to become competitors. Consider the current attempts of banks to keep savings and loan associations from offering equivalent financial services.

The best answer we can offer to the question, "Who is the proper audience for periodic corporate financial statements?" is the unsatisfying comment that large domestically based, publicly held corporations need to define an audience which goes far beyond the traditional needs of shareholders and creditors. Increasingly it seems that the audience should not be defined in terms of specific groups, but rather in terms of an ethical dimension such as the COMMONWEAL; that is, providing the greatest amount of useful information to the greatest number of interested citizens.

The good of society or the commonweal is a nebulous and difficult concept to use as a decision making criterion. But it is easier to work with than making subjective decisions about what parties constitute the "legitimate" groups to direct corporate financial accounting reports to. We have, after all, spent many years considering far more weighty issues, such as the justification for engaging in wars among nations, using the commonweal criterion. The foundation of this decision making criterion is more firmly anchored than a corporate financial reporting policy that excludes certain interested parties as members of the 'non-legitimate' group.

Objects to be Measured by Accountants

Besides considering the audience of corporate financial accounting communications in terms of specific groups or institutions, it also is necessary to ask "What are the proper objects to be measured by accountants?" Today accountants measure assets, liabilities, revenues and expenses. These objects are recognized and measured within the legal boundaries of the organization called the corporation. But several difficulties are inherent in deciding the confines of the corporation, and what is or is not an asset or liability.

Entity

Let us start with the legal fiction called the corporation. One has no doubt heard the saying that many companies do "80% of their business with 20% percent of their suppliers and customers." If this is so, there probably will be significant social interaction between the corporation and input suppliers and output customers. However, accountants have not measured these forms of interaction, at least, not until recently. Of late, the SEC is requiring corporations under its jurisdiction to describe the five largest customers of the reporting company if the amount of business transacted with anyone is greater than 5% of total annual revenues. Since this wedge has been driven into the corporate financial accounting disclosure policy for publicly held corporations, it is time to consider its extension to at least captive suppliers of materials and services.

Take, for example, the numerous small manufacturers who provide the vast majority of their production to one or a small number of large customers. The fortunes and strength of these suppliers should be combined with that of the larger publicly held company if one is to draw an accurate picture of the reporting corporation. For example, General Motors purchases many of its parts and sub-assemblies from suppliers while Ford does not. You see, Ford Motor owns iron ore deposits, iron smelters for converting ore into ingots, steel mills for converting iron into sheet steel and so forth. Thus, a proper comparison of these two automobile producers is difficult, if not impossible, without taking into account the differences in the way they acquire materials for the production of cars and trucks.

Our implied message has far reaching implications for the proper measurement of corporate activities. As fewer and fewer corporations dominate a given industrial sector or geographic locale, measurements based only on the legal boundaries of the corporation must become less and less relevant to those seeking to interpret the behavior and stature of the large corporation. Pointedly, we are nearing the end of an era where accountants can confine their measurement activities solely to the "legal" affairs of the corporation. It is time that those having the responsibility to measure corporate activities in financial terms begin to discuss different definitions of the boundaries of the corporate entity.

Effectiveness

What are some other measurements that should provide enlightment about the performance and financial condition of the large publicly held corporation?   One is the measurement of corporate performance during a fixed time interval. Today a corporation's performance is measured in terms of revenues and expenses or net income (loss).   But this profit measure is a much better indicator of short term efficiency than corporate productivity.

Currently when a customer agrees to pay for goods or services and the seller delivers them to the buyer, accountants record these activities as sales revenue.   Yet there is no measure of customer satisfaction recorded by the seller's accounting staff.   The result is that sales revenue can be very large in one period, and considerably smaller in the next if dissatisfied customers return items purchased earlier. What is needed are measurements of the efficiency of the seller's operations as well as indicators of the seller's effectiveness in providing goods and services which provide customer satisfaction.   Instances are too frequent where a seller has rung up impressive sales in one period and has gone bankrupt a quarter or two later because the items sold were returned by dissatisfied customers.

Fiscal Health

Along with measures of corporate productivity (efficiency and effectiviness) coupled with statements of net income or loss, the commonweal will benefit if decision makers review indicators of corporate fiscal health.   Today, the financial status of the corporation is described in terms of net assets or owners' equity.   Recall that owners' equity is the difference between assets and liabilities.   This is often a poor statement of the entity's financial health.   Although unusual, some companies have reported record levels of income and entered the bankruptcy courts in as few as thirty days.   It is possible to make a profit and go broke almost at the same time.   The trick is to earn income and maintain corporate solvency at the same time.   Thus management, to be successful, must manage sales and expenses as well as cash inflows and outflows or receipts and disbursements.

Unfortunately, the statement of financial condition or

balance sheet prepared by accountants often does not reveal the full extent of the liabilities the company is obliged to pay or the market value of assets its holds. Until about ten years ago, corporations seldom included all of its long-term obligations, such as pension benefit payments or long term leases for fixed assets such as trucks and airplanes, in the liabilities section of the balance sheet. But the rapid increase of inflation and interest rates during much of the 1970s led creditors, shareholders and employees to press for a more extensive definition of liabilities and considerably more disclosure about the nature, amount and timing of corporate obligations.

Extending the definition of "liability" leads to the consideration of how liquidity and solvency should be measured for the large corporation. Some accountants have concluded that financial solvency can be measured along two related dimensions: financial flexibility to alter the terms of repayment schedules and the capacity to repay amounts at regularly scheduled intervals.

Other dimensions that should be considered are:

> 1. the economic health of competitors in specific industrial settings,
> 2. the size of interest rate premiums above the so-called "prime" rate, and
> 3. the speed of technological change being encountered and expected.

A measure of corporate fiscal health is needed. Its attributes should be different from those included in current accounting measurements of income and financial position or condition in order to improve information user decision making.

Concluding Comments

We have demonstrated that it is not cost beneficial simply to provide more financial information about the objects now being routinely measured and communicated to shareholders, creditors, and others. To consider the proper

financial accounting disclosure policy for large publicly held
corporations, the audience of the accountant's reports as
well as the objects that might be measured should be studied. After identifying various parties having an interest in
the affairs of large corporations, we concluded that government is probably the heaviest user of published financial
information. But asking, "Who is the audience?" seems
impossible to resolve. We ended by characterizing the commonweal or the greatest good for the greatest number of citizens as an understandable and justifiable criterion to invoke
where accounting disclosure issues are being studied.

We also outlined some of the many objects that should be
measured in addition to the accountant's conventional measures of assets, liabilities, revenues and expenses. First, it
is time that accountants begin to measure the considerable
economic interaction that frequently occurs between companies and among clusters of suppliers, producers and customers. To understand the producer, it often is necessary to
know the type, size and volume of transactions that flow
between the supplier and the producer on the input side as
well as that which moves between the producer and large-
volume customers. This economic interaction can be
described in terms of transactions and other factors such as
industry concentration ratios or variants of measures of
interlocking organizational directorships.

Second, accountants need to develop measures of organizational productivity which incorporate customer satisfaction.
And because there have been too many Penn Centrals, International Harvesters and Continental Banks, accountants need
to develop indicators of corporate fiscal health that provide
earlier and clearer warning signals of impending acute or
terminal illness.

We have entered a period of economic interdependency
that demonstrates just how closely our fortunes are tied to
other highly industrialized nations. We can no longer continue the fiction that the corporation must be described by
accountants in terms of a legal entity which makes contracts
and conducts business. This is necessary, in part, because
industries are becoming more difficult to clearly specify,
and, in part, because traditional definitions of corporate
assets and especially liabilities are not providing decision
makers with useful information.

For the good of society, for the sake of the commonweal,

we need additional and different measurements of an organization's performance and status rather than more detailed
information derived from conventional financial accounting
measures.

We look forward to the day when financial accounting
reports describe the extent an organization is a good citizen,
measure how effective its performance is during a period,
and portray its fiscal health. Also needed will be indicators
of its interaction with important segments of the community
including suppliers and customers, as well as the assistance
it provides charitable and cultural enterprises. In time,
measures of organizational interaction hopefully will reflect
social as well as economic and financial attributes.

The Aim and Nature
of Business

THE PLACE OF PROFIT IN BUSINESS

Ronald Cordero

Not long ago, an Ivy League professor of mechanical and aerospace engineering was invited to Detroit to explain his new fuel-saving engine control system to the top executives of a major automotive corporation. But before he began, one of the executives volunteered some business-worldly advice: "One thing you should understand, Professor ... is that our business is making money, not automobiles."[1]

Now a remark of this kind, particularly coming from a successful executive of a successful corporation, is provocative as well as amusing, for it suggests that there either is or should be only one sort of business at all--that of making money. Looked at from this point of view, the particular area of activity of any commercial enterprise is not of any special importance. So long as a company makes money, it is not important whether it does so by making lightbulbs, records, or battleships. Different businesses may have various ways of working toward their goal, but they all have the same goal-- profit.

What I wish to consider here is the question of whether this notion of business as principally and inevitably profit oriented is not an oversimplification of the nature of commercial enterprise. Must the primary aim of any business be that of making money? It will be my contention that to give

---

1. J. I. Merritt, "Automakers Eye Durbin Engine Design," *Princeton Parent News*, Feb. 1, 1980, p. 1.

an affirmative answer would be not only to characterize business in an unfairly simplistic manner, but also to run the
risk of excluding *a priori* a whole range of potentially highly
satisfying business activity.

I. Is the Profit Motive Logically Essential in Business?

        Let me begin with the question of whether or not the
realization of profit is an aim that every business must have.
I do not believe that much work will be required to provide
the answer. The crux of the issue is whether or not we use
the term "business" in such a way that--because of the
meaning of the term--nothing can count as business unless it
involves the aim of making a profit. It might, after all, be
the case that the definition of "business" is such as to make
"We are in business," entail "We have the aim of turning a
profit,"--and to make the statement "He is in business,"
contradictory to the statement "He does not intend to make a
profit." The term *might* have such a meaning, but in fact it
does not.
        There may be an analytic connection between being in
business and charging for what one does, but there is no
analytic connection between being in business and planning
to come out ahead monetarily. An example or two may suffice to establish this point. Consider, to begin with, the
case of a group of monks who produce a flavorful liqueur
from the herbs growing around their monastery. Suppose
that they at first make about enough for their own consumption, with perhaps enough left over to be given to friends in
the village. At this point in the example, they are certainly
not in business. But suppose next that they decide to
increase their production and to charge those outside the
monastery for their product. Now they are in business.
There is no doubt of that: anyone can walk up to the monastery and buy a bottle of the liqueur. But does it follow
of necessity, just because they are in business, that they
have the intention of making a profit? This does not follow
at all. Suppose that they begin to charge for their product
only in order to be able to buy new bottles. Perhaps the
townsfolk are breaking containers, and the monks can not

afford to replace them. Suppose that the charge for each bottle of liqueur covers only the replacement cost of lost bottles, and that the monks are perfectly happy with the arrangement. They want to be able to furnish people in the village with the liqueur, and this is the only way they can continue. Does this change anything? Should we insist that because the monks are not planning on coming out of the transaction with more money (or even bottles) than they put in, they cannot be said to be in business? I think not. We have already agreed that the mere fact of charging for the bottles of liqueur puts them in business.

Or consider an example involving a one-person business. Suppose that an heiress falls in love with a small town in a poor country and decides to help the people there by opening a restaurant to sell nutritious meals for a price the people can afford. So she buys a building, arranges to buy meat, produce, and so forth, and begins to cook. As long as she charges something for the meals we cannot deny that she is in business; and we can be sure of this without inspecting her books or probing her intentions. She is operating a business whether or not she is making--or intends to make--a profit. The fact that she may intend to cover operating losses out of her own resources for as long as she is in the restuarant business does not keep her from being in business.

The profit motive, then, does not appear to be a logically necessary part of business. What is much more likely to be involved in our concept of business is the idea of charging for something on a more or less regular basis.

II.   The Centrality of the Profit Motive in Business

If we grant that the profit motive is not essential to the operation of a business--that it is logically possible to be in business without attempting to make a profit--must we not also grant that, as a matter of contingent fact, the profit motive is absolutely central in the conduct of most business? The answer, of course, is yes, but this is an affirmative answer which has to be understood with the greatest of caution. To say that the profit motive is generally central in

business is to say that the primary reason for the operation
of a business is generally the realization of profit. It is *not*
to say that in the conduct of business, the aim of realizing a
profit is generally given precedence over all other aims.
The difference is an important one.

When we speak of the realization of profit as central in
business, we are singling out the aim for which people usually engage in business. Our previous examples were of
cases in which the individuals involved were engaging in
their respective businesses for purposes other than profit.
The monks wanted the townsfolk to be able to share their
liqueur, and the heiress wanted good meals to be within
reach of the people in her adopted town. But these cases
were atypical ones, of course. More ordinarily, when people
engage in a business, it is because they want to make a
profit. Nations may go into the airline business on a nonprofit basis, and cities may remain in the mass-transit business in spite of continuing losses, but most entrepreneurs
would abandon a business that proved to be nonprofitable
and showed no signs of changing in that respect.

This fact, however, should not lead us to assert that
people who are engaged in the conduct of a business typically rank the aim of making a profit above all other aims in
importance. The centrality of the profit motive in business
does *not* involve the subordination of all other aims to that
of making a profit. In a similar manner, one might remark
that the centrality of the health motive in jogging does not
entail the subjugation of all other aims to that of maintaining
health. Most people may very well jog for the purpose of
maintaining health, but that does not mean that while they
are jogging they are ready to sacrifice all other aims to that
of maintaining health.

In fact, it is quite common--even the rule, rather than
the exception--for the aim of realizing a profit to be sacrificed to certain higher aims in the course of business. It
may seem at times as though people in business are not willing to accord greater importance to any other aim, but a little reflection should dispel that impression. There are several types of aims which, in the conduct of business, are
routinely given precedence over the aim of making a profit.

For one thing many, if not the great majority, of businesspeople rank the observance of many moral principles
above realization of profit. Suppose, for example, that the

directors of a typical corporation learn that the careful exe-
cution of just one murder would lead to a twenty-percent
increase in company profit for the year.   Suppose further
that the directors realize that the crime can be carried out
without any danger of detection.   What will they do?   Will
they order the murder?   I submit that even given the certainty of a perfect crime, most corporate directors would
reject the proposal on the grounds of its immorality.   They
would choose to make fewer profits and not be guilty of
murder.   They would refuse to subordinate the aim of avoiding immorality to that of realizing profit.

It should be understood that there are *many* moral rules
that most businesspeople would honor more than profit.
Suppose, for another example, that the owner of a
financially troubled department store learns that he can
almost certainly guarantee the profitability of his operation
by entering into a homosexual relationship with one of his
major suppliers.   He would in all likelihood refuse on moral
grounds--even if he could be sure that no one else would
ever know what he was doing.   Moreover, he would probably
refuse even if local laws permitted homosexual acts between
consenting adults.   This is a case, in other words, in which
a businessperson could well be expected to decide against a
course of action that would be legal as well as advisable from
the point of view of profit.   The average businessperson
may have gone into business for the purpose of making
money, but she or he would not be willing to do *anything* in
order to achieve that purpose.

Are there moral rules which are ordinarily sacrificed to
profit in the pursuit of business?   One must suppose that
there are.   It is probably not too common, for example, for
individuals in business to rank the aim of abiding by the
moral rule against deceit below the aim of making a profit.
The important point for the present discussion, however, is
that there *are* moral aims which in business are quite commonly ranked above the aim of making a profit.

Are moral aims, then, the only sort of aims that businesspeople place above that of realizing a profit?   The
answer is no, and the subject of treason provides a good
example.   It is highly unlikely that all who oppose treason
do so on moral grounds.   Many people, that is, see treason
as something devoutly to be avoided, without seeing it as
something immoral.   Accordingly, if many people in business

would resist participating in treasonable activities which would be both safe and profitable, we can say that they appear to value avoiding treason above obtaining profit. And I submit that in fact a great many people in business would reject a profitable, but treasonable proposition--even if it involved complete safety from detection. Suppose that a company is offered fabulous amounts of business from a foreign power in return for the use of its domestic facilities for espionage activities. Frankly, even apart from the question of safety from detection, I cannot imagine many managers acceding to such a proposal. Typical managers would dismiss the proposal without even considering the question of how safe the operation might be from detection. They would simply put loyalty to country above profit.

And what of the aim of legality--of abiding by the laws of country and locality? I would suggest that *many* businesspeople also rank avoidance of illegality above obtainment of profits. I am ready to admit, of course, that as in the case of the moral rule against deceit, there may be a certain number of people in business who would sacrifice legality for profit. But I still believe that it would be incorrect to describe the *typical* businessperson as ready to break laws if that would really prove profitable in the long run. Even if detection were out of the question--or, more realistically, even if the cost of legal defense, penalities, and sales lost from public disfavor were clearly going to be outweighed by increased profits--I still suspect that most businesspeople would choose to avoid serious illegality. Even in business, I submit, the aim of doing what is legal is commonly ranked above the aim of doing what is profitable.

Quite clearly, then, the centrality of the aim of making a profit in business does not involve the ranking of that aim above all other aims. The great majority of people in business *are* probably in business for the primary purpose of making a profit, but in the course of deciding how to make a profit, there are numerous aims which they typically rank above the profit aim.

III. Modeling Telic Hierarchies in Business

For clarity, it may be well at this point to review the conclusions reached so far about aims in business. And this can be done quite easily by speaking in the abstract of the "telic hierarchy" characteristic of business in general--where by "telic hierarchy" one means an ordered arrangement of aims. If, for example, one wanted to program a computer to make decisions in the manner of a businessperson, one would have to provide a list of aims. But simple identification of the aims to be used in making the business decisions would be insufficient. One would also have to specify the relative importance of the various aims, saying which are to take precedence over which, and so on. To specify all of this would be to specify the telic hierarchy. (And obviously, one could do this whether or not one were interested in using the information in a computer.)

Now, how are we to describe the telic hierarchy of a typical person in business? As we have just seen, that hierarchy includes several aims that are given *overriding* importance. This segment of the hierarchy will include the aims of not breaking (certain) moral rules, not becoming involved in illegality, not betraying one's country and so on. The actual list of aims of overriding importance for a typical businessperson could be obtained empirically. Collectively, the overridingly important aims can be thought of as a sub-tractive filter. Any proposed action which runs counter to any of them is immediately disqualified as an alternative. From all the possible ways of making a profit, they eliminate a great many.

Are there rankings among the aims of overriding impor-tance? After all, situations can arise in which one will have to frustrate one of these aims in order to satisfy another: to avoid immorality, one may have to break the law, for example. The fact that such cases are liable to be seen as posing *dilemmas* for the businessperson involved suggests that a hierarchical ranking among these aims is not always present before the problem arises. The person in question may have to establish the ranking when the case arises, by deciding which of the aims is to take precedence. If we were programming a computer, we could tell it to flash a

"dilemma" light if such a conflict arose--and then to wait for
input of the relative priority ranking.
     In addition to the segment consisting of aims given over-
riding importance, the telic hierarchy in question will contain, of course, the aim of making a profit. And how is this
to be described?   Since the overriding aims are specified
separately, there is no need to formulate the profit motive
with reference to limitations.   We do not, that is, have to
describe it as the aim of "making a profit without doing anything immoral, illegal, etc.".   We can simply state it as the
aim of making a profit--or as much profit as possible.   Quite
naturally, many businesspeople will posit the aim in the latter form--that of making as large a profit as possible.   And
the separately established overriding aims will help determine
what is possible.
     But is that all there is?   Does the telic hierarchy of a
typical businessperson contain only the overriding aims and
the aim of maximizing profit?   As a matter of fact, there is
usually more.   There are usually a number of aims which are
subsidiary to the aim of profit maximization in the precise
sense that they are established and maintained in the belief
that their fulfillment will further the realization of that aim.
While the exact nature of such aims may vary considerably
from business to business, examples are the aim of maintaining good relations with the public, the aim of minimizing tax
payments, the aim of maintaining the trust of the financial
community, the aim of getting the Acme contract, and the
aim of hiring Jones. (Note that subsidiary aims include both
general and particular aims.)   These subsidiary aims are
definitely *not* of independent importance.   If it ever becomes
apparent that the realization of an overriding aim conflicts
with one of them, it is the latter which is sacrificed.   That
is simply part of what is meant by calling them "subsidiary".
Moreover, if two subsidiary aims conflict, the resolution is
made by reference to the aim of making a profit.   The aim
whose frustration will least endanger the realization of profit
is sacrificed.
     Thus the telic hierarchy in business can be described as
consisting of a segment of overriding aims on the one hand
and a profit-motive segment on the other hand, composed of
the aim of maximizing profit and its subsidiary aims.   To be
sure, the average decision maker in business will have other
aims as a *person*-- the aim of visiting a friend on the

weekend or making spaghetti for dinner, for example. But such personal aims are not properly considered as part of the telic hierarchy used in making decisions in business. They are not the aims of the individual *qua* businessperson.

IV. Diversifying Central Purposes in Business

We have already established that there can be businesses in which the central purpose is not the realization of profit, (let alone its maximization). The monks' liqueur business illustrated that. The telic hierarchies in such cases are atypical for business in that they do not even contain the aim of making a profit. What I should like to consider now is something a little different: the case of a business which has the aim of making a profit, but has it in addition to one or more other central aims. Such a business could be described as having diversified central aims.

Suppose that a company is founded to make a profit *and* to accomplish something else. In addition to the usual overriding aims, the telic structure of such a company will include *two* central aims, along with their respective subsidiary aims. There is nothing logically impossible about such an arrangement. And as a matter of fact, I suspect that a number of existing businesses could be shown to be of this type. Any such business, of course, would encounter special problems because of its two central aims. It is only reasonable to suppose that situations would arise in which a choice would have to be made between an alternative that would tend to increase profit and one that would tend to further realization of the other aim. Would not such dilemmas make the conduct of business extremely difficult?

I think that this need not be the case. Problems of conflict between two central aims can be minimized by the careful choice of a general procedure for "meshing" the two aims. A company of the type in question might decide, for example, to aim for a profit of x percent (high enough, perhaps, to insure the availability of funds when needed). Resources not required for the realization of that amount of profit would then be directed toward realization of the other central goal.

It is important to note that a company's performance with respect to its second central aim could be measured just as precisely as its profit-making performance. Previously, it may have been impossible to obtain a precise rating of company performance with respect to any goal other than profit. Now, however, with advanced opinion-sampling techniques and computer systems, it *is* possible to have more than one numerically precise "bottom line". Company--and managerial--performance can thus be evaluated with respect to more than one central aim.

Suppose, for example, that the owners of a business wish both to make a profit and to contribute to the clean-up of the environment in a certain section of the country. The telic hierarchy of this company would involve certain overriding aims and the dual central aims of making a profit and contributing to the cleanup, together with the various subsidiary aims. The company might, for example, engage in the manufacture of pollution-control and recycling machinery. Each year, a decision could be made as to how much profit would be sought. The central aim of profitability could be specified, that is, as one of making an *x* percent profit. Then, so long as that aim was observed, decisions could be reached with an eye to achieving the environmental aim.

Or someone might operate a business with the dual central aims of making a (central minimum) profit and improving the lives of customers. A certain food product might be sold, that is, not just to make a profit, but also to improve the health of consumers. A resort hotel complex might be operated both to obtain a profit and to enhance the lives of vacationers. And an automobile company might have the simultaneous central aims of making money *and* making vehicles that would decrease the country's dependence on foreign fuel.

While the existence of multiple central aims would inevitably introduce complexities, it should be noted in all fairness that it would also bring certain advantages. For one thing, pursuit of a non-profit central aim might well advance the central aim of profitability. Customers might be attracted, that is, by the other central aim. They might prefer to do business with a company that was trying (and not just incidentally to its attempts to make profit) to raise the standard of living of people in a third-world country, conserve natural resources, or even just provide fulfilling jobs for its employees. Furthermore, the existence of another central aim, in addition to that of profitability, could change the way employees felt about a particular business and their participation in it. Instead of perceiving themselves as part of an organization totally directed toward the realization of profit, they could see themselves as part of an organization trying to make money *and* to do something else. Participation in such a business might be significantly more satisfying for many people.

V.   The Place of Profit

The place of profit in business, as should now be clear, is a matter of choice. Those who are engaged in business *decide* where to place the aim of making a profit in the telic hierarchy they establish and use as their basis for making decisions *qua* businesspeople. They do not *have* to have the aim of making profit at all. If they do adopt that aim, they certainly do not have to give it sufficient importance to override all other aims. They do not even have to give it a unique place of centrality in their telic structure.

The fact that the aim of making a profit is so often made the only central aim in business may simply reflect the strength of the desire for profit on the part of those who found and direct businesses. But there is also a chance that what it reflects, in many cases, is *tradition*. Many people in business may establish and maintain the aim of making a profit as the only central aim simply because they do not realize that alternatives are possible. Business is so often described as an activity concerned with profit and courses in business schools are so often taught on the assumption that profit maximization will be the only central aim, that those who *make* it uniquely central may do so without realizing that they could do otherwise.

I would suggest that the possibilities for businesses with diversified central purposes need to be explored. As I have said, I believe that many such businesses would be found to exist already. And I think that once the possibility of diversified central purposes is generally understood, the public's attitude toward business may improve. It should

become easier for people to give business credit for its good
effects, when they realize that those good effects are not
necessarily incidental.

LIST OF CONTRIBUTORS

The Editors

KENDALL D'ANDRADE is a Lecturer in Philosophy at Loyola University of Chicago. His publications include "Hegel on Affirmative Action," "Which Logic Should You Use?" and "Bribery,"

PATRICIA H. WERHANE received her Ph.D. from Northwestern University. She is the author of several articles on business ethics, coeditor (with Tom Donaldson) of *Ethical Issues in Business* (Prentice-Hall, Second Edition, 1983), author of *Persons, Rights and Corporations* (Prentice-Hall 1984), coeditor (with David Ozar and A. R. Gini) of *Philosophical Issues in Human Rights* (Random House, forthcoming.) She is currently Associate Professor of Philosophy and Associate Dean at Loyola University of Chicago.

The Contributors

KENNETH D. ALPERN received his Ph.D. in Philosophy from the University of Pittsburgh and teaches at Virginia Polytechnic Institute and State University. He writes primarily in the areas of ethics and political philosophy. Among his most recent publications are "Aristotle on the Friendships of Utility and Pleasure" and "Moral Responsibilities for Engineers."

MICHAEL J. BARRETT is currently Professor of Accounting at the University of Illinois at Chicago. His corporate involvement includes consulting engagements with Standard Oil of Indiana and The First National Bank of Chicago, and active commiteee membership of the Institute of Internal Auditors, the Band Administration Institute and the Health Care Internal Audit Group. Combining his professional experience and his academic knowledge, Barrett's *Standards for the Professional Practice of Internal Auditing* were adopted and published by the Institute of Internal Auditors in 1978. His most recent publication, *Auditing Procedures Study No. 1*, was published by the AICPA in 1984 as a guidance for the confirmation of receivables.

THOMAS M. CALERO, Ph.D., is Associate Professor of Management at Illinois Institute of Technology, Chicago. His areas of teaching experience are organization theory and behavior, human resource management, social issues in business and business ethics. His research interests include the special management problems of owner-managed enterprises; morale, leadership and productivity relationships; and employee quality of work life. Consulting assignments have taken him into major corporations, government agencies and health care institutions. His publications include: *A Handbook for Health Care Institutions, Technology and Managerial Careers, Mangerial Manpower Development, and Perils of the Family Firm.*

BARRY R. CHISWICK is Research Professor in the Department of Economics and Survey Research Laboratory at the University of Illinois at Chicago. Professor Chiswick has published numerous articles and books on labor markets, immigrant and ethnic groups, and health facilities utilization. He has also had extensive public policy experience, including service at the President's Council of Economic Advisers. He authored "The Demand of Nursing Home Care: An Analysis of the Substitution of Institutional for Non-Institutional Care" *Journal of Human Resources*. His two most recent books are on immigration issues, *The Gateway* and *The Dilemma of American Immigration*.

RONALD A. CORDERO obtained the Ph.D. in philosophy at the University of Illinois at Urbana. His work has centered largely in the field of ethics. Recently delivered papers include "International Business and the Happy Exploited" and "General Education Requirements and the Imposition of Culture". Articles include "Moral Aspects of the Allocation of Public Health Care Funds" (Transactions of the *Wisconsin Academy of Sciences, Arts, & Letters*, 1981), "'Ought'" (*Midwestern Journal of Philosophy*, Spring, 1977), and "The emise of Morality" (*The Journal of Value Inquiry, Fall, 1974*).

WILLIAM C. FREDERICK teaches courses on business and society relationships, corporate social responsibility, and business ethics at the Graduate School of Business, University of Pittsburgh. He has conducted research on corporations, and business values. He has taught business ethics at the University of Santa Clara (1980-1981) and in the Institute for Ethics in Management at Yale University (1981 and 1982). He is coauthor of *Social Auditing: Evaluating the Impact of Corporate* Programs (Praeger, 1976) and *Business and Society: Management, Public Policy, Ethics* (McGraw-Hill, 1984).

JOHN H. HADDOX, Ph.D. from the University of Notre Dame, has taught at The University of Texas at El Paso for 26 years, including 9 as Chairman of the Department of Philosophy. Among his publications are numerous journal articles, Chapters in 10 books, and 3 books, including *Antionio Caso: Mexican Philosopher* and *Vasconcelos of Mexico, Philosopher and Prophet* (both University of Texas Press).

MICHAEL HOOKER received his Doctor of Philosophy degree from the University of Massachusetts at Amherst. Dr.

Hooker has taught philosophy at Harvard University
and Johns Hopkins University. He currently serves as
President of Bennington College and prior to that he
was the Dean of Graduate and Undergraduate Studies at
Johns Hopkins. He is the editor of two books, the
author of two books and over twenty articles on philosophy.

MICHAEL KEELEY is Associate Professor of Management at
Loyola University of Chicago. He received his Ph.D. in
organizational behavior from Northwestern University.
His articles have appeared in journals such as *Administrative Science Quartersly, Academy of Management
Review, Journal of Value Inquiry,* and in other edited
volumes. His current research concerns the integration
of political philosophy and organizational theory, particularly with respect to models of corporate effectiveness.
Issues raised in his conference paper are further developed in "Impartiality and Participant-Interest Theories
of Organizational Effectiveness" *Administrative Science
Quarterly,* 1984.

LARRY MAY is Associate Professor of Philosophy at Purdue
University where he teaches ethics and political philosophy. He has written dozen articles over the last six
years, and presented many conference papers, several
directly relevant to the main topics of this volume. At
present he is working on a book-length treatment of
groups and ethical theory which will provide the metaphysical and epistemological underpinnings for the various theories of organizational responsibility he has
developed.

THOMAS F. McMAHON, C.S.V., Professor of Socio-Legal
Studies, teaches in the School of Business Administration of Loyola University of Chicago and is the Director
of the Loyola Center for Values in Business. His
degrees include a doctorate in moral theology (University of St. Thomas Aquinas, Rome, Italy) and an MBA
in   marketing   (George   Washington   University,

Washington, D.C.). Having published over fifty articles on business ethics and corporate social responsibility, he has received honors from Beta Gamma Sigma, Loyola MBA Alumni Association and the Better Business Bureau of Metropolitan Chicago. Father McMahon was ordained a Roman Catholic priest in 1954 and is a member of the Clerics of St. Viator, a religious community.

CHRISTOPHER MORRIS is currently visiting Assistant Professor at UCLA. In recent years he has taught government at the University of Texas at Austin and he has been a consultant for the University of San Francisco, program in professional studies. Recent publications include an article on nuclear deterrence forthcoming in *Ethics* and in an anthology (Prentice-Hall), an article on redistribution in *Social Justice*.

MARK PASTIN is Director of the Center for Private and Public Sector Ethics and Professor of Philosophy, Business, and Public Affairs at Arizona State University. He was formerly Associate Professor of Philosophy, Indiana University, and he had visiting appointments at Wayne State University, the University of Michigan, Harvard University, and the University of Maryland. His publications include "Strategic Planning for Science" *The Research System in the 1980's*, edited by John Logsdon (Franklin Institute Press, 1982), "The Multi-Perspectival Theory of Knowledge," *Midwest Studies in Philosophy: Volume V* (University of Minnesota Press, 1980), and "Meaning and Perception," *Journal of Philosophy* (October 1976).

WILLIAM Y. PENN, JR. is Associate Professor of Philosophy and Relig- ious Studies at St. Edwards University. For the past ten years his major interests have been in the application of the empirical and theoretical work of Piaget and Kohlberg to applied ethics and the philosophy of religion, and he has presented a number of papers on the methods he has developed. His publications include "Business Ethics at St. Edward's, Parts I and II," authored with Barbara Lau, *The Austin Business Executive*, June-July, 1984, and "Current Research in Moral Development as a Decision Support System," with Boyd Collier, *Journal of Business Ethics*, forthcoming.

MICHAEL PHILIPS received his Ph.D. from the Johns Hopkins University in 1971. He has held visiting positions at the University of Hawaii and the University of Miami and is currently an Associate Professor of Philosophy at Portland State University. Professor Philips most recent papers include "Racist Acts and Racist Humor" (*Canadian Journal of Philosophy, Spring 1984*), "On the Transition from Ideal to Non-Ideal Theory," (forthcoming, *Nous*), "Are Coerced Agreements Involuntary?" (Law and Philosophy, Spring 1984), and "Normative Contexts and Moral Decisions," (*Journal of Business Ethics, 1985*). Professor Philips' book *Philosophy and Science Fiction* was published by Prometheus Books in the Spring of 1984.

TAL SCRIVEN is Associate Professor of Philosophy at the California Polytechnic State University in San Luis Obispo. He received his Ph.D. from the University of Southern California in 1980 and is the author of "Preference, Rational Choice and Arrow's Theorem" which appeared in the December 1981 issue of the *Journal of Philosophy*.

JAMES VALONE is Associate Professor of Philosophy at the Bellarmine College in Louisville, Kentucky. He is the author of a recent book *The Ethics and Existentialism of Kierkegaard: Outlines for a Philosophy of Life*. He has also published articles in the area of business ethics, social philosophy, phenomenology, and philosophy of the social sciences. In addition, Professor Valone writes and publishes poetry.

LETICIA VERASTEGUI has earned a Bachelor of Science in

Accounting at the University of Illinois at Chicago. She is currently a professional staff member of Continental Bank's Internal Audit Division.

STUDIES IN RELIGION AND SOCIETY